THE LONGER VIEW

Harvey Jackins

RATIONAL ISLAND PUBLISHERS
Seattle

THE LONGER VIEW
First edition. Copyright © 1987 by Harvey Jackins. All rights reserved. No part of this book may be used or reproduced in any manner whatsoever without written permission except in the case of brief quotations embodied in critical articles and reviews. For information, address Rational Island Publishers, P.O. Box 2081, Main Office Station, Seattle, Washington 98111, U.S.A.

Library of Congress Card Number: 87-26429
International Standard Book Number: Cloth Binding: 0-913937-17-7
Paperback: 0-913937-18-5

Jackins, Harvey.
  The longer view.

  1. Counseling.   2. Leadership.   I. Title.
BF637.C6J323 1987   158'.3   87-26429
ISBN 0-913937-17-7
ISBN 0-913937-18-5 (pbk.)

Manufactured in the United States of America

Technology and knowledge are exploding.
Potentials for producing wealth, enormous.
Our re-emergence is accelerating.
The theory opens bright new vistas for us.

The crumbling system cracks and strains and falters.
Wilder and wilder schemes for war are financed.
The smallest social problems can't be handled.
Billions are hungry in a world of plenty.

How fortunate we are to face this prospect,
Gifted to have this long view of the future,
To see the dangers in perspective, challenged
To take charge of it all and find solutions.

— *Harvey Jackins*

Table of Contents

Poem v
Foreword ix

Part One — ADVANCES IN THEORY AND POLICY
"Caring" Between Humans..3
Clarifying and Summarizing...7
No Ancestors, No Descendants......................................25
Try to Become a Trusted Leader, Not a "Guru"......................29
Taking Key Actions That Trigger Other Desirable Actions...........33
Who is in Charge of a Session?....................................39
Cleaning Up Some Concepts...45
The Successful Contradiction and Discharge of Heavy Fear;
   Helpful Hints for Experienced Clients..........................49
Make a Special Effort to Develop Working-Class Leaders............53
Wygelian Leading of RC Areas......................................57
What Does "Policy" Mean in RC?....................................63
Shouldn't Good Language Always Be Creative?.......................67
Counseling Owning-Class People Well...............................71

Part Two — QUESTIONS AND REPLIES
Cleaning Up Distress Completely...................................75
"Away From Distress" Doesn't Mean Repressing Discharge............81
The Meaning of Contradiction......................................85
When to Decide Not to Be Restimulated?............................89
Staying Human Through Deep Tragedy................................93
Are Oppressed People Really Welcome in RC?........................97
Visitors' Policy...101
"Re-emergence" and "Growth"......................................103
Loving Good Language...105
No Tolerance of Any Oppression...................................109
How Can We Handle Unemployment?..................................113
Is Damaging the Environment "Oppression"?........................115
Deciding How to Feel...121
Can You Counsel Away Disabilities?...............................123
What Is Reasonable and Possible?.................................127
"Criticism" of the Artist..131
Stuttering...133
Bereavement..135
What Are the Seattle "Intensives"?...............................137
How Does Oppression Start?.......................................141
Comments and Questions at the First International
   Mental Health System Survivors' Workshop.....................145

Part Three — LEADERSHIP
The Enjoyment of Leadership..............................165

Part Four — COMMITMENTS
Commitments Refreshed and Up-Dated......................201

Part Five — THE 1985 WORLD CONFERENCE
The World Conference.......................................213
Outline: State of the World Report, The 1985 World Conference....215
Taking Our Bearings..219
Outline: Organizational Report, The 1985 World Conference.......239
Outline: The Clarification and Generalization of the Fundamentals
   of Co-Counseling, The 1985 World Conference...............243
Outline: The Frontiers of Re-evaluation Counseling Theory,
   The 1985 World Conference................................247
Outline: Decisive Counseling and Leadership,
   The 1985 World Conference................................251
Graduation Day, The 1985 World Conference..................255

Part Six — GENTILES AND JEWISH LIBERATION
How Can We Develop More Jewish Leaders?
   Dialogue between M— and Harvey Jackins...................279
Counseling Between Jews and Gentiles......................299
Seeking An Effective Gentile Voice.........................329

Part Seven — REPORTS
A General "Upbeat" Report..................................339
Report on Recent Activities................................345
Latin American RC!...349
Jewish Leaders' Conference, 1986...........................351

Part Eight — ORGANIZING
Understanding and Using Organizational Forms................355
A Realistic Conference, For members of organizations
   or enterprises...365

Foreword

This volume contains most of the important insights that developed during 1985-87 in the widespread activity of the Re-evaluation Counseling Communities.

In this period a number of individuals were able to grasp the use of decision for accelerating their re-emergence from distress, and assume critical leadership roles in the wide world at the same time. These two years saw the achievement by a substantial number of Co-Counselors, of "having their lives exactly as they wish to have them."

If this book is your first contact with the ideas of Co-Counseling and you are interested in putting these ideas to *use*, you may write to me at 719 Second Avenue North, Seattle, Washington 98109, USA, for information on whom to contact for classes in your locality.

This book is number eight in the central development of Co-Counseling. The previous books, in the order of their publication, are: **The Fundamentals of Co-Counseling Manual, The Human Side of Human Beings, The Human Situation, The Upward Trend, The Benign Reality, The Reclaiming of Power,** and **The Rest of Our Lives**. Some of these have been published in nineteen languages other than English.

There are also six other books on auxiliary topics within Re-evaluation Counseling. Twenty-nine special journals are published for particular groups of Co-Counselors.

—Harvey Jackins
July 22, 1987

Typesetting and layout were by Valerie Jaworski. Paste-up was by Katie Kauffman. Proofreading was by Personal Counselors staff and Gloria Berman. The cover photograph is by Harvey Jackins. Typefaces are Baskerville II medium, italic, and bold face, and Helios in bold face, set on a Compugraphic Editwriter 7500.

THE

LONGER

VIEW

Advances in
Theory and Policy

"Caring" Between Humans

"Caring" between humans interests me. To be clear and effective in "caring for" each other seems to me a key to enhancing the quality of human life and functioning. What does human "caring" consist of? How did it come about?

Some simpler, more primitive attitudes and relationships might be described as forerunners of "caring."

I would consider coexistence as the most primitive forerunner of caring. Rocks coexist. To be an entity in the universe already creates some sort of a relationship to all other entities in the universe.

Two entities can actively inter-relate to each other as prey and predator, as food and feeder. Biologists speak of a predator as being "useful" to the *species* of its prey, even though destructive of the individuals.

The word "symbiosis" as applied to two living entities indicates some advantage to each of the entities through their interaction with each other. Sometimes one entity may eat the other, but, in the process, scatter some of the other's seeds to new ground. Sometimes one entity devours the pollen produced by the other but spills enough that the first entity becomes an effective pollinator and is crucial for the production of future generations of the second entity. Many such relationships have been described between moths or bees and flowering plants. Biological research reports of the last few years indicate that symbiosis is a common phenomenon in the world of living

Appeared in **Present Time** No. 67, April 1987.

things. Symbiosis is a higher level forerunner of "caring" than is coexistence or predation.

Adults of many species of living things "care for" the young of their species with great persistence and effectiveness. Termite workers care for termite eggs and larvae. Adult bees and wasps care for their immature forms. The scent or taste of the coating exuded by the eggs or the larvae is rewarding to the adult worker in some programmed way. To handle and lick the immature forms gives the adult physical satisfaction. When something goes wrong so that the exudate is not produced, the previously "caring" adult lapses to predation and promptly eats the eggs or the larvae instead of enhancing their survival. Nevertheless, this is a more advanced step toward "caring" than strict symbiosis. It is mutually rewarding. The reward to the larvae is in being nourished and handled and thereby enabled to live. The reward to the adults is the gratification of the rewarding taste or smell.

The care given by mammal mothers (and sometimes fathers) to their offspring also seems to be "built in." The mammal mother, for example, licks the newborn mammal infant clean, apparently for the pleasure of the taste of the waxy coating on the newborn's fur. To nurse the infant seems to be rewarding and pleasant in ways that human mothers can describe, and is pleasurable beyond merely avoiding the pain of swollen breasts and nipples. There is a clear and mutual reward in that the mammal infant receives nourishment necessary for its survival and growth while the mother is rewarded by avoiding painful sensations and receiving sensual gratification.

With human mothers and fathers, there are many higher levels of sense gratification than merely good taste or freedom from pain. All of us have experienced the gratifying smell of a baby's skin or the touch of a baby's hands or cheeks. When we adults are aware enough to look into a baby's eyes and grasp that another human intelligence is looking back at us, we are likely to find it satisfying. This is, I think, "caring" on a higher level than the cow and calf experience it.

There is certainly some kind of mutual gratification built into participation in sex at all evolutionary levels. It is celebrated in *human* song and story but is usually difficult to distinguish clearly from the distress patterns with which the society has infested it.

Humans also experience gratification from being with each other, from being in a group with each other, from physically touching. We in RC have concluded that this is a rational human need built into our species, to touch each other, to see each other, to be in each other's company, to hear each other's voices, and that this is inherently mutually rewarding unless obscured by distress. This is quite apart from sexual gratification or from any patterned gratification of "having power over someone else" or "feeling that we're important" because "someone else depends on us."

There is gratification on the intellectual level. Human intelligence observably yearns for interaction with other human intelligences. I have speculated earlier that "nothing in the universe is complex enough to be really challenging, satisfying, and delightful at the highest level to a human intelligence except another human intelligence." This interaction with each other is mutually gratifying.

I propose, however, that *human* "caring" embraces all of the more primitive levels, but is by no means fulfilled by them. The essence of *human* caring stems from our own essential natures, the high-level natures that we have evolved with the development of our elaborate central nervous systems with their potential functions of *intelligence, awareness, complete freedom of decision,* and *power.*

We inherently care that things be "right." (I will not try to define here what is meant by "right." This, like "caring," will be an undefined term in the mathematicians' use of the word "undefined." You either know what I am talking about or you don't.) We recognize the superb "rightness" of other intelligent humans. If we were not distressed, all humans would clearly "care about each other." We would passionately, deeply wish for, and assist in, the survival and flourishing of every other human, and, to lesser degrees, of every form of life and of every real entity in the universe, simply because that is "right."

(Humans often get crunched back by distress patterns to more primitive attitudes than this and sometimes human caring is occluded entirely and *functionally* replaced by destructive and vicious attitudes, producing child abusers, racists, and even assassins, murderers, rapists, and war-makers. This we in RC already understand and are determined to remedy.)

Introspecting, I know that I yearn for other people to "care" about me in ways that want me to be successful, want me to flourish in every possible way, just because I am what I am. I am enhanced by caring that takes pleasure in thinking about me and seeing that I flourish because it is the "right" state of things, because it is the "right" way for things to be. For me to be as far along the upward trend as I am (that is, being an intelligent human) seems to me to mean that my survival and flourishing naturally gives pleasure and satisfaction to every other human being that is aware enough to notice it.

I propose, as we re-emerge, that we seek to "care" about each other just because it is the right way for things to be; that we discharge any blocks to doing this; that we assume this to be our inherent attitude and that we not settle for anything less. I propose that we win our way back to taking great pleasure in enhancing the life of another human being regardless of whether anyone knows we are doing it or not, or whether there is any other reward or satisfaction in it for us except just the knowledge we did the "right" thing.

Clarifying and Summarizing

I want to review the remarkable clarification of the fundamentals of counseling that has taken place in the recent period. As advanced concepts have broken through, they have illuminated what we'd been doing previously, so that we can now better summarize the fundamentals of RC.

THE FUNDAMENTAL THEOREM

The first clarification of the basic theory is what I call the "Fundamental Theorem of RC." This is the realization that what everyone in the world is trying to do, intuitively and spontaneously, all the time when they're with other people, **will work** if they will **just take turns**. That's the fundamental theorem. Clarity for me on this came at the last general Arab workshop that we held. We held it on the island of Cyprus so that people of various Arab nations could come together. Most of them were almost completely inexperienced in RC. They had friends who had told them to come but they had little practical experience at all. In an effort to base the instruction on their own experience, I took time in the beginning to ask them what, in their opinion, were people doing when they were with each other in any situation where work or other attention-compelling activity wasn't demanding all their attention. How did they spend their time with each other?

They had a variety of suggestions at first, but I kept the discussion going, and finally they reached complete agreement, out of their own experiences. They agreed that whenever people were together, in the coffee shop, or the bazaar, or what-

From a lecture on September 7, 1985 at a workshop in Anchorage, Alaska, USA. Appeared in **RC Teacher** No. 21.

ever the particular culture provided for contact, they were all **trying to get someone to pay attention to them**. After a lot of discussion, they reached agreement on this. Whenever people are together, they spend their time seeking to have someone else pay attention to them, to listen to them. This fit all my experience, too.

Then I asked them, "And are the people paying attention to each other?" At first they said, "Yes," but the discussion went on, and finally they reached the conclusion, "No, no one pays attention; no one is ever really listening. They're all waiting impatiently for their chance to interrupt and try to get someone to listen to them."

I think this is the situation around the world. Four-point-eight billion people are spending whatever slack they have in the company of others trying to get someone to pay attention to them, trying to get someone to listen to them. We know why. They're trying to get a chance to discharge some of the distress that their attention has been wrapped up in ever since they were first hurt. In general, no one is paying attention because everyone else is also preoccupied with trying to **get** attention. So the fundamental theorem of RC can be re-stated: What everyone in the world is trying to do, all the time, intuitively and spontaneously, that is, claim someone else's attention so they can discharge and re-evaluate, will work, if they will **just take turns**.

It probably should be no surprise that, at our most advanced levels of RC, we still run into the problem that people do not **really** pay attention to each other. We now know why. This is the second great clarification of the fundamentals of RC theory. The breakthrough came at a "Counseling with Supervision" workshop in October, 1982, in New Jersey, a workshop that had been specially called to try to see if we could locate the answer to this problem.

THE ANCIENT HABIT-PATTERN

It was plain, even in '82, that the theory was advanced

enough and furnished all the tools necessary to make possible tremendous advancements in people's lives. This theory was also being lived up to occasionally in brilliant counseling demonstrations at workshops. Yet the general level of counseling in our Communities, including that of the most experienced counselors, was very erratic. The practice of counseling was just not living up to the possibilities, and we didn't know why.

We had made various guesses. We had tried various devices without much success. We still had to cope with the phenomenon of a brilliant theory and occasional brilliant demonstrations co-existing with a generally low and unsatisfactory level of counseling. So we gathered there in New Jersey, fifty-some of the best Co-Counselors that we could gather together, and we set up two video cameras. Everyone was committed to counsel before the cameras and then examine the sessions critically. We were determined to put our finger on the reason why counseling practice was so far below the level of theory.

It worked. We had many experiences, some humiliating, some amusing. By the end of the workshop, we were confident that we knew what the sought-after factor was, the mysterious factor that had kept counseling practice so unsatisfactory. The problem all along had been an "Ancient Habit-Pattern" of keeping our attention on our own distresses **all** the time, even when we have promised to put our attention on our client in our role as counselor.

What had been keeping counseling so sloppy was this ancient habit-pattern of being preoccupied with our own distresses even when we were counselor. The basic definition of Co-Counseling, which had always been "two intelligences paying attention to one person, or to one person's distress," was being violated. Two people had usually been paying attention to **two** people's distresses, by and large. The occasional brilliant counseling had come when, for some reason, the counselor had lived up to the fundamental definition and had kept his or her attention on the client.

After the workshop Nancy Kline wrote a couple of articles pointing out that, having not had any other resource when small, we could be proud of ourselves that we had, after our first undischarged hurt, kept our attention on the distress in order to have it ready to hand out if anybody came by who would pay any attention and help us get some discharge. Intuitively knowing that this could work, we could be proud that we had tried to make it work. Then, though it may have worked a few times when we were very small (which probably reinforced our decision to keep our attention on our old distress in case we ever had a chance to haul it out for discharge), it had not worked well enough. Frustration and disappointment accumulated, and what began as a choice and became a habit, went on to become a habit-pattern, rigid and loaded up with distress. Thus, all people have been preoccupied with their own distress ever since they were first hurt, and that preoccupation has become rigid, has become a pattern. This is the primary reason why counseling had remained at such a low level compared to the possibilities revealed by the theory. Meanwhile, however, the theory had progressed pretty steadily and was then and is today at a high level. We have all the tools and information necessary for complete, rapid re-emergence available in print and video today.

THE REPEATED DECISION

We've created a tool for dealing with the "ancient habit-pattern." This is simply a **repeated decision** to give up this habit-pattern and substitute for it a posture or attitude of paying attention only to interesting and profitable concerns. This is a slow, sometimes seemingly cumbersome technique, but it's what we have so far, **and it works.**

With your permission to be client, I will now demonstrate it:

It is logically possible and certainly desirable to end this ancient habit-pattern of paying attention to my old distresses all the time and substitute for it a new attitude of paying attention to interesting concerns. This certainly would include present time—the lake out there and the birches on the shore, and all those good things; the fact that I'm in the middle of a semi-circle of interesting people whose attitudes toward me seem largely benign; the poetry that I have memorized, the songs; the existence of my family. And so, I now decide to end this ancient habit-pattern and adopt a new attitude and posture of paying attention to workable matters. And I do this for a number of reasons. The first reason is that the old preoccupation with distress hasn't worked. Not only have I not profited by this preoccupation, but I don't know any one of the 4.8 billion people in the world that has gotten anywhere with it. I'm going to keep on making this decision, because it obviously doesn't work to do it only once; much of our re-emergence is like melting a big block of ice slowly. And so, I now again decide to give up this ancient posture of being preoccupied with my old distresses all the time and substitute for it a new attitude of paying attention to interesting things. I will persist in doing this because, so far, after nearly three years of doing it, I've never failed to yawn whenever I've done it, and, as experienced counselors, you know to treasure yawns; these are the pulling up of the roots of a pattern, and they have profound results. It works if I make the decision before a workshop like this demonstration, it works if I do it as a client in a two-way session, it works if I do it in a group, and it even works if I do it by myself. For years, I've fought the anxiety pattern that wakes me up at four o'clock some mornings, to wonder if I failed to do something yesterday that will eventually lead to nuclear holocaust because I failed to do it. (You know that kind of thing.) I previously had all kinds of other devices for resuming sleep. I'd read RC literature and yawn and go back to sleep; but now I don't even have to turn on the light. I make the decision about three times, and the yawns start coming, and about the fifth yawn I wake up the right time in the morning. Ahhh!

We have a little group at Personal Counselors in Seattle who meet once a week before work and take turns making this decision. We've learned that after we've gone around the circle making the decision three times at each turn, it works well to go

THE LONGER VIEW

around saying what we've been thinking of during the previous circuit. It turns out, of course, that often what we've been thinking about is our old distresses, but by now we're immune to embarrassment about that. It's also true that that isn't all we've been thinkng about. Some very interesting thinking comes out of that circle. Then, we go around once again with each person making the decision three times, and after that each one says once again what he or she has been thinking, and so we continue until it is time to go to work. I yawn steadily and others discharge in every possible way.

And so, once again, I decide to change this ancient habit-pattern of paying attention to my old distresses all the time into a new attitude or posture; and I don't care how slowly it goes, it's going; it's getting there. And I'm encouraged to keep doing it, and I encourage all of you to join me in doing it, because it seems to be solving the problem. Ever since I've been doing this, people have been saying spontaneously, "Hey, your counseling has improved a **lot** since last year!" It seems to be making a difference. I know that I'm a tougher counselor by far. And so, I will continue to make this decision. It **does** work. The habit has been installed and re-installed for sixty-nine years, so it's not surprising it's taking a while to get it completely out, but the improvement is steady, and so I highly recommend it. It will seem **boring**, over and over and over again. I yawn, and yawn, but many other people have other kinds of discharge. It does work, and I suggest you do it routinely, that you do it under all kinds of circumstances, in order to move steadily out of this preoccupation that has kept us such poor counselors for each other compared to what we could be. That's the second great clarification of the fundamentals.

REVISING OUR PREOCCUPATION

At this point, I ask you to take a very advanced step with me. All of us, as far as I can tell, have been preoccupied with **getting** good counseling. I would like to ask you to join me in making a decision to give up this preoccupation with **getting** good counseling, to just give it up. (After discussion, almost everyone joins in the decision.) Now, I would like you to join me in another preoccupation instead. I would like you to join me in a preoccupation with **giving** good counseling. Giving good counseling is extremely rewarding. You have the delight in giving effective help to somebody when they need assistance. (After discussion, there is agreement and decision by the group.)

THE EXACT TOOLS OF THE COUNSELOR

The third great clarification of the fundamentals of Co-Counseling is the definition of exactly what the counselor needs to do in order to help the client discharge. Now, not **everything** the client needs from the counselor is help in discharging, not everything. There are times when the client needs information. There are times when the client needs other kinds of assistance. Standing guard is partly assistance with discharge and partly assisting people to rest deeply. There are other things a client can need from a counselor besides help in discharging; but at least 95% of what the client needs from the counselor **is** help in discharging, because where the whole re-emergence and recovery process has been held up is in the blocks on discharge. In the development of RC we have correctly put our emphasis on what the counselor can do to help the client discharge.

Now, we know **exactly** how to help the client discharge under any conditions. The counselor needs to do three things:
1. Pay anough attention to the client to see **clearly** what the distresses are.
2. **Think** of all possible ways to contradict those distresses.
3. Contradict the distresses **sufficiently**. The client will always discharge.

THE FIRST POINT

On the first point, the key word is "clearly," to see clearly what the distresses are **this** session, **this** time. Now, the most common substitute for doing this is, of course, to "know" what

THE LONGER VIEW

the client's problem is because you "understand" — "I feel that way myself" — to project your distress on the client. There are many other patterned substitutes for paying this attention, as well.

THE SECOND POINT

The second point is to think of all possible ways to contradict that distress, **and keep thinking!** It is not sufficient to come up with one notion. (Well, often it has been, or apparently has been. The way counseling has worked, let's face it, is that, in a great many sessions, the counselor, in great confusion, fires a bullet at what they think the client's distress is, and the client, in his or her great eagerness to make it work, picks up the target and runs over and puts it where the bullet lands and manages to discharge. I remember, in the early years of professional counseling, that I would sometimes offer a client a phrase and the client would burst into wild discharge, and I'd sit there kind of smug, thinking "I really hit that one," and the client would discharge and discharge and pause to mumble the phrase, and I'd lean over to hear, and they weren't mumbling **my** phrase. They'd misunderstood me just enough to get a lot of discharge.)

We might as well be good counselors and try to think of **all** possible ways to contradict the distress. Words are a weak contradiction to a pattern, yet this is often as far as you see the counselor's mind go. The client says, "I don't feel anybody likes me." "Okay, say everybody likes you," says the counselor, in an offhand tone. Every pattern in existence has been argued with thousands of times already. The pattern is used to words; it's calloused to words, numb to words. Words are the least effective contradiction. Because of the rigidity of our chronic patterns of voice and posture and facial expression, the pattern has hardly had **any** contradiction in those areas, and it's completely vulnerable there. If you tell me that nobody likes you, I can even **agree** in words — "You know, that's **right**!" (In a bright tone of voice) The patten is disarmed by my verbal agreement, but my cheerfulness contradicts the patterns completely so discharge follows.

Think of **all** possible ways to contradict the distress. Think of tone of voice; think of facial expression; think of posture, think of anything else. You should have five or six contradictions in mind. Get in the habit of thinking of at least five or six ways of contradicting the distress. Once the client starts discharging, revealing more details of the pattern, you can add all kinds of other contradictions. Don't go unaware when the client's discharging. This is a chance to think of additional contradictions so the discharge can proceed from a trickle to a thunderous roar.

I don't know anyone yet who's thought of all possible ways to contradict a distress, but in the spirit of no limits, say **"all** possible ways," and then don't start until you have three or four of them in mind at least. Don't just think of one contradiction and then quit thinking.

THE THIRD POINT

For the third point, the key word is "sufficiently." Contradict the distress **sufficiently**. The client will always discharge. If you have thought of four or five contradictions, and you've put them in, and the client still isn't discharging, it isn't time to give up. It's time to contradict the distress more. As soon as you've contradicted it sufficiently, the client will always discharge.

Every one of the 4.8 billion people in the world, hardly any of whom have ever heard of RC or the word "discharge," is waiting, patiently or impatiently, for another one of the 4.8 billion people to come up to them, pay enough attention to them to see clearly what the distress is, think of all possible ways to contradict that distress, and then contradict it sufficiently. Each one will immediately burst into as much discharge as the distress is contradicted. They don't need to have any sessions on theory. This is completely built-in for every human being. Every one of the 4.8 billion people is waiting for you to do just that. Every one. It'll take a while to get around to 4.8 billion people, but you can enlist others to do it with you.

To read this is helpful; to hear it said is helpful; but remember the three pseudo-abilities that a pattern has. The pattern has the ability to persist, it has the ability to confuse you, and it has the ability to make you forget. Anything that is as anti-pattern as these three directions gets obscured. I know it gets obscured because we have brilliant leaders of the RC Community, who do good jobs; when I do a supervised counseling demonstration with a couple of them, and I say, "Counselor, why don't you turn to the audience and say out loud the three things that a counselor must do to let the client discharge?", the counselor turns to the audience and says, "Um, ah..." and has forgotten the three conditions. When you go into a counseling situation as a counselor, the pull to be client yourself makes it easy to forget. So I suggest that you burn these words into your brains in letters of fire. To make a start of it, I'm going to ask you to repeat them rote fashion with me:

1. Pay enough attention to the client to see clearly what the distresses are.
2. Think of all possible ways to contradict those distresses.
3. Contradict the distresses sufficiently. The client will always discharge.

THE GREAT CLARIFICATIONS

These are the great clarifications of the fundamentals of counseling: First, the fundamental theorem that it's a completely spontaneous process; that what everybody is trying to do will work if you can just introduce the notion of taking turns.

Second, that the obstacle to applying our theory is the existence of an ancient habit-pattern in each of us of being preoccupied with our own distresses all the time in the hopes that having our attention on them will enable us to pull them out and put them before someone and get some discharge. It's understandable how we got into that habit, and it's also possible to give it up.

Third, the clarification of exactly what the counselor needs to do for 95% of the counselor's job, which is to help the client discharge: Pay enough attention to the client to see clearly what the distresses are; think of all possible ways to contradict those distresses; contradict the distresses sufficiently. The client will always discharge.

THE RE-DEFINITION OF "RESTIMULATION"

Now, there have been all kinds of brilliant insights breaking through on the frontiers of counseling, all based on these fundamental clarifications. One of the great insights on the frontiers is the re-definition of restimulation. Our original definition of restimulation was "the involuntary association of old distress with something in the present." We found this useful and very helpful. Instead of being reproached for being upset, we were not. To hear about restimulation as an involuntary association relieved us of a lot of guilt, but the old definition began to show strain. As things progressed, Co-Counselors were talking about **resisting** restimulation. If we decided to resist the restimulation, what happened to the involuntary business? It became voluntary. People were saying that they **decided** not to be restimulated.

The new definition of restimulation is "the usually unaware, but nevertheless intentional, bringing up of past distress, with the excuse of some similarity in the present, in the hope of claiming someone else's attention and securing some discharge." This puts us in the position of saying that we have to decide to be restimulated. If we get the definition internalized and integrated into our thinking, it gives us a chance to decide not to be restimulated ahead of time, to establish habits of resisting restimulation.

It hasn't worked well to decide to be restimulated. Sometimes people in the Communities have seemed to make it work.

I remember, early on, how some people were competing with each other about discovering new restimulations. What they were doing was using their upset as a way of imposing the role of counselor on someone else. A lot of that's gone on in the Community, the unaware clienting, the forcing ourselves on people, forcing other people to be our counselors without their agreement. It hasn't **really** worked, even though it apparently worked for a few people who assumed the role of a kind of nuisance within the Communities for a while and got lots of discharge, but not to any enduring purpose, because they ruined their relationships as they went.

The point of deciding not to be restimulated ties right in with giving up the ancient preoccupation with our old distress. This has been an important clarification, that restimulation is something that we decide to do. In general, we will have a better session if we decide not to be restimulated but contradict the distress instead of plunging into it. The fact that we have sometimes gotten restimulated and then been able to claim support from someone else and have a great session doesn't mean that that's the best way to do it. If we completely forget all our advanced theory, we can still lurch along like that, but we won't have a responsible relationship between ourselves. We won't have the most supportive Community. To accept the new definition of restimulation and, hopefully, decide not to be restimulated, every time we manage it, is going to improve things all the way around.

INTELLIGENCE PLUS OTHER CAPACITIES

Another important insight is the realization that we have many profound capacities besides our intelligence. The universe is dynamic, observably. Everything is in change, always. That supposedly eternal rock out there is vibrating in every crystal, atoms are creeping through the lattice structure, and weathering is taking place. Lichens are etching away the surface. The supposedly immutable is actually in constant change. It's a universal characteristic of the universe, to be in dynamic change all the time.

QUANTITATIVE CHANGES ALTERNATE WITH QUALITATIVE ONES

Observably, change occurs in alternating forms. Small, quantitative changes occur over a period and then reach a certain nodal point, and a sharp qualitative change occurs. The simple, familiar example of this is ice. Ice can be at a very, very low temperature, and then you allow it to warm. The water molecules are in a crystal lattice, but they're vibrating in the lattice, and, as the ice warms, they vibrate faster, they move more, until you get to 0° Centigrade, and then the slow quantitative changes produce a qualitative change, and the molecules break loose from the crystal relationships and start sliding over each other, and you have the liquid form of water, a different relationship, a critical, qualitative change. Then, as you increase the temperature, the molecules slide over each other faster and faster, till at 100° Centigrade (at normal atmospheric pressure), they slide so fast that the quantitative changes lead to a qualitative one, and they quit sliding and start bouncing. They assume a different relationship to each other and become a gas. Molecules rebound from each other and have all the characteristics of a gas. The slow, quantitative changes reach a certain point and qualitative change occurs. The dynamism of the universe expresses itself in the alternation of quantitative change and qualitative change.

This takes place on all levels of complexity. As life evolved, there were many qualitative shifts. As central nervous systems developed, they started out very simple and became more complex as life evolved. At some point, the quantitative change in increasingly large central nervous systems reached such a point that qualitative change occurred. The last article I read on our brains said that our central nervous system has 100 billion neurons. Observably, only a few hundred of these bring information into our central nervous system from our sensors, and only a few hundred of the neurons take commands out from our central nervous system to our muscles and glands. Do you know what the rest of those 100 billion or so do? They sit and talk to each other. Tremendous interplay. The development of central nervous systems reached a point, somewhere in evolution, that a critical, qualitative change occurred—the emergence of intelligence as a completely different way of functioning. We define intelligence as the ability to come up with fresh, new, accurate, successful responses to each new situation, not ever having to be limited to inherited responses or the conditioned warping of inherited responses.

THE DISTRESS PATTERN IS A REVERSION

Actually, the distress pattern is a reversion to that earlier kind of functioning, which, for our pre-human ancestors, constituted a crude form of learning. The deer that gets stuck in the quicksand and manages to escape acquires a warpage of the familiar pattern of approaching a water hole because of this distress and avoids that spot, a crude form of learning. The use of this patterned conditioning, which we do with our horses and dogs and call it training, installs patterns. In general, the patterns installed are not any worse than the ones they replace. The animal's functioning is not degraded by the substitution of a new stress pattern for the inherited instinctive pattern. But for human beings, the imposition of the distress pattern is enormously degrading. It shoves us down, at best to the level of stupids and at worst to the level of monsters whose exploits are celebrated in newspaper headlines.

AWARENESS

The qualitative shift in central nervous systems brought intelligence, which we treasure and value and seek to recover by getting the distress patterns off it through discharge. It brought not only intelligence but also a super-function of **awareness**, which seems to arise out of intelligence but is more than intelligence, because a lot of our intelligent thinking goes on below awareness.

POWER

The same complexity which developed so that billions of neurons interact with each other all the time, continually, awake or asleep, also brought us a couple of other capacities that have been obscured from us by the accumulation of distress patterns. One is **inherent power**. There seems no question now that power is inherent, that all of us were conceived and most of us born with an inherent expectation that the universe would be responsive to our wishes. If you observe the occasional child who had a wonderful pregnancy and easy delivery and has been encouraged to discharge, there's no question: They expect everything to go according to their wishes. They're friendly about it, not dictatorial or arrogant, but they really expect it.

There are some grounds for this. Notice, in a group of adults, when a child raises its voice, cries, demands attention, every adult within earshot takes notice. We can not ignore that greatest voice in the animal kindgom. Unfortunately, in the grip of a pattern, the adult may go over and slug the child or something like that, but the child's expectation and the nature of their relationship with adults is that they have power. They have power to call adult human beings to their support and to get what they want, and that's power. If the adults were all rational, this power would be plain.

Apparently, power, complete power, is inherent in the complexity of our central nervous systems. It's inherent, just as intelligence is. The realization that power is inherent simplifies our job, because it doesn't mean that we have to pump up our muscles or get six Ph.D.s in order to have power. It means that we have to discharge the powerlessness patterns that have been imposed upon us.

FREEDOM OF DECISION

Another capacity is apparently inherent: This is a **complete, absolute freedom of decision**. We can decide anything. We're absolutely free to decide intelligently or decide unintelligently. We're free to decide on the basis of the evidence; we're free to decide in the teeth of the evidence. We're free to make a good decision or a perverse decision. This may not sound very progressive, but I think we have to face this absolute freedom of decision or we won't reach for our power. This freedom of decision means we can decide, right now, not to indulge in a single bit of patterned behavior from now on. I don't know how **often** we're going to have to decide, but we have the freedom to decide and make it stick. Apparently, the complexity of our central nervous system, once it attained a certain level, not only brought us intelligence and the super component of awareness, but also brought us inherent, complete power and inherent, complete freedom of decision. We can make any decision we want, regardless of circumstances. Now, the conditioning of this society, of course, has told us ten billion times, with fear and cruelty and interference and everything else, that we don't have any power; we've got to do what we're told; we don't have any freedom of decision; we have to do what our parents said, or what the church said, or what God told us or God told somebody else, who told us. The reality has been hidden, has been denied to us, and so we have thousands of distress experiences of being told we can't decide and we have no power.

The situation is such, and the operation of the oppressive societies is such, that at least two of us are going to have to do enough trenchant work, counseling each other, discharging powerlessness, and discharging the notion that we're not free to decide, that we can act on these clear insights.

A FRESH, CLEAN FUTURE

Each new moment brings the beginning of a fresh, clean future that we do not need to allow to be contaminated by past distress. We can keep it clear and clean by decision.

If we succumb to carelessness and slip and allow that new future to be messed up, all is not lost. Here comes another new moment beginning another clear, clean future that we can have just the way we want it.

And if we mess up that one, there's an endless series of such fresh starts still coming.

It's a very exciting time. We're on the edge of having everything we want.

No Ancestors, No Descendants

A microgeneticist has recently said that the common idea that humans produce genes in order to produce more humans is a distortion of reality. He said that anyone familiar with the interactions of genes in humans would agree that it's much more the case of the genes producing humans in order to produce more genes. (The genes are sections of the giant molecules of deoxyribonucleic acid that reproduce themselves by assembling a replica of themselves from the material in their environments and then separating from it. These giant molecules also produce all the ribonucleic acid, proteins, and other molecules necessary to assemble the replicas of themselves, and they do produce all other living things, in our case, humans, so that the replicas of themselves are spread widely and have an opportunity to vary and form new combinations with each other. The gene line or the gene pool or the gene network is the channel of heredity, and we humans are just twigs off this main stem.)

When I read this at first, I was amused at the opportunity this gave us humans to be more modest about our role in the scheme of things but did not think of any more useful consequences of the information.

Then a number of other factors began to come together in my mind. Because we seem to issue from within our parents' bodies, it has been easy for us to believe that we are *descended* from them. Our parents, grandparents, and others have believed this too. Rules, expectations, obligations, and requirements have been laid upon us by relatives, religions, cultures, and societies in the name of this apparent reality.

Appeared in **Present Time** No. 68, July 1987.

THE LONGER VIEW

"Children, obey your parents in the Lord, for this is right!" "Honor thy father and thy mother that it may be well with thee and thou mayest live long on the earth."

Now, I began to think of us grandparents, parents, children, and grandchildren as adjacent twigs branching off the main genetic stem or network on which the genes are actually descending from each other. I remembered a number of clients with deep distress rooted in heavy, irrational assumptions or obligations that had been implanted and accepted by the clients only because of the taken-for-granted relationship of the clients to fathers and mothers and grandparents.

Next, I remembered the considerable number of RCers who have tackled "establishing a rational relationship with their parents" and succeeded; and how, in every such successful case, the RCer has informed me with delight and with the parents' concurrence that "we are no longer parents and children, but good friends."

I realized I have been saying for years that the most satisfying achievement of my life is that four very fine people who used to be my children are now my good friends.

I recalled listening to Polynesians from various parts of the Pacific over my lifetime, beginning with a longshoreman I worked with fifty years ago, each one of whom told me how marvelous it was in their cultures not to "belong" to their "natural parents" as we seemed to do in Western cultures, but to have every adult in the village available as a "parent." Whenever they chose, they moved from one house to another, knowing that their "original" parents had no particular claim on them and that they would be welcomed just for being themselves in every household into which they moved.

Over at least the last ten years, in certain situations with certain clients, I have been using a kind of fantasy. This consists of informing them "seriously" that it was time that they were told that the people they had been calling their parents were not their real parents, that their real parents were "star people" who had to leave earth and did not dare take them with them because the space ship was damaged, and so they had left them with these earthling foster parents, knowing that as "star children" they could somehow survive no matter how miserable it was, and if the space ship made it, their "star parents" would be back for them at a later time.

Usually I say that I have had word from their real parents that they will be returning to earth next month to pick up the star children they left and that they will then take the client back to her or his "own people."

Almost every client to whom this is said discharges voluminously. If listened to after the discharge, they will express a great sense of freedom at being "released" from the relationship with the people they had considered their real parents until now.

All these things, considered together, made me realize what an unfortunate vehicle the so-called parent-child or ancestor-descendant relationship is for the oppressive society and the patterned cultures to impose hurtful nonsense on us in the form of these expectations, obligations, and assumptions that we would never accept if we were free to think for ourselves.

In the older cultures tremendous obligations were and are laid on children to "take care" of their parents, I suspect so that the society would not have to take any responsibility for them. This has been diluted somewhat in recent years in the West, although not so much but that we feel guilty about our parents being abandoned in nursing homes, even if we are still too timid to insist that society create an alternative.

The notion is still almost unchallenged that one is "of course" obligated to one's children. After all, the parents brought the children into the world without consulting them; the parents

THE LONGER VIEW

must certainly be obligated to take care of them, yes? It was an enormous relief to me a few years ago when my discharge and re-evaluation led me to the realization that anything my children would need from me I would, of course, do for them because I wanted to. I did not need any *obligations* to make me perform rational acts in this area.

The whole notion that we "descend" from each other, pounded in heavily by the educational institutions and the cultures, by the patterns of the people around us and by the appearance of us issuing from our parents' bodies, can now be dispensed with. Those whom we have regarded as our ancestors or our descendants are simply fellow branches growing on the genetic trunk somewhat adjacent to us, fully human and delightful and able to be enjoyed and cherished, but having no other real relationship with us than that of friend, acquaintance, and fellow human, just as do all other humans.

To realize this can free us from an enormous load of taken-for-granted notions that have burdened our thinking and functioning. It can set us free to think for ourselves, to start our relationships over and to live as delightful friends with every human being with whom we wish to be friends. Starting completely fresh, what kind of relationship would you like to have with me?

Try To Become A Trusted Leader, Not A "Guru"

Can a leader secure, enjoy, and make use of growing trust and confidence from the people whom he or she is leading without dependency patterns and declining-to-think-for-oneself patterns developing among these people?

In the early years of the Re-evaluation Counseling Communities there seemed to be a tendency for people, when hearing me propose new developments of theory, to immediately voice intense criticism of the proposals. It seemed that people who supported the proposals were quiet while people who spoke were critical. It was not because the proposals were bad, because the critics almost always later came to be enthusiastic supporters and users of the proposals they had criticized.

This has changed in the last seven or eight years. Currently, large numbers of people respond positively to the initiatives I propose. If the proposals are contained in an article in **Present Time** or some other publication, people write to me with enthusiasm about the new suggestions. If I advance a new idea at a workshop the workshop attenders usually applaud and often start applying the idea at once.

Feeling-wise, I find this pleasant, of course. Everyone likes to be appreciated. Everyone likes to be supported. Everyone likes their thinking to be agreed with. I also become a bit uneasy. I wonder if a kind of rigid pattern is intruding into the relationship between me and the people who agree with me and applaud me so easily.

Appeared in **Present Time** No. 66, January 1987.

THE LONGER VIEW

Oppressive societies in many cultures of the world have demanded agreement with, and unquestioning loyalty to, the rulers. Soldiers in feudal nobles' armies were conditioned to be ready to give their lives at a leader's command. These are obviously patterns installed by oppression and are not likely to confuse us.

We have also heard about "gurus," the well-publicized leaders of various movements, cults, and ashrams who are simply "adored" by their followers. A long "profile" article appeared in **The New Yorker** magazine describing the relationship between the Rajneesh and his Oregon commune of followers. There have been good detailed accounts of the functioning of Chassidic communities around their rabbis. More on the fringe, the horror of the Jonestown affair caused us all to flinch at the unquestioning "willingness" of hundreds of people to commit suicide at a leader's suggestion.

A possibly much more subtle example of unthinking support concerns me. Chou En Lai was a brilliant thinker and thought independently for many years. However, at one point in the famous Long March, after Mao Tse Tung's policies had been rejected repeatedly by the central committee, with disastrous results, Chou En Lai made a statement something like this:

"I have opposed Comrade Mao's thinking on many occasions in the past and have come to different conclusions than he has done. I have supported him sometimes also; but every time that I have opposed him he has been right and I have been wrong. Henceforth he will have my complete support in the leadership of the Central Committee and of the Eighth Route army."

This was a turning point for China in that Chou En Lai's commitment put leadership of the liberation forces of China firmly in Mao's hands. Chou En Lai's support for Mao from then on was unstinting.

This certainly had many good results, but, as far as I can

tell, Chou never thought *independently* from then on. It seems to me this was a mistake. It seems to me that it must have been possible to have given wholehearted, unstinting support to Mao's correct positions and still gone on making contributions of his own. I speculate that this could have strengthened the liberation forces and perhaps have prevented the counter-revolutionary policies which followed Mao's death.

There seems to be some kind of addictive allure to finding someone you can trust, someone who appears intelligent, and then *letting that person do your thinking for you.* Since RC leaders are becoming more and more dependable and intelligent, this phenomenon is likely to attach to them.

This concerns me. I am speculating about it in print in the hopes of drawing attention to it and discussion about it by other RC leaders. How can we accept and use the support which our correct policies and our consistent actions have earned us and will earn us and which certainly strengthens our efforts for world-wide liberation and the prevention of nuclear holocaust, yet, at the same time, prevent the people who have come to trust us from simply accepting our thinking and stopping doing their own independent thinking?

The enthusiasm of supporters is not a dependable indication of the thoughtfulness of supporters. The accounts of Chassidic males' devotions to their beloved rabbi's sermons indicate that they thoroughly enjoy their enthusiasm for the thinking of someone for whom they hold such affection, but they show no indication of thinking independently for themselves or doing anything beyond accepting the thinking of the rabbi. The rabbis, by all accounts, often think well, at least in a limited way, but operate on certain fundamental assumptions which narrow their area of interest far too much in a world as complex and dangerous as today's is.

How can we RC leaders accept the support, the unity that comes with it, the focused activity that an agreed-upon pro-

THE LONGER VIEW

gram brings; how can we enjoy the comfort of being appreciated and still keep clearly before our associates and assistant leaders the necessity of them continuing to think independently and critically themselves?

Possibilities I have thought of so far include:

1) When we propose policy, we use language such as "I would like your critical appraisal of the following ideas," or "Here's a proposal that needs to be thought about."

2) We ask such questions as, "Where do you think this will lead us if we put it into operation?", "Are there some possible dangers or difficulties that will appear if we follow these policies that I am proposing?", "Can you see another route that will have as good or better effects if we follow it?"

3) We make such statements as, "I know you have different viewpoints than I do because you have different backgrounds. If you examine this situation from your background, what policies do you come up with? What similarities are there between your policies and the ones I am proposing here, and what differences?"

Perhaps we can use large posters over our workplaces that remind us and our associates, "There is at least one elegant solution to any real problem, *and probably an infinity of them*," or "I need your *thoughtful* support, not your unthinking agreement."

Taking Key Actions That Trigger Other Desirable Actions

As we become more effective and more influential in the dual process of our individual re-emergences and the building of world-class communities centered upon our individual leaderships, we will occasionally be faced with the apparent difficulty (and sometimes the reality) of there being too much for us to do. Many of us by now have already had the experience of taking on responsibilities beyond what we had been doing, eagerly carrying them out, and then finding that we are working long hours and getting inadequate rest, exercise, and recreation as a result. The phenomenon of over-fatigue and "burn-out" is an almost universal accompaniment to the job of leader in the institutions of the oppressive society. It has been far too frequent a companion to our most responsible and effective leaders in RC as well.

Two years ago we evolved the counseling technique of "standing guard" as a way of helping each other discharge *recorded fatigue* patterns. These, because they are able to be restimulated by new tiredness, can make a little new fatigue seem overwhelming. The "standing guard" technique, when utilized by an effective counselor, has dependably led to discharge of the recorded fatigue patterns and to recovery of one's inherent zest and endurance.

OTHER PATTERNS

There is often more to the difficulty, however, than old recordings of fatigue. There are other patterns such as "having to do it all one's self" or "feeling no one else can be depended

Appeared in **Present Time** No. 66, January 1987.

upon." These can be discharged and eliminated, too, with good counseling.

There often is also the *reality* of there being far too much work within the usual operation of a leadership role for one individual to carry it out adequately, given only one person's time and strength.

LEADING LEADERS

Here one helpful approach to date has been the realization that a leader who wishes to lead a world-class community must lead leaders; that leaders can be produced from followers and followers thus trained to be leaders can in the process be trained to become leaders who train other leaders. Each generation of leaders can learn the possibility, the necessity, and the means for training and enhancing additional leaders and leadership.

STILL LOTS TO DO

There is a residue of difficulty, however. The onrushing proliferation of nuclear arms and the accelerating collapse of the oppressive society produces, within the ruling classes of the society, an enormous pull toward war and the use of nuclear weapons. The more aware we become, the more tasks we see that need doing. There is a great deal more to do than one individual, acting alone, can hope to accomplish.

Fortunately the dynamic nature of reality offers some clues to a workable solution of this dilemma. The development of the future proceeds with great complexity, influenced by all the past events that created the preconditions of the present and the future, but with a continuing interaction with the events that are taking place currently and with our anticipations of the future. In this complexity, certain "key" events can be located or estimated, events which, if accomplished, will necessarily trigger the carrying out of other desired events or courses of action.

THE RELEASING OF OBSTACLES

These key events will sometimes be the *releasing of obstacles* that have developed in the work.

In past years in the northern United States, logs were often cut in the woods in winter and sent to market by floating them down river in the spring. Lumberjacks would shepherd and guide vast quantities of timber down the fresheted rivers. On occasion the mass of logs would jam at some point in the river and great pile-ups would develop. It became a crucial skill to find the "key log" in the jam, the removal of which, with peavey, pry bar, or dynamite, would free the whole mass of logs to continue on their course downstream.

The progress of events and the development of movements are subject to similar obstacles. The untangling of "key difficulties" which are holding up progress on a broad front can be compared to the freeing of the "key log" in a log jam on a river. If a person playing an important role in a movement becomes non-functional through accident, illness, preoccupation with distress, or unforeseen circumstances, to restore that person to functioning or to replace that person in the role with a functioning person is a key activity that releases the development of many other activities.

THE CREATION OF PRE-CONDITIONS

Creation of pre-conditions for events which one desires to take place has a similar effect.

If one wishes to produce a motor car, for example, it will be necessary to find (or even construct) an iron mining operation, smelting of the iron, mills to produce steel, and the casting or forging or machining of parts in order that the manufacture of an automobile can proceed. In other kinds of manufacturing the transportation, warehousing, and sub-assembling of materials are pre-conditions that must be met for the desired product to be attained.

Leading a large number of people in a world-class community organized around one's self to achieve mass re-emergence, eliminate nuclear hazards and construct a rational society will certainly have analogous pre-conditions at every stage.

INCISIVE COUNSELING

One pre-condition that comes quickly to mind is establishing communication and association with other able, rational individuals. The key steps to this pre-condition will include the counseling of otherwise able people who are limited by distress patterns. We know how often this has marvelous results in freeing and enhancing the abilities of the person counseled to perform, to act, to lead.

(This is one of the great advantages that the RC leader enjoys above all other leaders, the possession of the tools and skills of counseling. This often enables one to solve problems with considerable ease that are regarded as insoluble in the wide world.)

TRAINING AND EXPECTING

Another triggering action which creates the pre-condition for desired activity is the training and production of new leaders. Almost all humans are leading difficult, despairing lives at present because of a lack of leaders and leadership. The skills and knowledge about producing new leaders that we are acquiring are priceless. We are learning to provide the safety, the modeling, the encouragement, the counseling, and the relaxed high expectations that develop additional leaders quickly.

MANY OTHERS

There are many other obvious types and examples of "key actions" which a leader can take to multiply the effects of his or her efforts. All will lead to the recruitment of additional forces and the enhancement of desired activity, including the building of one's own world-class community.

We have much to learn about this process, but the insights we have so far are valuable. I conjecture that if you and I as leaders actually correctly determine the "key actions" or the "nodal points" of our situations, and move on them we can indeed live every moment well.

We can take only actions that we enjoy taking, we can avoid fatigue and burn-out, we can retain sufficient leisure for rest, recreation, and enjoyment.

We can, at the same time, operate with ever-increasing effectiveness as leaders of an ever-increasing throng of other leaders who are leading other leaders who are constructing and developing world-class communities and, in the process, solving the key difficulties confronting the human race.

Who is in Charge of a Session?

I have heard discussions at workshops and have had the question raised in correspondence as to "Who is in charge of the session?" It has sometimes been proclaimed that "the client is in charge of the session." Various irresponsibilities on the part of counselors or poor results from counseling have sometimes been excused on that basis.

On the other hand, from the time of the early article "Who's In Charge?" we have held to a general position that each person is in charge of **everything**, as the only possible rational attitude for entities possessed of intelligence. Also people have applauded and admired "tough," demanding counseling which broke through difficulties for the client.

Who is really in charge of the session, the client or the counselor? I would say **both**.

If we look at the session process as a whole, I think we're bound to recognize that **two** (or more) intelligences being involved is the central feature of effective counseling. We've been emphasizing that the ineffectiveness of much past counseling was caused by the counselor having his or her attention on the counselor's distress instead of on the client's during the session. We now have a commitment, that has had fine results in the last three years, to end this ancient habit-pattern.

If two intelligences are involved in a process, can one intelligence be subordinate to the other and **only** carry out the thinking of the other person? I think not. It's true that a person **can**

Appeared in **Present Time** No. 65, October 1986.

THE LONGER VIEW

function as a helper to another person. It's true that one person can function under another person's direction. Any symphony player knows that the exquisite cooperation between a hundred people present in a good performance only comes when the directing is done by the director and individual players don't set their own tempo or interpretation. Nevertheless, the violin players are in charge of playing the violins, each one of them, and the trumpet player is in charge of playing his or her trumpet. The full intelligent in-chargeness of each person is required in this kind of relationship.

The same thing is true of the counseling relationship. It is an exquisite and extremely rewarding cooperation between two intelligences. Each one of the people is necessarily going to be in charge of the session if the session is to be optimally effective. The client is in complete charge of the session **from the client's point of view and in terms of the client's functions**. The counselor is in complete charge of the session **from the counselor's point of view and in terms of the counselor's functions**. Any idea that one should be subordinate to the other misses the fact that there are two distinct roles which have to be carried out here.

What are the specific roles of the counselor and of the client? What in-chargeness lies in each one's domain?

THE CLIENT

The client is in charge of anticipating and planning his or her role in the session; is in charge of combatting the three tendencies of patterns to confuse you, to persist, and to make you forget; is in charge of assembling and keeping in touch with written directions, frameworks, and commitments that have worked well; is in charge of thinking about what can be the most crucial factor for the client's re-emergence if it can be worked on successfully. The client is in charge of recalling and reviewing (before the session or at the beginning of it) the importance of **decision**, not necessarily decision following discharge but, more powerfully, decision preceding and amplifying discharge. The client is in charge of thinking about the particular counselor, and about what distress, if any, is likely to not be handled successfully by the particular counselor. The client can choose to work on distress that is likely to be handled successfully rather than be unrealistic and push a kind of distress at the particular counselor which he or she is unlikely to handle well and so weaken the relationship and accumulate disappointment.

It is the client's responsibility **to choose** to be a successful client as far as the client's own role will carry the day. The client is in charge of **trying** each direction the counselor offers at least a time or two **before** arguing or rehearsing the distress the direction is intended to contradict. The client is in charge of thinking or remembering that the counselor is another human being with complete goodness, power, and freedom of decision. The client is in charge of not writing the counselor off or "being disappointed" in him or her.

The client can properly keep in mind the possibility of exchanging roles, at least briefly, (or, if one is engaged in "training one's own counselor," for an extended series of times) in dealing with any of the counselor's difficulties.

The client is very much in charge of being on time, being courteous to the counselor, being appreciative, and, in reviewing the session after it is over, being sure to emphasize the positive aspects of the session, the counseling, and the counselor **before** making any "helpful" suggestions as to how they could have been better.

THE COUNSELOR

The counselor is in complete charge of coming to the session determined to take (and practiced in taking) his or her attention away from his or her own past distress (using the commitment against the "ancient habit pattern," or the commitment against lending a pattern one's own power or influence.)

THE LONGER VIEW

The counselor is in charge of reviewing his or her memories of the client and what he or she has heard about the client from other counselors or teachers. The counselor is in charge of coming to the session with a clear expectation of paying enough attention to the client to see the distress clearly, of thinking of all possible contradictions to the distress, and of helping to contradict it sufficiently to bring discharge by the client. The counselor is in charge of realizing that a good counselor thinks about the client not only for the one session but for the client's entire existence. The counselor not only thinks of what attitudes, directions, or commitments will bring discharge right then, but also which series of actions or perspectives will move the client toward continuing re-emergence. The counselor needs to think of the client from the perspective of the rest of the life of the client and plan on leaving the client with attitudes, commitments, directions, and relationships that will enhance the client's continued re-emergence after the session, towards having more sessions, and towards good work in later sessions.

The counselor is in charge of putting aside any other feelings in order to love the client deeply, depending, if necessary, on the theoretical assumptions about what any human being is like underneath the distress. With that unpatterned human being in mind, and loving that human being, the counselor's thinking will be enhanced. The counselor is in charge of having relaxed, but high, expectations of the client. The counselor assumes that **this client** has a full capacity to be the greatest thinker the world has ever known, and to function in the most loving and totally supportive way toward other human beings, the world of life, and the upward trend in the universe. The counselor assumes that the client has complete freedom to make decisions and carry them out, and that the client has an inherent sense of complete power which needs only to be challenged and uncovered for it to begin to operate.

The counselor is in charge of remembering and holding the seven attitudes toward the client of approval, delight, respect, confidence in and for the client, relaxed high expectations, commitment to the client, and love to and of the client.

The counselor is in charge of challenging any patterned attitudes **toward being a client** that have accumulated on a client.

I find, for example, that I often work at workshops with clients who, in the absence of effective counseling support, have worked out a routine of "running their own sessions" in an effort to make their counseling work without much support. They often, unawarely, rehearse their distress over and over thinking they are contradicting it.

Confronted by a good counselor they then will tend to make one of two kinds of mistakes. (1) Feeling that there is now support against their distress, they abandon the effort to contradict the distress themselves. This leaves the situation pretty much where it was previously when the client was trying to contradict the client's distresses alone. Again only one of the team is contributing. It is now the counselor alone trying to contradict the client's distresses, while the client rehearses the distress over and over. (2) The other tendency is for the embattled client, who has been trying to "counsel herself" because of lack of adequate participation by previous counselors, to stay in the rigid routine of "counseling herself" by arguing with every direction the counselor offers before trying it. In these cases I find it is part of my role as counselor to "retrain" the client to reassume the client's role by offering information about theory, by persuasion, by formulating good directions or commitments that define the client's contradiction to the distress. (Directions and commitments are, basically, tools for helping the client function well in the client's roles.)

A top-notch session will have **both** the client and the counselor contradicting the client's distress, the client in the client's roles and the counselor in the counselor's roles.

Who is in charge of the session? The client is in complete

THE LONGER VIEW

charge of the session. The counselor is in complete charge of the session. Each has completely distinct roles to play. When both sets of roles are well-played, then memorable sessions take place and re-emergence is rapid.

Cleaning Up Some Concepts

We have been emerging from confusion left upon us in our lives and our cultures by the long-time accumulation of distress patterns. We have been learning to resist the enforcement of that distress by the oppressive society and the resulting confusion caused by that. To assist this emergence and resistance we have occasionally proposed new concepts as a way of clarifying what we've observed and as a way of communicating with each other.

Some of these concepts have been very useful over a particular period, but in communication between Co-Counselors have tended to acquire patterned connotations that aren't helpful and generate additional confusion. Also new developments in the same area often bring greater clarity and make it possible to view the same phenomenon more broadly and from a better perspective than we did when we began using the original concept. Then the limited character of the original concept becomes an impediment to our broader view and the concept needs clarification, redefinition, or replacement.

"CONTROL PATTERNS"

One such concept is that of "control patterns." In first learning to counsel another person and assist that person to discharge, and in communicating this information between Co-Counselors, it seemed helpful to particularly notice the part of the patterns which interfered with discharging. These had accumulated on almost every one of our distresses from the social conditioning against discharge. Often these took the form of

Appeared in **Present Time** No. 63, April 1986.

certain physical manifestations. Clients would observably grip their fists, or bite their lips, or hook their feet against each other in a patterned effort to remain "controlled," to not discharge. When the counselor would ask the client to contradict this by ungripping fists, unbiting lips, unhooking legs or ankles, or by adopting a relaxed posture, more voluminous discharge would ensue. We came to speak of these particular manifestations of the total pattern as "control patterns." Since discharge was enhanced and the counseling was made more effective by the counselor noticing, naming, and contradicting these, the concept of "control patterns" seemed like a worthwhile development and a useful addition to the tools of the counselor.

As time went by, however, in counseling practice, it became noticeable that the concept "control pattern" had sometimes come to have a pejorative or "blaming" connotation. Any patterns of invalidation, scolding, or criticizing, which were part of the distress of the person acting as counselor, would sometimes seize on this concept and use it to criticize or poke fun at the client. "You've got a control pattern!" became a too-familiar cry of triumph from a dramatizing counselor as if he or she had just won a victory "over" the client. In practice such confused counselors sometimes manipulated their clients incessantly, justifying it by the tiny spurts of embarrassed laughter wrung from the uncomfortable client. The main thrust of re-emergence would become sidetracked by the counselor's dramatizations around the concept of "control patterns."

It's worthwhile to remind ourselves that any pattern is a very *total* phenomenon. The distress recording includes *everything* that went on at the time of the distress and at the times of the successive restimulated rehearsals of the original recording. To focus on only one, or a few, of the particular aspects of a distress recording which is gripping the client, and become preoccupied with it, is to dull ourselves to the tremendous opportunities for securing contradictions to the great variety of manifestations of the pattern. It's also good to remember and remind each other, that any client must be treated with respect, that the client is *not* the pattern. It is too easy to give the impression to a client who is fighting hard to get out of a distressed condition that the counselor is viewing the client as the pattern and is criticizing or rehearsing some kind of a superiority attitude at him or her.

I have not used the term "control pattern" (at least awarely) in my counseling for some time. It's true that I will seek the contradiction of a pattern in any aspect I can, including encouraging the client not to "hold on" to himself or herself in any physical way. I will ask a client to modify her facial expression, or use a tone of voice different than the content of the distress. I don't think, though, that to go on speaking of "control patterns" as if they were a separate phenomenon and with the term's apparent invitation to poor manners on the part of the counselor, is useful. I would suggest we consider dropping any preoccupation with, or frequent use of, the phrase.

"FROZEN NEEDS"

Another concept that certainly has been useful, and still is, is the concept of "frozen needs." To observe that clients would expend much effort in continuing, fruitless attempts to secure "parenting," or "nurturing," or "loving," or "approval" from the current environment was useful. To further observe that counselors committed to such a client would often attempt to furnish these in the hopes of securing discharge or at least making the client "feel better" and that doing this provided little re-emergence from the pattern and always had diminishing effectiveness, was an important step forward. We realized that if a need is present at the time of a distress recording, that need can be and often is recorded as part of the distress recording and will replace rational motivations during its restimulation in later periods or in its chronic operation, and this was a valuable understanding. We came up with the principle that "A frozen need cannot be met. It can only be discharged." This has certainly saved a lot of time and prevented wasted effort in Co-Counseling in the years since it has been circulated widely. I'm sure it will continue to do so.

Also, around this concept, however, there has crept in a kind of "blaming" or "critical" attitude on the part of some counselors. Clients have been told triumphantly, "That's just a frozen need of yours!", or "Quit rehearsing your frozen needs at me!" Such "triumphant criticism" has not improved the counseling climate or been helpful to clients.

I think a possible correction to this would be to realize clearly that the frozen need, although part of the pattern, is being held out by the client as a request for contradiction to the distress itself, and in order to secure discharge. Viewed in this manner, there is certainly no justification for having a critical or "blaming" attitude toward the client who is expressing the frozen need.

This does not mean that the counselor is now encouraged to try to fill the "frozen need," at least beyond the common technique of "over-filling" it (an initial massive, surprise contradiction to get the discharge started). There are techniques that have worked out well. Saying, "Goodbye forever to any hope of the parenting that I didn't get when I was little. I will have to be my own parent," and similar ways of contradicting the frozen need with an attitude of reality are still workable. But we need to recognize that the client was not being foolish in holding out the frozen need, but was holding it out, as in any dramatization, for the counselor's examination and in the hope that the counselor would recognize it as a call for help. Seeing the "frozen need" this way and carefully finding ways to contradict it and bring about its discharge should "clean up our act" a little bit in terms of our attitudes as counselors toward our clients.

The Successful Contradiction and Discharge of Heavy Fear
Helpful Hints for Experienced Clients

Many experienced Co-Counselors currently have made the transition from discharge of tears to confronting heavy fear. This sort of progression is natural and normal in the overall process, just as shaking follows tears in the discharge of any particular distress incident.

In most of our lives the distress and oppression have been heavy enough that a great majority of our distress begins on the level of "accepted loss," which needs to be discharged in tears. Only a few of us seem to be so fortunate that most of our distress never got lower than terror. I think by now the great preponderance of us experienced Co-Counselors (those with three to fifteen years experience) have begun our systematic re-emergence with a great deal of shedding of tears, and have persisted in this successfully over much of our time in Co-Counseling.

I still meet a few experienced Co-Counselors who are shedding a few new tears each session, which have accumulated because of their failure to break over into the fear discharge that they are subjectively ready for but have not objectively found the contradiction nor the effective counseling to begin. Most experienced Co-Counselors are currently, I think, shaking in their sessions, but many of them want to become more efficient and accelerate their re-emergence.

Effective techniques for discharging heavy fear efficiently are known and have been demonstrated at workshops and on videocassettes for some time. The overall contradiction to terror or

Appeared in **Present Time** No. 68, July 1987.

heavy fear is, of course, *safety*. What *is* safety for the particular client dealing with a particular terror varies widely.

One possible manifestation of safety is a reminder that the danger is usually not present in the session, but happened a long time ago. In some other cases the danger will not be present in the session but will only have to be faced in the future. (Even if the client has "terminal" cancer or AIDS, he or she is unlikely to die during the session and probably has a great deal of time still to live.)

Isolation is a crucial component of almost all terror, and to actually get the client to meet your relaxed, friendly gaze is often enough to bring discharge. Having the client hold you tight while you respond with equal pressure from your arms contradicts the isolation on the tactile or physical level.

The counselor can offer "guarantees" to the client which may allow the shaking to begin: "I promise you that I will not let the boogy-man get you during this session at all. You will be completely safe from him at least until the end of the session"; "I will go with you to meet your nemesis, and we will face him, her, or it together," for examples.

A very useful contradiction that I did not recognize until about a year ago is to express the fear or terror *cheerfully* and *enthusiastically* (as always, words may not be enough; it may require cheerful facial expressions and cheerful tone of voice). Just as deliberately exhibiting embarrassment brings laughter discharge because it contradicts the almost universal pseudo-dignity concealment which we have attached to our embarrassment patterns, so acting cheerful and enthusiastic about the feelings that horrify us leads to a short fuse of laughter and then easy continual shaking as long as the contradiction is continued. As always, of course, the counselor will do far more modeling of the tone of voice, the facial expression, and the enthusiastic, cheerful words than the client will be able to do, but the client will be discharging while the counselor models this over and over again with the apparent confident expectation each time that the client will do it also.

This technique works wondrously well, but it does require the counselor to step out of his or her own chronic terror in order to really furnish the expression and tone of voice that goes with the delighted sounds such as "Whee! I am terrified!! Oh joy! Oh joy!"

The client's own first creativity toward contradicting heavy fear often takes the form of reaching for the next lighter painful emotion and dramatizing that. This is perfectly valid. The discharge achieved in this way can often open the client to the other techniques in a good and useful way. Sometimes the client reaches for embarrassment. The counselor should enthusiastically help with this because if they can begin to laugh, especially on the subject connected with the heavy fear (such as in an embarrassed tone of voice, "Oh I'm so embarrassed to be so terrified"), the laughter will open the door to the shaking without the client even noticing that the shaking has begun.

More commonly, the client reaches for an anger dramatization. Most experienced counselors are already familiar with this. A great amount of so-called "discharging anger" has taken place which was not discharging anger at all, but which has helped generations of us to *act angry so that we could cry*. Oceans of tears have been shed in this way. (Also, pages of print have been used in explaining over and over that this is not *anger* discharge but a clever way to begin the discharge of *grief* by putting your attention on a lighter, contradictory kind of distress.)

This works just as well for heavy fear. Some useful model dramatizations of this kind are: "No more! I am not going to be intimidated any longer!" (with pounding of fist in palm, stabbing motions of finger, or stamping of foot as an accompaniment); "You're much too nice a person to act like that and I'm not going to allow it any more"; "From now on you're going to treat me with respect. Do you hear?"

In other words, it's possible to borrow a little anger and make a dramatizing ladder out of it to climb up out of the heavy fear far enough that the contradiction will allow the shaking to begin.

The cheerful celebrating of the heavy fear or terror is the best and most dependable technique I have found, however, and I heartily recommend that all experienced counselors begin experimenting with it. It is a little more demanding of effort and of stepping outside of his or her own chronic distress by the counselor than other techniques, but it is likely to get the client "really rolling" with fear discharge. Try it.

Make a Special Effort to Develop Working-Class Leaders

A sizable portion of the present members of the RC Communities are working-class in their present status and in their origins. The organization of the working-class liberation movement within Re-evaluation Counseling has not, however, kept pace. This is probably because other groups have, in the nature of their oppression, been left free to be more demanding of attention and help in getting organized than has the working class. Even though the working class is, in every sense, the most important group of people in Re-evaluation Counseling and in the world, we have, up until now, allowed various pressures to lead us to neglect its organization.

This is paralleled by the current disorganization of the working class in the wide world. In the great profiteering rip-off of the last decade, by the most greedy sections of international capital led by the Reagan administration and its supporters, working people have suffered drastic reductions in their incomes, living standards, security, and well-being. Women workers and Third World workers and colonial workers have had the most severe oppression, but the crucial organizations of the working class, the trade unions, are also suffering severe setbacks.

I think this will require that all of us, whatever our class backgrounds or our particular interests, take initiative toward the organization of working-class people. I ask all Reference People — Area Reference Persons, Regional Reference Persons, and International Liberation Reference Persons — to

Appeared in **Reference Point** No. 26, 1987.

begin finding and establishing working-class leaders on every level of responsibility.

In doing this myself, I have found that the title of "Apprentice" Liberation Working-Class Person seems to be much more easily accepted by potential working-class leaders than the title without the "Apprentice" prefix, probably because it doesn't seem like such a demanding and drastic challenge. So, if you can find individuals in any group who are working-class in their lives or outlook and are willing to take initiative and leadership, will you please appoint them Apprentice Working-Class Liberation Reference Persons on an Area level, on a neighborhood level, on a factory level, on a trade union level, on a Wygelian level. If you are a Regional Reference Person, you may make temporary appointments of Regional Working-Class Liberation Reference Persons whose job is to establish Area and other level people. (We plan no Regional bureaucracy in any section of the population; Regions will still simply have a Regional Reference Person as the only permanent fixture, at least in this historical period.)

The main job of each of these people is to organize support groups of working-class people, help them get established and set up leadership, and then set up Wygelian Working-Class *Leaders'* Groups to bring together the leaders of the support groups and any other working-class leaders that come forward. Please make it a responsibility that anyone named an Apprentice Reference Person or leader of a support group will have their name, address, and phone number mailed to me in Seattle for inclusion on the roster of working-class leaders in our computer so that we can establish better communication with them and between them.

(The organization of trade unionists is proceeding well, and all trade union members will receive a warm welcome, but we don't want to limit the organization of the working class to trade unionists, because at present only about 10% of the working class is affiliated with unions.)

I will very much appreciate your attention to seeing that this receives a high priority in our organizing. When so many smaller sections of the population are developing programs and good policies within RC, we cannot afford to neglect the majority of our members, and our greatest source of strength.

Wygelian Leading of RC Areas

The Wygelian Leaders' Group developed out of our efforts to reach the different sections of the population adequately and enhance the development of leadership. It has correctly been estimated to be a major development in both leadership and in organization. It is being used widely and is reaching many different sections of the population. Even international conferences of particular groups of RC leaders are being organized in roughly the same way.

APPLY WITHIN RC

We have been slow, however, to realize and implement its application to leadership *within the RC Community itself*. In many of our Areas, we are still caught up in various semi-workable rigidities. A Reference Committee, for example, is treated as if it were the old-style "executive committee" that we have become used to in the functioning of the society around us. Area Reference Persons are often regarded as "executive officers" leading and pushing members of the Area as if the Area were a business corporation or a church sodality or a sports club. The development of *all* RCers into leadership is still inhibited by the ways that some Areas continue to function.

It is true that the development of the Leadership Functions Chart and its use (where it has been used) have clarified the many different leadership functions that need to be filled by many different leaders, but there's still a tendency for the ARP or the Alternate ARP to hold (and feel burdened by) an unduly large number of these functions.

Appeared in **Reference Point** No. 26, 1987.

THE LONGER VIEW

I think it is time to review and revise our leadership operations in our Areas, Sub-Areas, *and incipient Areas* of our Community.

I propose that every Community where there are a number of RCers calls an occasional meeting of everyone who has taken even a little responsibility for the functioning of RC in that location, and other RCers who are willing, upon being asked, to take even a little leadership and responsibility for the development of RC and that this meeting function on the Wygelian leaders' agenda.

THE AGENDA

News and goods as people come in.

First point: each person reports on what they have been doing in the recent period which has contributed to the development of the RC Community. This is without comment or discussion, just each person being listened to in turn.

Second point: each person has a turn sharing information and opinions he or she has about the situation confronting the development of RC in the neighborhood. This can include: what opportunities exist, any possible difficulties, what populations are available, what organizations exist in which RC could become a functioning tool, and any other information or opinions which people have.

Third point: each person has a turn saying what he or she intends to do in the next period to contribute to the growth and development of the Community.

On these first three points, the best counselor, the most experienced leader, who is present as a Consultant to the group, participates and has a turn. On the fourth point, the Consultant becomes a counselor. If the Consultant is to be counseled, it will be at another time, not during this meeting.

Fourth point: each person is asked, in turn, where he or she will be having difficulty in carrying out his or her plans and proposals as a leader. Each then receives the best demonstration counseling session the Consultant is able to give. When possible, other counselors will commit themselves to follow up the demonstration with persistent counseling of the person in the same difficulty. When each person has had a turn at being counseled by the Consultant, the meeting simply concludes with a circle in which each person says what he or she liked best about the meeting.

These meetings can take place in very small Communities, where there is only one teacher or potential teacher, and only a few others interested. Such a small meeting will serve useful purposes. As the group becomes larger, but not yet large enough to qualify as an Organized Area (that is, it does not yet have thirty or more active Co-Counselors, two or more teachers, and one person able and willing to become Area Reference Person), such occasional meetings will constitute all the leadership body there is. The teachers, if there is more than one, will confer and designate which of these acts as the custodian of Outreach funds (The Re-evaluation Foundation treats every incipient Area as if it's already an Area, each one maintaining its own store of Outreach funds and its own account with the Foundation), but all other leadership functions will be served by the occasional Wygelian Leaders' Group meeting.

Meetings are called only when there is something to meet about. They can be called on the request of any member or the initiative of the person chosen as Convener, or at the request of the person who has been invited to be the Consultant.

When the group has become large enough to qualify as an Organized Area, and wishes to, there should be one meeting of all RCers to set themselves up as an Organized Area. The key step here is to choose one person to be the Area Reference Person and another to be the Alternate Area Reference Person.

It needs to be made very clear at this point that the Area Ref-

THE LONGER VIEW

erence Person is only one of many leaders, is just the one who takes on certain specific functions that are required by the Guidelines. The Area Reference Person does not become the sole leader, does not become the dominator or dictator or work horse of the Area, but simply carries out the following functions:

(1) Participate in the certification and decertification of teachers.

(2) Approve of the scheduling of any Area workshops that draw more than one teacher's students.

(3) Approve of printed material, which purports to represent Re-evaluation Counseling, that goes out on an Area level. (If such material goes out more widely than one Area, it must have the approval of the International Reference Person.)

(4) Give the final approval to suggested uses of Area Outreach funds, through signing grant applications to the Foundation if in the United States, or by taking it out of the sugar bowl or bank account where Area Outreach funds are kept in other countries.

(5) Make an occasional decision for the Community on a rare occasion when a decision needs to be made more quickly than consensus can be reached.

(6) The Area Reference Person will approve applications to Regional or International workshops. This is the same function that a teacher performs outside of an organized Area.

These are minor chores and do not take a great deal of time on the part of the Area Reference Person at all. It is an honor to be an Area Reference Person, but it's no huge job. Most Area Reference People also teach and organize and lead and set up support groups and do other things because they enjoy leading and desire the growth of the Re-evaluation Counseling Community, but all these other functions devolve upon every person who is or aspires to be a leader of RC. Everyone who attends the Wygelian Leaders' Groups meeting, which constitutes the basic leadership body of an Area, is fully qualified to undertake any and all of them.

The Guidelines say, "The basic job of the Area Reference Person is to think about the Area as a whole and to exercise judgment on which activities are consistent with Re-evaluation Counseling theory and policy." In this period we want to release much more individual initiative and so we invite all leaders to participate in this. Consensus on such matters develops easily out of the Wygelian Leaders' Groups meetings.

Only if unyielding controversy develops and persists will the Area Reference Person have to make a final decision.

Actually, of course, since the 1985 World Conference, each experienced Co-Counselor is urged to build and lead a world-class community around his or her individual leadership. The sharing and conferring offered by the Wygelian Leaders' Group meeting structure makes this easy to develop.

What Does "Policy" Mean in RC?

Jaap Sanders of Amsterdam asked me to try to define what "policy" in RC means. The question arose when a leader at a workshop referred to her very firm opinion about some matter as "policy" and someone who disagreed with her felt that she was insisting that the matter was not open for discussion.

"Policy" in RC is a little different than it has been in most organizations. It's a little more difficult to define, but I think it's also a little closer to a rational concept.

On the one hand, our efforts and our activities are much more fruitful and effective if the members of the Re-evaluation Counseling Communities are in agreement with each other and are working consistently towards the same goals. On the other hand, we cherish flexible thinking and freedom of initiative. We are theoretically agreed that no future situation can be exactly anticipated ahead of time and that a person needs to be free to adjust and modify any plans in the light of the eventualities that actually turn up. In an attempt to express this we've called our basic agreements "Guidelines" instead of "laws" or "by-laws" or "constitutions." We've clearly agreed that *any* policy is a draft policy, to be periodically reviewed and modified in the light of accumulated experience.

On the other hand, we have recognized that agreements that *are* entered into need to be kept. People joining the Community as new members will be expected to keep the agreements that were established by the other members and expressed in the Guidelines. Even though the new member did not participate

Appeared in **Present Time** No. 67, April 1987.

in the framing of the Guidelines and policy, the new member's joining the Community implies that he or she is expected to follow the Guidelines and policies. If any Co-Counselor feels a change is needed he or she can use the procedures for change set out in the agreements themselves. In terms of the Guidelines there are two:

> (1) To convince the International Reference Person to suspend or change a portion of the Guidelines prior to the next World Conference. He is granted authority to do this by the Guidelines themselves.
>
> (2) To propose and secure the adoption of a change in these Guidelines at the next World Conference itself.

Since we encourage all RCers to think about and try to reach rational positions on all issues confronting humanity—including the most controversial (Guidelines, Proposal 4)—our attempts to evolve correct policies are reaching farther and farther into more and more fields of human activity and into more and more detailed applications. A considerable number of new draft policy statements are drawn up each year for various groups of RCers who share some commonality, either ethnic, racial, gender, occupational, or "oppressional." The existing draft policies are discussed regularly and have revisions proposed, agreed upon, and published.

In essence none of these policy statements (other than those adopted at the World Conference) are "binding" on anyone. They are expressions of the clearest agreements that the people who tackled thinking about these areas were so far able to reach. In the wide-world sense of the term "policy" the numerous women's policy statements, men's policy statements, blacks' policy statements, young people's policy statements, and so on, are not policies of the RC Community as a whole. They are the best proposed policies that people who have paid attention to the topic have been able to come up with, so far. These are honored by the rest of us by publication and circulation as worthwhile endeavors. Critical responses to them are always desired and expected and it is out of these responses that the periodic revisions of these "policy statements" take place.

In practice, this mode of thinking and discussion and publication has worked so well that the great majority of RCers probably think of the policy statements printed in **Present Time** for particular groups as their own and, in some vague sense, actually "binding" on them. Generally these statements are responded to with considerable enthusiasm by the people who read them. In RC there exists a very high degree of not only agreement, but even enthusiasm for the wide reaching "draft policy statements" that we have in print. The casual observer might think that we have a thoroughly controlled and highly managed intellectual climate. This, however, is only the appearance. All of these draft statements are the opinions of the individuals in the groups that draw them up.

In terms of publication the Area Reference Person is responsible to check and make certain, as far as she or he can, that any publication on the Area level that purports to represent RC is not in conflict with our fundamental literature or the basic areas of agreement expressed in the Guidelines. Anything published more widely than an Area requires the approval of the International Reference Person before it can purport to publicly represent an RC position. The International Reference Person is charged with the responsibility of not okaying such publication unless it is consistent with our fundamental literature and the agreements that we have made in our Guidelines.

This has, in general, been carried out well. There have been some violations, of course. Messes have occurred and had to be cleaned up and the torturous process of clarifying confusions once they are engendered by a contradictory policy being published as RC has wasted some of our time, but, overall, the record is good.

Shouldn't Good Language Always Be Creative?

The other day during a client's session the client and myself were struggling to communicate to each other about her situation. I was trying (probably wrongly) to suggest formulations or words that might express for the client exactly what she was trying to say. Suddenly she came up with a sentence that perfectly described the situation for herself and one that I could hear well also. I felt a great surge of communication. It eliminated the temporary difficulties between us and ended the danger of my speaking "for" her.

Following my satisfaction at hearing the situation described so clearly, I had a flash of understanding about language that was different than any I had previously had. It may not be new to any of you readers, but it was new and important to me.

THE "RIGHT" WORD

I had been "educated" to think that there was always one exactly right way of expressing any particular idea, any particular thought, and that within that context the problem was largely one of "finding the right words." I had grown up on a farm speaking a fairly limited dialect of U.S. English. In the ninth grade I attended the first school that had any proper equipment. I became very enamored of the great Webster's Dictionary. Sometimes the teacher would allow me to take it to my desk if I finished my work early. I read through much of the dictionary just delighting in the enormous number of words there and to some extent memorizing them.

Appeared in **Present Time** No. 66, January 1987.

(Unfortunately, I had never been taught to interpret the marks which indicated pronunciation so I usually invented my own pronunciation for the ones I memorized. I have ever since embarrassed myself regularly by mis-pronouncing words for which my audience knew the correct pronunciation. That embarrassment has lessened somewhat in recent years. I've discovered that many English words are pronounced differently in different English-speaking countries. If I just look confident when I attempt my own uninformed pronunciation, people in England will assume it's a U.S. pronunciation, and people in the U.S. will assume that I've "picked up" an English pronunciation. As I say, the embarrassment has lessened.)

I did accept the attitude in these school years that to communicate well required finding the "right words" or the "right word." For a long time I sought to improve my communication by finding a larger stock of words and wider array of synonyms. I have felt fortunate for many years that I have learned at least some varieties of English, a language of a great many words and a great many synonyms. I didn't realize the great difference between languages in this respect until some of my own books began to be translated into the languages of the smaller countries of Europe. The translators often begged me to use "standard English," not only because my dialect was difficult, but because I was using a wide array of synonyms. The translators would expostulate with me that English often had twenty synonyms for a particular word but their language had only two or three and it made their task of translation difficult if I used less common English words.

CREATIVE EXPRESSION

What I realized in that flash after my client's beautiful formulation of her thinking, however, was that really human use of language must at all times be creative. I finally saw that repeating the "right word" is almost always done by a pattern. It may be a broad chronic pattern which uses "proper English," for example, or it may be a limited narrow pattern, which repeats the same phrase over and over on all occasions, but it will be patterned and less than intelligent in either case. Using language well will mean to reach for a *new* set of words with a *new* modifying effect upon each other in the sentence or paragraph or article or talk, that communicates the whole idea frankly and well. The words and phrases can and do modify each other in the context in which they are used and this mutual influence gives to the whole a distinctly different and inflective meaning than the words and the phrases would have had by themselves or in other contexts.

To achieve a fine piece of communication once in a well-thought out lecture or article or conversation or poem certainly deserves respect and, sometimes, repetition. There is nothing wrong in quoting and repeating an excellent formulation. We all intuitively recognize this in our enjoyment of certain pieces of poetry. We quote them correctly or read them accurately when we can.

FREE OUR USE OF LANGUAGE

As we are communicating with each other, however, as we are thinking afresh, we must also turn our language loose to be continually creative. Every word we use reflects on and modifies its neighbors; and not only from the present. It has connotations from past use of the word in poems or other masterpieces of thought and literature. There may be a "right word" but only in this particular context. It will not be "right" for a similar communication at a later time. If we think it is (as I had been educated to think) we will be slipping into a pattern and failing to communicate at our best.

I think that I have sometimes been intuitively creative in the past. I have sometimes spoken well. People have enjoyed my use of language. I have written a poem or two which expressed an important idea creatively. I think, however, that I have been hampered and inhibited in doing this all the time or doing this at my best by the unaware notion that I had accepted from my early education that there was always a "right word" or a "right way of saying things." I was dragging along an unaware assumption that I would necessarily use the same words that Abraham Lincoln did if *I* were to give the Gettysburg address, that I would fall short of Shakespeare's eloquence if I did not use his identical words in my treatment of a subject which he had already treated in a sonnet or a passage in a play.

I would like to hear your thinking about this. How can we encourage each other to master the use of language by being continually creative, continually flexible, not only in our choice of words but in our tones of voice and our vocal inflections and the expressions on our faces as we speak? How can we use cadence, loudness, pitch, and all the other characteristics which can be impressed on language to make our use of language and our communication be eloquently fresh?

Counseling Owning-Class People Well
(An Introduction to Nancy Kline's Article, "Transcending Owning-Class Distress")

For the last few months I have been challenging a number of individual leaders in RC Communities who have owning-class backgrounds to begin to contradict and discharge some of the more "comfortable" patterns which the oppression of owning-class people, particularly as children, has left upon them. These are patterns which are often resented by non-owning-class people, but because they are contradictory to the patterns imposed on working-class people, are sometimes emulated by middle-class individuals and working-class individuals. They have begun to hold back the growth of the RC Communities, and the recruitment of large numbers of working-class people into them, because of the resentment often felt toward these patterns.

Among these patterns are a kind of arrogance, condescension, "taking over," the assumption that what is good for the owning-class individual is automatically good for everybody, and seeing the main issue in progress to be reaching of the "unenlightened" owning-class people by the "enlightened" owning-class individuals. I would suggest that just as any rational society will be class-less, that is, everyone who works manually will also work intellectually and will manage and will own the means of production, so the job of owning-class leaders in RC (and we have a number of them and they have done some excellent leading) is primarily to bring the working class *into* RC and into *leadership* of RC in large numbers and that if this is neglected, all the other good things they are doing are largely ineffective.

Appeared in **Present Time** No. 65, October 1986.

THE LONGER VIEW

Below are some thinking and some actions in response to these challenges by our cherished Nancy Kline. I think you will find her thinking very interesting, certainly if you are owning-class, and I think even if you are working-class-raised-poor, as are the majority of us.

Questions and Replies

Cleaning Up Distress Completely

Dear Harvey,

I went to Judy Lazarus Yellon's workshop on incest near Seattle about a month ago. There was something she kept saying clearly, with no hesitation and over and over again — that was how one can clean up an incident of distress. She talked very matter-of-factly about how she'd cleaned up incidents. Somewhere in the workshop I really internalized the reality of being able to clean up an incident. She spoke so clearly and was so sure about how she had accomplished these feats! I think somewhere in my Co-Counseling career I had forgotten about the fantastic ability to get rid of all the distress around an incident. Maybe I never really accepted or understood that if I pulled the patterns, distresses, or whatevers up by the roots, there would be nothing left to be restimulated. Wherever I've been, I'm sure excited about it now. And I'd be extremely pleased if you'd take time to pen something to me and other Co-Counselors who are thirsty for a reminder about this quencher (what was that?). Anyhow, I'd like to hear or read some inspiration from you. I'm quite excited. One thing I appreciated that Judy said was that one has to get their counselor to remind them in their session to stick with cleaning up the distresses rather than working on something else.

Rachel Noble
Portland, Oregon, USA

Dear Rachel,

This was a very important question for us in the very early days of RC. Could a client's distress be completely eliminated or could it only be alleviated? As we evolved the concept of the distress *recording* the question re-phrased itself. Could a distress

Appeared in **Present Time** No. 67, April 1987.

THE LONGER VIEW

recording be completely erased or would there always remain some trace or residue of it, modifying in at least a slight degree the client's behavior, feelings, and "thoughts"?

The changes we were achieving (when this early, primitive counseling "worked") were so exciting that we were motivated to continue in any case, but as we early Co-Counselors made decisive gains the longing quickly appeared in all of us to be "completely free," to be completely rational, to have no distress recordings or rigidities at all.

Fortunately, we had (or took) time in those days to pursue questions like that. Co-Counseling sessions were two or three hours each way, often on successive days. My one-way, paying clients never had sessions shorter than two hours, and four-and six-hour sessions were common. (I once stayed with a man who came in for an interview for fourteen hours of very heavy grief discharge.) Demonstrations in classes sometimes began at 7:30 PM and ended at 3:00 AM.

We pursued single areas of distress in our Co-Counseling, also. Once I began crying about the death of my older brother, I stayed with it (or came back to it) for at least two hundred hours of hard crying, before the shaking began. I had a pact with my counselors that they would bring me back to that topic, no matter what else I had to work on in between times.

This kind of persistence was what led to the discovery of the "natural order" of discharging. Although it may be obscured by particular volumes or characteristics of the distress in any individual case, every human follows a fundamental order of discharging, to whatever extent he or she can. Once the person can begin crying, he or she will continue crying (as long as the safety, support, and contradiction permit) until the tears are all discharged, or nearly so. Then, if there is safety, support, and contradiction to the exposed heavy fear, the person will begin to shake (tremble). When the trembling is done, laughter ensues. With this laughter exhausted, the "righteous" vocaliza—

tions and "decisive" physical movements begin. These give way to laughter of a slightly different quality, and this to reluctant talk, then eager talk, then a little laughter, and, finally, the evaporation of the memory or topic *as a distress memory*. (It can still be recalled if asked for as information.) The yawning, which indicates the discharge of the physical part of the distress, appears erratically in the midst of the emotional discharge or, sometimes, for long periods by itself. It tends to be more common later, rather than earlier, in the process.

We checked on this phenomenon thoroughly. There is no question, as far as I am concerned, but that the effects of any particular distress *can be erased completely*.

The level of persistence typical of most Co-Counseling in our present Communities will not, however, *clean up* distresses. Such un-rigorous Co-Counseling has brought, and does bring, lots of benefits to the participants, and Co-Counselors seem willing to settle for these (perhaps for lack of modeling of the other). I have only been able to demonstrate the cleaning up of a distress at a workshop on one occasion (**Present Time** No. 46, pp. 21-22) because of time restraints.

Pretense can certainly raise its unlovely head around this. After this workshop demonstration I received many reports by mail and phone that "we have cleaned up an incident." Most, at least, of these were obvious agreements between the client and counselor to pretend to have done so, to fill some kind of a frozen need for recognition, excitement, or "keeping up with the Joneses."

To clean up an incident requires real commitment to sticking with it. The client needs to agree ahead of time, but once the process is begun, the persistence must be furnished by the counselor. The client will feel enormous pulls to discharge on other, more "urgent" topics, and will sometimes have to do so for a while before the counselor can bring his or her attention back to the committed topic or incident.

THE LONGER VIEW

(You are melting a hole down through a glacier and the surrounding ice becomes much easier to reach than the bottom of the hole as the hole gets deeper, and also has a tendency to melt and run into your hole.)

It is the counselor's responsibility to bring the client back, bring the client back, bring the client back to the agreed-upon area.

The counselor can easily allow himself or herself to be re-stimulated or rationalize away from the commitment to persistence, as unfamiliar kinds of discharge appear. (The only time I ever demonstrated counseling through *boredom* at an International workshop, half the workshop was leaving the meeting or signaling me to stop before we were half through.)

If the counselor furnishes the persistence and good counseling (1. Pay enough attention to the client to see clearly what the distresses are. 2. Think of all possible ways to contradict that distress. 3. Contradict the distress *sufficiently*. The client will always discharge.) any particular distress incident or related series of incidents *can be cleaned up*. It may take many, many sessions, but it can be done. Even a chronic pattern can be erased completely, and it has been done.

Can an individual clean up *all* of his or her distress and re-emerge completely? I see no unsolvable reason why not, and I intend to do so.

It has not yet been done, however. Certain difficulties have appeared for those of us who have worked hardest at this. One is that our attention has been pulled hard to doing something about the state of the world before it blows up, rather than concentrate on our own re-emergence. Another is an unexpectedly heavy tendency on the part of our counselors to "turn client" in our sessions, at least to the extent of not really thinking about us. This has not yet been solved, although I am reasonably sure it is explained as the "ancient habit pattern" being lured by the reality or at least the reputation of our having so much free attention that our counselors find it hard to resist forcing themselves upon us as clients.

I think these, and other, difficulties will be solved, however. In the last short period I have been able to be with the same group of people consistently for the first time in years, and I am seeing some possibilities of getting *complete re-emergence* under way once more.

Harvey

"Away From Distress" Doesn't Mean Repressing Discharge

Dear Harvey,

I think there is quite a lot of confusion within the Communities about just how to counsel with attention away from distress. It seems that some counsellors insist that clients focus solely on the beauty of the world and not be permitted to voice any of their unpleasant, "bad" thoughts. Whilst I know that working in this way can bring copious discharge for some people from a position of feeling good and knowing the reality of the world, I think that for many people it is inappropriate not to allow them to say how hard things have been. It silences some clients and can leave them with a sense of futility and frustration. (It may, of course, leave the counsellor feeling comfortable as they have not had to listen to the client's pain.) With some types of hurt experience where there is an extra, deep layer of denial and silence imposed (incest, for example) it is essential that the client be allowed to talk, tell the story, and have a sense of being heard. Of course, it is quite correct to ensure attention is kept in the present, safe reality and not allow clients to stay stuck with lots of "bad" feelings. But to not allow complete expression of incidents of hurt I believe can leave unfinished business, hopelessness, and a further pull to rehearse distress in order to get someone to pay attention to us.

For some clients, telling details and discharging about how they feel suicidal is working with attention away from distress, as paying attention to the distress would be to die.

The counsellors that work with attention away from distress successfully, seem to manage to combine irreverence and a sense of fun with gentleness and compassion — truly communicating their understanding of the client.

Appeared in **Present Time** No. 62, January 1986.

THE LONGER VIEW

I have seen counsellors "mock" or exaggerate a pattern and, whilst I've seen this practised effectively in demonstrations by experienced counsellors, I see many who forget that there is a whole load of painful emotion behind the pattern. Many of us have been humiliated and teased in the past and this can just serve to restimulate and is basically disrespectful. It's fine to be tough, creative, and resourceful when counselling, but we must remember that we are privileged to be assisting another human being and must work with an attitude of love and respect.

I would like to see more clarification of this in workshops, especially communicated to teachers and leaders, so they can then disseminate the information. Part of the oppression of mental health system survivors, which I believe includes all of us, is that discharge is severely interrupted, should it be seen as anything outside of "normal." The person is led to believe they are ill, or "mad," or, in RC, "too deeply distressed."

I believe that some of us have internalised this so much that we find it hard to accept or remember the need for heavy discharge. Possibly there are other factors operating as well. Because of unawareness of how severely this oppression operates, I think it is important especially at workshops and classes to state clearly that it is right and correct for humans to discharge from beginning to end if necessary. Maybe for some people it would be necessary to clarify the difference between discharge and dramatisation, or disruption may occur. I appreciate that lots of noisy discharge would interrupt a time when information was being given. It may be appropriate for people to go discharge elsewhere for a while with the attention of a counsellor. I think the important point is the making visible (giving permission) of it being fine to discharge. Shaking, crying, trembling, and laughter make a workshop a wonderfully safe and inspiring place to be. We need to model in our workshops and classes something of how our world will be when people are freed of the need to hide away their tears and trembling. In order to contradict the controls that keep discharge inhibited, people need to know it's okay again and again.

Sue Lemon
Merseyside, England

"Away From Distress" Doesn't Mean Repressing Discharge

Dear Sue,

Thanks for your long and interesting letter. On what you are saying about the need for clear application of the attention away from distress, I agree with you entirely, and you say it very well. We have tried to clarify this over and over again in workshops, and the fact that it doesn't get communicated well is, I guess, just an example of the fact that patterns do interfere with and substitute for communication, whenever there is any leeway allowed them. All breakthrough notions in counseling seem to be miscommunicated a lot at first, and then gradually become clarified. I think I will print this portion of your letter in the January **Present Time**, perhaps with my approving answer as a contribution to clarification.

Harvey

The Meaning of Contradiction

Dear Harvey,

I took my fundamentals class about a year ago, and since then I've been reading as much literature as I could get my hands on. I'm in an ongoing class now, and I've recently started assistant teaching a fundamentals class. RC has become a major part of my life and the theory is something I'd like to share with the world.

There is one thing, however, that has confused me ever since I first read about the basics of RC. That is the word "contradiction." I have never gotten a satisfying answer from anyone when I asked for a definition. I was only given more examples of "contradictions." I looked the word up in the dictionary, but that did not help. So, I amassed as many examples of "contradictions" as I could, and I moved on.

When I agreed to assistant teach, the confusion about the word re-surfaced because I now had to communicate this important concept which I was unclear about myself.

My problem is that the word does not adequately describe what I say to my clients and yet they discharge and they tell me I'm a good counselor. From my not receiving a good definition early on and from recent talks with my fellow Co-Counselors, I suspect that others are confused about this word too.

Recently, I began reading a book about a "certain German scholar living in England" because I was curious about classism and wide world changing. In my reading, up popped this word, "contradiction"! But the author was very clear to provide the information that in Marxian and

Appeared in **Present Time** No. 63, April 1986.

85

THE LONGER VIEW

earlier Hegelian philosophy the word had a precise meaning that could lead to confusion if one didn't know this. That sounded familiar! It seemed to me that everyone in RC was trying to re-define the word "contradiction" to fit "what-they-did-as-counselor," instead of finding a word that really did fit.

The author of this book defined Marxian contradictions as "inner pressures and stresses" which brought about development, social transformation and metamorphosis, transition from one form to another. This definition of "pressure and stress" seemed a more accurate way of looking at what a counselor does to a pattern than my mental dictionary definition of contradiction as an opposite or denial. I also noticed a nice metaphorical relationship between an RC session and Marxian social development. In both a session and society "stresses and pressures" — i.e., Marxian contradictions — bring about transformation. Discharge could be seen as an outward manifestation of internal transformation. Is that where "contradiction" came from?

As counselor, I've tried thinking in terms of "pressuring," "stressing," "pushing," "jiggling" the pattern, and I've felt more clear and effective. The word "contradict" seems to carry too much negative meaning like "denial," "oppose," and "inconsistent." "Contradiction" seems to make me think in terms of "diametrically opposing" a pattern and that doesn't leave much room for often-needed sneaking up and surprising the pattern with a hit on its flanks or a poke from underneath or a kick from the back. Or sometimes it's even effective, as you know, to go along with the pattern and outdo it. Now, I can contort my mind and call that a "contradiction" or "diametrical opposition" and maybe in some ways it is, but there's got to be a better word. (I'm beginning to sound like I'm from the Society to Ban the Word "Contradiction.")

What do you think of all this? Has this already been discussed? My ideas seem to have helped a few other people. Does it make sense to you?

Meanwhile, it's fun to write to you.

Tom Boulet
San Diego, California, USA

Dear Tom,

Thanks for your letter. Your questions around the word "contradiction" are interesting.

We have frequently had to take an existing word in the English language and re-define it for our use in RC because many of the concepts we're dealing with have never been dealt with in the language before. "Counseling" itself, when we began, had the most common meaning of giving advice, and in the thirty-five years since we began using it in another way, the other meaning has spread till many other groups think of counseling as different than advice-giving.

A clearer definition of the way we use the word might help. A possible one is "any action which illuminates the pattern as being a pattern, as being non-reality." In other words, that "a contradiction exposes the pattern's insidious claim to be reality, or to be present-time reality." This fits what we've said earlier, that whenever a pattern can be seen to be a pattern, discharge ensues.

What do you think of that? Does it help?

Harvey

When to Decide Not to Be Restimulated?

Beste Harvey,

Een aantal maanden geleden besloot ik je te schrijven over een onderwerp wat mij al een hele tijd bezig houd, nu pas kan ik de tijd vinden om dit te doen. Het gaat om het principe "Je kan kiezen om niet gerestimuleerd te worden." "Blik gericht op de goede werkelijkheid enz." Ik vind dit een zeer juiste levenshouding en inderdaad een garantie tot uren ontlading. Er is echter een probleem wat ik je graag wil voorleggen.

Om bewust te zijn, dat je gerestimuleerd bent moet je het eerst onderkennen en vervolgens erkennen. Dan kan pas kan je besluiten om het niet te doen. Vaak is de kern van systematische onderdrukking, dat de onderdrukte niet meer "weet en herkend, dat hij/zij onderdrukt is." Immers bevrijding begint daar waar je inzicht krijgt in je eigen onderdrukking.

Vaak maak ik mee, dat counselors denken, dat ze niet gerestimuleerd zijn en dat ook beweren, terwijl ze midden in hun pijn zitten. Ik merk, dat dit weinig effecktief is. De samenwerking of kommunikatie wat degene beoogd werkt niet, zij/hij raakt hierdoor in de war en meestal (afhankelijk van haar/zijn pijn) voelt hij/zij zich schuldig of raakt verstrikt verstrikt in haar/zijn specifieke geinternaliseerde onderdrukking en komt zo alleen maar verder van huis.

Ik zou willen vragen of jij hier jouw gedachte over willen laten gaan. Ik pleit ook, dat de nieuwe inzichten niet te pas en e onpas gepropageerd worden, want het werkt niet onder alle omstandigheden. Wel is het zo, dat je zaken moet proberen, de mankementen kom je dan tegen, om ze te kunnen korrigeren.

Ik verheug me op je antwoord. Is dit misschien iets voor **Present**

Appeared in **Present Time** No. 64, July 1986.

THE LONGER VIEW

Time? *Ik zou het leuk vinden om gedachten en ervaringen van anderen hierover te horen. Zou het mogelijk zijn om deze Nederlandstalige brief in de PT op te nemen. Het is leuk om verschillende talen in het blad te zien.*

Veel liefs en groeten,
OEI, Ien Siang
Hengelo, Nederland

Dear Harvey,

Months ago I decide to write you about an issue that occupied my thinking. It is the idea "to choose not to be restimulated" and "be in the benign reality." I think this is a good and valuable attitude, that will guarantee hours of discharge, which is just what must happen. Yet there is some little problem here I want to discuss with you.

To be aware that you are restimulated, you must know this and want to admit it. Then you can decide not to be restimulated. Often the heart of the systematic oppression is that the oppressed is not aware or does not identify the situation as "oppression." You should know first and admit that you are oppressed before you begin to free yourself of it.

Often in practice I see RCers think they are not restimulated and say they are not, while they are restimulated completely and act in the middle of their hurt. It then does not work. The communication or working relation that the person is trying to manage does not work, they become frustrated, feel guilty and bad about themselves (exactly how depends on the oppression that they have gotten), the internalised oppression runs, and people get lost.

I want your opinion about this phenomenon. Often people are so enthusiastic about the new frontiers that they want to share with others and begin to propagate it; often this new idea is not working under all circumstances. But on the other side, it is better to make mistakes than to do nothing. You then have the opportunity to correct them.

I look forward to your thinking on this issue. Is this something that can be published in the next **Present Time?** I like to know also what *experiences others have with this subject and want to hear some of the thinking. Is it possible to print both the Dutch and English letter from me? It is great to see* **Present Time** *multilinguistic.*

Oei, Ien Siang
Hengelo, The Netherlands

Dear Ien,

I am delighted to have your letter and thank you for taking the trouble to send the English translation as well as the Dutch. I think your suggestion to have the question and my answer in **Present Time** would be a good one.

The problem, I think, lies in your sentence "that to be aware that you are restimulated you must know this and want to admit it. Then you can decide not to be restimulated." I think this is the unworkable approach. One can understand the phenomenon of restimulation and decide not to be restimulated ahead of time, and make this decision over and over again. This is what works. To wait until you are restimulated, and having difficulty in thinking, in order to make the decision is very, very difficult. It is worth doing, but both on reclaiming power and on keeping one's attention out of distress and refusing to be restimulated, the decision is made effectively when one is thinking clearly. And this is the time to do it, rather than expect that one can pull oneself out by oneself, or at least do it very well, once the difficulty is in progress.

Harvey

Staying Human Through Deep Tragedy

Dear Harvey,

On January 7th my son, F—, ten years old, died in an awful way. He and his twelve-year-old sister (my daughter) N— were staying with his father for a few days; he lives elsewhere. There was a fire in the house. N— escaped in an heroic way by the roof, but F— could not get out of the house; nobody could get into the house to rescue him. He was choked and had burns and charred feet when they got him out of the house.

And here I am: mother of a beautiful, lovable daughter and mother of a beautiful, lovable son, who is as dead as a stone.

I wanted to tell you about F—. He was a wonderful young person who never accepted any oppressive pattern. It was great to live with him. Thanks to RC, I had learned so much already about how to respect and love him and play and have fun with him. I am so glad that you're alive, Harvey, and that you started RC and made it possible for me to discharge my terror and despair and grief about what happened to my dearest F—. Most of the time I can feel that I am really a happy person, my life is worth living and I am so very, very glad I had the opportunity to live ten years close to F— and I hope a lot more with N—.

The last weeks I've used the direction, "I am the happy mother of F—," or "I am a happy woman," "Living is great," in my sessions; it works very well and I discharge deeply. Writing this I wonder: Does this really matter to you? But whatever it feels I know it does.

The funeral was very inspiring. Three hundred fifty young people and adult people saying true things about F— and their relationship with him

Appeared in **Present Time** No. 68, July 1987.

or just crying all the time; there was singing and laughing also and lots of flowers and a white coffin with nice coloured animals on it for F—.

I've got lots of clients now here in my little village. People start discharging right away when they see me and remember F— and the funeral, where so many RC people supported us in having an honest atmosphere where everyone discharged easily. So I am going to write something about my feelings, about F—, about discharging, in the village paper. (It is read by most of the 900 people here.)

My support group is going well. There is another couple in it who lost their son of sixteen years also recently. We make lots of fun — especially about the terrifying events that caused the death of our beloved ones. It is a good way to discharge heavily. Sometimes N— wants to assist in the group. It is a good contradiction for her that there are adult people who know that it is an important issue for her and want to support her as counselors. Most of the people here (non-RC) used to say. "Oh, for a child it is not that bad. She forgets soon and is happy as before as if nothing has happened."

I enjoy also working towards a closer relationship with N—. It's a great challenge, especially now; she needs me more than ever to love her and be her ally. She never stops showing me what I have to work on and is interested in how I find out how to get rid of my distress patterns. She also discharges a lot. The past weeks I am thinking of her wisdom: she is so smart, but I wonder if she really trusts anybody besides herself and, most of the time, me? She really trusted adult people to save F—, and I think she decided to trust nobody — because they did not.

She is aware of the confusion of so many people and I suppose she's right to take charge. It is painful to see how difficult it is for her to rest deeply, especially when I am not around to watch out. I suppose I have to learn to rest deeply myself. I am very "awake" even at night. Do you have some suggestions?

R—
Garrelsweer, The Netherlands

Dear R—,

I am terribly sorry about F—'s death and I send my deepest regrets to you and N—. I think that N— is quite right to have reservations about whom she can trust, and that she will check out adults instead of assuming that they can all be trusted, and that is okay. She can trust you, and there will be others that she will trust as she finds that they are trustworthy. If she keeps discharging about the loss of F—, then any irrational distrust will discharge along with it.

I am going to extract part of your letter about F— for **Present Time**, since I think it will mean a lot to other people to hear how well such a tragedy is being handled, and I hope you do not mind.

I would give N— some "standing guard" time when you just promise for an hour or half hour or whatever to see that nothing bad happens and she can really rest, and she will discharge and rest and will come out of that part of the hurt. There must a great deal of terror there. Get your Co-Counselors to stand guard for you, too.

Please give N— my love and tell her that I'm very proud of her. Both of you take time to talk to F— as if he were sitting on the edge of a cloud in heaven with his little golden harp beside him, and tell him all the things that you never got around to saying to him when he was alive. He will be a perfect counselor for you, and I think you will both discharge a lot and the F— that you still have, that is, the picture of him in your minds, will straighten out and become very clear and dear, and the grief will cease to hold either one of you back.

Harvey

Are Oppressed People Really Welcome in RC?

Dear Harvey,

I'm writing to clarify my standing in the International RC Community and the Minneapolis/St. Paul Community.

Since 1981 I have organized and led classes, support groups, and workshops on women's oppression issues, classism, and racism — for women, in the wide world, always multi-racial.

After attending the Native Teachers' and Leaders' Conference in Vancouver, I have consistently attempted to draw more Native people into RC, either into the formalized Community or by leading all-Native support groups.

I have attended the World Conference, three Midwest USA Teachers' and Leaders' Workshops, Mary Hodgson's classism workshops in the local Area, and Co-Counsel regularly with John Sellen and Judy St. Claire.

I am currently leading an all-Native women's support group — four women consistently attend. This is my second all-Native group. Two weeks ago I started a formal RC class with six Native people who have made a six-week commitment to attend.

Problems, sorry, Challenges:

1. Money — none — me or them. I can't charge and they can't afford the books. Can I get some free? They can't afford the classes or workshops. Can some or all go free?

Appeared in **Present Time** No. 67, April 1987.

THE LONGER VIEW

2. Second challenge — recognition that what I am in fact doing is RC. When I've tried to get people invited to local RC classes and workshops it always comes up, "What's their previous experience in RC?" I say this group, class, workshop I led, and the response is usually no response. It seems I'm recognized as a Native leader in RC, but not necessarily as a teacher and I'd like some clarification around that.

3. My classes are a "little" different. For instance, in my women's group we have five women (including myself) and approximately eight young people (all under three years old). We do it, and we do it well. They not only can't afford daycare, they don't want to leave their babies. Sometimes I think the RC Community here gets intimidated by our involvement with our young people. What I do is counsel and teach the women themselves and either counsel them to parent well or deal with the young people myself. So it's not this well-structured, ordered setting, but it works with Native women. Judy St. Claire has agreed to come to our group in February or early March. I need a bridge between the two Communities: Native people who have attended RC classes have quit or withdrawn, so I'm going to try an opposite tactic.

With the RC class I hope John will agree to do a mini-workshop with the group.

I recognize the value of formal classes, lectures, theory, reading — I need to create safe enough openings to allow and facilitate that happening.

In Minneapolis there's a core group of 200 to 300 Native people in Alcoholics Anonymous. Three of the treatment centers are showing the Four Worlds Development Project video about Alkali Lake. The time is right for me to move on this.

I'd like support and guidance around what I'm already doing, and start planning for Phil Lane to come here for a two-day workshop training later in 1987 if that's possible.

I've also been in contact with Tim about doing a parenting workshop next fall — primarily Native American/Jewish young people — Native adults and some key RC leaders who have been my (and my children's) strongest allies.

My work is going great — lots of forward movement. My three daughters are as beautiful as ever.

Any help, suggestions, direction, guidance will be greatly appreciated.
Marcie Rendon
Minneapolis, Minnesota, USA

Dear Marcie,

The question about money comes down to simply spending what Outreach money we have in the way that brings the biggest return. I try never to make any commitment to indefinitely finance any group of people for classes, literature, or workshops, but always try to lay out Outreach money as "seed money" to be used until the particular group gets themselves organized in order to "live off the country as they go." I think in this case this means that I will apply for a grant from International Outreach to give you a lending library of all RC literature for your work in reaching out to Natives and will trust that you can find some way to take up small collections for new literature so that it's kept up-to-date. I can send you, say, twenty **Fundamentals Manuals** or **The Human Side of Human Beings** providing you can organize them in the lending library so that people use them while they're taking a class and put them back in the library for others to use who take the class for the first time. (I would assume that people will buy their own literature once they get interested enough.)

I would also pay John a small fee to do the workshop that you propose if he is not willing to do it for free, but I suspect he would be.

International Outreach will be available to pay for the first general workshop and first general class for anyone from your classes.

In other words, we'll make initial outlays from Outreach Funds to get things started, but will not take on a permanent subsidy.

THE LONGER VIEW

I think the way you've organized your class is excellent, and if the group can continue to be cooperative they can probably pay you something in terms of housework, babysitting, or other services. No one should be subsidized permanently. It leads to dependency.

As far as your people not being accepted in classes and workshops, that sounds bad, although if the people who are leading the classes and workshops are going to turn your people off with uptightness and unaware racism, then it's probably a lucky thing. The idea of having people from the white community sit in your classes in order to learn to teach that way is probably a good idea. Have you thought of Vera Matich? The working class is generally more relaxed about learning how to work in a new situation.

I think I will print part of your letter in the next **Present Time** so the issue gets looked at more widely. Please send me the names, addresses, and phone numbers of all the Native people that you've taught RC to. We need to keep our computer list up-to-date now that our computer is working well.

Harvey

Visitors' Policy

Dear Harvey,

In June I may be coming for a visit in the US, and I would like to meet with the RC Communities, mainly with the Jews. In my meeting in New York in November, I was successful, and, in a meeting I had in Boston and later in Amsterdam, people were impressed with my way as a counselor. The information I gave was vital. I hope that you agree that I make contact with counselors to lead groups on Jews and Jews, Jews and Arabs, Jews and Israel.

Avi Butavia
Jerusalem, Israel

Dear Avi,

On your meeting with the Communities outside Israel in June or doing workshops or meetings, it is important that this be agreed to and handled by the leaders of the Areas and Regions where you are going. There has often been a problem in RC of people liking to go abroad and doing meetings and workshops and either inviting themselves or being invited by a personal friend or enthusiastic partisan. It should be checked with the Regional Reference Persons, the Area Reference Persons, and local Jewish leaders if you were to come and do such meetings. What I will do is put a notice in the journal that goes to Regional Reference People, which will be the paragraph in which you discuss this in your letter and this paragraph in which I am replying to you.

You can see how it would be if people came to Jerusalem and

Appeared in **Reference Point** No. 26, May 1987.

THE LONGER VIEW

set up meetings or activities there without clearing with you and Sara. In fact, I think in the past people probably did some of this.

Harvey

"Re-emergence" and "Growth"

Dear Harvey,

I have been struggling a bit with the term "re-emergence" in RC and would appreciate hearing your response to my concern. There are two parts to my concern. One is that the term re-emergence sounds like an attainable state of being completely distress-free. While that would certainly be nice, I don't see that as exactly my goal. As far as I'm concerned, I might as well consider myself re-emerged right now. I am not distress-free, nor have I licked "the ancient habit pattern." However, there really isn't anything I couldn't do right now if I chose (given enough time and information, of course), and I have enough free attention that when I am acting in a distressed manner, I generally can see that and know what to do to return to my more rational self. I guess what I am saying is that I see my life as a process, not a state, and no matter how close to re-emergence I may get, the process will keep expanding and there will be new growth. I suspect that this is the intended meaning of re-emergence and it is its misuse that I am reacting to.

My second concern with the word is that, to me, it implies that we were born "emerged" and got messed up. I think that is too simple. I agree that infants are born completely intelligent, etc., but it takes such enormous amounts of nurturing and new information for them to grow, that I see a continuous process of "emerging" in growing up. Obviously for most of us, that emerging took some detours, got slowed down, was tramped on, but I don't think humans ever stop emerging.

Clare Foreman
Mansfield, Pennsylvania, USA

Appeared in **Present Time** No. 67, April 1987.

THE LONGER VIEW

Dear Clare,

On your concern about the word "re-emergence," I share your concerns if the word meant what you assume it means, but I believe it's simply that you assume that re-emergence means a state, while I assume and wanted everyone else to assume that it means a process. In this sense, I think it is a very real and useful word, and it is quite accurate. It's true that *growth* takes place continually throughout our lives and that this is a process that would go on if there were no distress. But there was a time *before* distresses were laid in, even if it was 'way back to conception. Then distresses got laid in. The process of re-emergence from those distresses is a meaningful and important process even though separate from and parallelling in time the process of growth. So I don't know if anyone will ever attain an end to the process of re-emergence from distress, but I certainly have that as a goal, and I rather think it should be possible. We certainly are able to accelerate the process as our theory becomes clearer and our information replaces the misinformation that was dumped on us by the huge accumulation of patterns and oppression. So I'm going to keep trying for the completion of the re-emergence *process* and the closer I come to it, the better I will grow in the parallel process of growth alongside it. How does that sound to you?

Harvey

Loving Good Language

Dear Harvey,

I liked your discussion of good language (**Present Time**, *January 1987*), but it also raised questions which have troubled me for some time. When do good habits become chronic patterns? When is care in the use of language pedantry? When does trying for the best become elitism? Is distress always bad or does it, like pain, have survival value?

I am old enough to have gone to school when rhetoric meant, not political bombast, but the art of speaking and writing effectively. I was fortunate enough to have several teachers who trained me to write as clearly and concisely as possible, to use care in the selection of words which would express my thoughts forcefully. I also had a father who, an excellent mechanic himself, taught me to have respect for and to use well good tools. I can still remember his saying, when I grasped a hammer handle too close to the head, "John, do you have something against that hammer, that you are trying to choke it to death?" I am not aware of any distress tied to these experiences. I was taught to use tools, both manual and verbal, effectively and I am often annoyed to see the misuse of either.

I agree that there is seldom one solely right word to express a given thought. Rather, I think we should take care to avoid the wrong word. There are several kinds of wrong words, as I see them. There is the word with a mistaken meaning, as in the recent frequent use of *reticent for reluctant*. Sometimes the wrong word is a good one put to a bad use. *Prior to once* had the sense of logical or temporal necessity. Now most use it exclusively for the simpler *before*. The wrong word may be what Follett calls a vogue word, a good word that is overused in place of other good words which add variety, e.g. I find *total* and *enhance* overused in much writing and speaking. The wrong word may be a technical term

Appeared in **Present Time** No. 67, April 1987.

THE LONGER VIEW

or jargon used outside its field, like the careless use of parameter *in a non-mathematical context. When we use these wrong words, we set up stumbling blocks in the path of understanding. The reader breaks stride, wondering exactly what we meant.*

It is useful to have descriptive works, like the recently published **The Story of English**, *telling of the wealth of borrowing in the English language. But if we wish to convince others that we are thinking clearly, we also need prescriptive works like* **The American Heritage Dictionary**, *Strunk and White's* **Elements of Style**, *and Follett's* **Modern American Usage**.

There can well be many styles in which to express the ideas of Abraham Lincoln's Gettysburg Address. "There are nine and sixty ways of constructing tribal lays," says Kipling, "And-every-single-one-of-them-is-right." Who, however, would want the Gettysburg Address parody, in President Eisenhower's style, which was put out about thirty years ago? In politics and ethics, the means determine the end; so in rhetoric results are shaped by style. We do the best we can with the abilities we have. Let us be sure it is our best.

John Leininger
Waverly, Ohio, USA

Dear John,

Thanks for your excellent letter of February second. I am pleased that you wrote that way and I have marked it for **Present Time** for sure. That's real thinking from someone who has thought in the field, which seems to me to be these days a rare jewel.

On your question of when do good habits become chronic patterns, I think only when they acquire tension and distress. Almost everything we do well requires the construction of sub-routines so that we do the right thing without having to put aware attention on it, but we can change when the situation requires it. There would be the same answer to your next two questions: when is care in the use of language pedantry? And when does trying for the best become elitism? Only when distress wraps around it does it become rigid and non-survival. To try for the best always seems to me to be our inherent, flexible structure.

I think "distress" as we use the term, that is, stored-up recorded hurt that leaves us rigid where we were previously flexible is always "bad." It is something to get rid of as fast as possible. Pain has survival value when it's current pain. When it is recorded, it's only something to discharge as fast as possible.

Thanks again for an elegant letter.

Harvey

No Tolerance of Any Oppression

Dear Harvey,

It was great to read of the trip to China, and of the Regional workshops for Latin America.

It was also exciting to see your interest and concern that we always use independent thinking. Your example about Chou En Lai is perfect. I have been in counseling for over two years and I have gotten the message that it is not okay to have intellectual disagreements with areas of counseling. And although some of this may be my own distress, I doubt it as I have spent the last six years in various academic environments where critical thinking has always been encouraged.

One of the main ways that my thinking has been discounted is with the circular argument, "That's your distress," or, "Counsel on it." I've also seen that the tendency within counseling is to say that disagreement means distress. So thanks for writing the article.

I have a few areas about counseling theory and wide world changing strategy I'd like to discuss with you. One is that I believe that it is theoretically important to say that no one can be re-emerged until the whole society is re-emerged. It's an abstract question, but I have learned in counseling classes that individuals can become increasingly re-emerged and then still bring the society patterns with them. As we know from counseling racism theory, white people are conditioned to be chronically and unawarely racist simply through their bad experience of growing up white. Re-emergence should mean an end to acting out oppressor roles. This is also a crucial point in distinguishing counseling from religions such as Buddhism where individual *liberation is the goal. We can of*

Appeared in **Present Time** No. 67, April 1987.

course regain our power, but our re-emergence can not be achieved until the society is free from racism and all forms of oppression.

Another point: I heard recently in a class that "there really is no oppressor group, that white people suffer from racism and people of color suffer from racism." It's of course true that racism is a catastrophe for white people for a variety of reasons, but it trivializes the oppression of people of color to equate the experience of whites with the experience of people of color. And as you've written about, agents of oppression do suffer, but they also do achieve concrete privileges from oppression. Owning-class people, for example, here in New York are able to afford decent housing — something which many of us cannot. This is a real concrete gain from being owning-class, which gives them a tolerance to allowing class oppression to continue. Another example is being able to telephone friends long distance if they need to. This is a simple, real thing, to contact friends in other cities. I can't afford to do that. On the whole, I would agree that it is not in the interest of owning-class people to see class oppression continue, but I think that we must recognize that they do have real benefits from their class position.

I also question your insistence that the industrial working class is the primary class to win over to the need for wide world structural change. What about women house workers? Or white-collar workers? I agree with the primacy of workers, as if workers don't work, the whole society will not function. But I don't understand why industrial workers are primary. If house workers refuse to work, then the society will not function. If white-collar office workers refuse to work, then the society will not function. I understand that you've stated the need to organize all sectors of the population, but why primarily industrial workers?

What class do you think that housewives (women house workers) are? What class would a housewife married to an owning-class man be? My thinking says working class, unless she doesn't have to work because they buy domestic servant labor. What do you think?

I am very excited by your work on a Gentile voice in combatting anti-Jewish oppression. In fact, I am using the form and much of the writing of the program for a Committee Against Sexism with a membership of men. Is it okay with you that I use some of your writing without crediting you for the program (of course changing "women" for "Jews")? I'll send you the final copy when I am finished.

I am looking forward to your New York City open workshop this spring. Michael Sweringen is a great teacher of men. Dorothy Stoneman is leading an excellent Wygelian leaders' group on the area of Nicaragua. I just spent five successful months teaching high school in Manhattan and performed so well that I was fired last week. I'm excited at the prospect of finding a new teaching job: perhaps in night school, or maybe in the city's prison system. As always, my teaching concentrates on liberation.

John Goetz
Brooklyn, New York, USA

Dear John,

On your question about why I emphasize the importance of the industrial working class, it's simply that they are the major producers of wealth under the present system. They produce at a vastly greater rate than service workers do and their conditions of life push them in the direction of organization and of using their crucial position so that they can be decisive in requiring social change while all the other people need a far greater level of awareness and organization to be equally effective.

You certainly have my permission to use my ideas and claim them as your own any time you wish. I agree that a working housewife is working class, regardless of who her husband is.

Sorry you were fired from your teaching job. I would not quite take pride in it. The next time you must be clever and skillful enough to hold onto the job and take over the situation.

Harvey

How Can We Handle Unemployment?

Dear Harvey,
We have a working-class support group in San Diego. What thinking is going on now on the issue of unemployment? We see it as devastating to working-class people much more than the temporary financial hardships — a scar seems to form. Being unemployed does a head job on working-class people — we recognize that it seems to affect us differently (and, we think, much more profoundly) than we can observe it affecting middle-class, or owning-class people.

Lillian B. Rubin wrote a book for college people on the working class, **Worlds of Pain**. *It's a pretty good book and she got the right idea on working class. We're not a group to climb out of — she's not hung up on upward and downward mobility: what a crazy way to see the world.*

Jose Carvajal
San Diego, California, USA

Dear Jose,
Unemployment is a huge issue, and it was discussed, but no program was worked out, at the trade union activists' conference. Some of the people who were there are trying to get programs going in their particular unions.

The reality is that large numbers of perfectly competent people will never again have a job until this society is replaced. Since we're so far along in its final collapse, if we survive the collapsing society's tendency to use nuclear weapons, we will probably have full employment again only in the new society.

Appeared in **Present Time** No. 67, April 1987.

Meanwhile, of course, it's good to get in lots of practice organizing to combat the effects of the unemployment. In the 1930's, here in the State of Washington, we had a big organization called the Workers' Alliance of Washington, organized on a trade union model with locals in different places, for unemployed people. It played a very, very good role in getting better unemployment compensation, better old age pensions, better injury and accident compensation, etc. It went out of existence during the period of full employment which came with World War II. World War III, of course, would wipe us all out, but since we're not going to let that happen, I think organization of the unemployed is an immediate, important job.

I have heard of Lillian Rubin's book. People have told me that it's good. I will read it when I get a chance.

Harvey

Is Damaging the Environment "Oppression"?

Dear Harvey,

At the Ste. Anne de Bellevue workshop, I convened a topic group that I called "Planet Earth Liberation." Another participant in the topic group and I later reported to the whole workshop. I convened the group because I had been thinking about this subject and counselling on my related material, and I wanted to discuss it with other Co-Counsellors. Since the workshop, I have continued to think and discharge on this material.

I observe a human use of the natural landscape (including lands, waters, plants, and animals) that is systematically abusive and even destructive. In Re-evaluation Counselling, we have defined "oppression" as the systematic mistreatment of one group by another. If we broaden our concept of "group" to include non-humans, I think that it is reasonable to conclude that humans are oppressive toward the natural landscape.

Consider, for example, human relationships to (non-human) big mammals. Most human cultures (certainly the big and "successful" ones) genetically manipulate them to serve that culture's needs. Many human cultures consider it acceptable to kill them for sport — only because they are animals. I propose that such activities are systematic mistreatment and patterned; hence oppressive.

If it is true that there is an oppression system happening in this way, then we humans must be locked into an oppressor role. What is this role? What are some of the effects? One example: there appears to be a compulsive pull in affluent, technologically-advanced cultures to eat meat (it has been demonstrated that as GNP rises, so does the consumption of meat). One negative result of this is that many thousands of humans die of star-

Appeared in **Present Time** No. 63, April 1986.

vation each year. I propose that this result is directly, although perhaps not uniquely, due to this oppression system.

In "The Elements of Oppression and The Struggle for Liberation" **(The Upward Trend,** *p. 297), you wrote the following: "Oppression of one group of people by another group of people originates in, and is perpetuated by economic exploitation, by the organized taking... of the value produced by the work of one person or group of persons by another person or group of persons. Thus, the slaveowner takes the value produced by the slave and returns only the minimum necessary to keep the slave alive." Can one write, with truth, the following: Oppression of the natural landscape by humans originates in, and is perpetuated by, economic exploitation, by the organized taking of the value produced by non-humans (including work by non-humans) by humans. Thus, the human takes the value produced by the non-human and returns only the minimum necessary to keep the non-human alive.*

Some thinkers in the wide world have called this oppression "resourcism," and in particular toward non-human animals "speciesism." Some have proposed that the process of this oppression (how it operates) is "development."

In the topic group at the Ste. Anne de Bellevue workshop, I hypothesized that the true danger to the natural landscape, and to humans, is the day-to-day playing out of the oppression. The result is a continuing degradation of ecological quality (or richness). (Upon ecological richness depends human sustenance, well-being, and often identity.) I also hypothesized that a preoccupation with nuclear arms buildup and a potential nuclear holocaust acts to divert attention from, or obscure, this situation.

There is an alternative to the idea of the human oppression of the natural landscape, as follows: human interaction with the natural landscape is not oppression as we have defined it in Re-evaluation Counselling but something similar, with economic exploitation undoubtedly a significant part of it. If this is the case, then it is perhaps because humans are so accustomed to the oppression patterns that operate between groups of humans, that interaction between humans and the natural landscape takes the same patterns — in other words, the distressed interaction is transferred from one situation to the other.

The purpose of developing theory and setting policy on this subject is two-fold: to help focus Co-Counselling, contradict chronic patterns, and facilitate discharge; and to guide effective action in the wide world. In this respect, I think that you have made a good start with "A 'Framework' for Humanity" (in **The Benign Reality***, p. 673).*

Harvey, I believe that there is undischarged distress in the above, as well as a lot of good thinking. I would like to hear your clear thinking on the matter, specifically on the idea of the operation of an oppression by humans of the natural landscape, and on how to pursue this matter in my Co-Counselling and in the Co-Counselling Community.

For your information, some personal background — I began to Co-Counsel in Ottawa in 1979 and I hold a Bachelor of Design in Environmental Planning and am pursuing a career in landscape ecology.

Geoffrey Katz
Halifax, Nova Scotia, Canada

Dear Geoffrey,

The questions you raise are important questions, and you've obviously been thinking about them. I do not think your tentative conclusions are the best, however, because I think it would put us humans in the position of being "natural" oppressors, and I think that is wrong. First of all, a good definition of oppression is not just "the systematic mistreatment of one group by another," but, more correctly, "the systematic mistreatment of one group of people often, but not always, with another serving as the agent of the oppression, *with the mistreatment being organized and supported by the society.*" In the case of parents and men, for example, the oppression of men as men or of parents as parents seems to stem directly from the society without other groups intervening as agents of the oppression. I think the oppression always is by the society, not by other humans.

The environment is something that human beings will necessarily have to be supported by and, in a sense, "exploit." All forms of life live from other forms of life in a sense. All forms of life (except the green plants and a few sulphur bacteria) are directly parasitic or predatory upon green plants and a few sulphur bacteria, the original synthesizers of energy compounds. This is not, in itself, oppressive. The whole ecosystem depends on this interaction, the feeding of one group upon another, and if this were oppression and in that sense a negative thing, the entire system of life would be wrong.

I think oppression takes place only on the social level and with humans and to use the same word to describe phenomena at another level is to confuse things rather than clarify them. I think it is quite all right for human beings to feed off and be nurtured by the environment or in a sense to "exploit" the environment. There is nothing wrong about that. In fact, it's necessary. The people who become so righteous about being vegetarian simply ignore the fact that we are almost as closely related to the plants that they eat as we are related to the animals the use of whose meat they decry. All life is closely related. Every cell has the same sort of DNA. Even subcellular life operates on the same kind of life molecules as we ourselves do and all plants and animals.

In practice, many of the more primitive groups of people that we know, who have not yet entered into a state of organized society, live in considerable harmony with the environment. Even under certain class societies, very stable agricultural relationships evolved in the environment over long periods of time without marked destruction. The present society has been so extremely destructive of the environment simply because profit is its only motive, and the fastest profit is given the highest priority. The destruction of the environment is always approved in the name of profit.

It isn't technology that destroys the environment. Technology could just as well support and improve the ecology. All living species could be maintained and new ones created by the use of our present knowledge and our present technology. When we are free from this, almost certainly the last, oppressive society, our technology and knowledge will surely be used toward that purpose.

I personally think we will eventually place all dwellings and transportation underground and allow the surface of the earth to be free for other forms of life to share with us. Sometimes people flinch at the thought of living underground, but of course most present buildings are caves above ground and pavement, as such, does little to improve the livability of the world.

We all have a real stake in working out a clear policy for the preservation and enhancement of the ecological environment. RCers such as yourself (and there are many who have written and published on this already) need to organize, work out policies, and take action in the wide world, but not by identifying what you're trying to do as "resistance to oppression by humans of the environment" (except as oppression of humans by the society interferes with care for the environment and spoils the environment in the interest of quick profit). It would be best to treat it rather as the separate problem that it is in order to continue to rouse people and organize politically and see that the environment is protected.

The labor movement in some countries has, at least for brief periods, taken a position of striking rather than participate in the degradation of the environment. This shows that allies can be won on this. The environmental movement, which basically seeks to care for the ecological environment, is a natural ally to the labor movement, the feminist movement, and all the other liberation movements against oppression.

How does that sound to you?

Harvey

Deciding How to Feel

Dear Harvey,

I appreciate the boost I've gotten from theory around the power of decision. It seems that we still place a limit on it: "We can't decide how to feel." I wonder about that. I wonder if we can decide how to feel. (Wouldn't anything else — settling for feelings of being helpless or unworthy or unloved — be paying attention to our distress?) Deciding how to feel will undoubtedly have mixed success at first, but we will probably get better and better at it, just as we do with decisions about how we are going to act. I'm having fun thinking about this and playing with it in sessions.

John Schmieding
Amesville, Ohio, USA

Dear John,

I agree that we can decide how to feel *if we decide ahead of time* by making and repeating various commitments and decisions. I don't think it is very useful to tell this to someone who has slipped into the restimulation soup — at least not until after he or she has gotten out.

Harvey

Appeared in **Present Time** No. 63, April 1986.

Can You Counsel Away Disabilities?

Dear Harvey,

I would like to ask you a question for the benefit of my hidden disabilities class, which is going splendidly into its second series. It's an amazing class. It always works, and it's always a little magical.

We were discussing the question of discharging disabilities. I talked about not blaming the client for not discharging the disability, discharging what gets in the way of taking care of the disability (exercising, etc.), and then moved on to the frontier where we are not sure what will discharge. I've been excited by the post-polio patients who have been able to retrain their muscles to walk, seemingly by having a particular doctor assure them it's possible and contradict hopelessness. I know from your work with me, much less from Lourdes, that it is possible to have a very quick healing.

Some things "seem" clear. I would be very surprised if a human grew back an amputated limb. But then I was reading something yesterday about the large amounts of sexually-reproducing life-forms that sometimes have parthenogenesis. This evidently even happens in very early stages with humans though no known birth is known to result. (Jesus doesn't fit because such a child would have to be female.) So who knows?

It also seems clear that we can lessen the effects of some disabilities by discharging, whether that can be through mitigating pain, or taking appropriate care, or discharging the effects of oppression that make a disabled life difficult. It also seems that some disabilities grow out of emotional stress, like stuttering and many colds and sore throats.

Someone said that you had said, at a disabilities workshop, "Discharge your disabilities," (meaning to get rid of them?). I think I was at that

Appeared in **Present Time** No. 63, April 1986.

same workshop, but I don't remember that, but it might have gone by me. So my questions are: Did you say that? What did you mean? Are you talking about trying to lift sentences of gloom or just trying it as an experiment? I guess my other question is: If you didn't say it, why didn't you?

The other experimental counseling I'm doing is treating a distress I have as a disability. I have an inability (sometimes a total inability, other times a difficulty) to hear people when they spell or give directions to me. This comes from years of reciting the multiplication tables in my head when my mother was "talking," i.e., berating me. I'd counseled on it a little before with success but didn't finish the work. I've committed myself now to do it. It doesn't seem like a physical disability, but it seems like by now there certainly is a physical component to it, in that certain neuron paths or connections are differentiated out. I don't know that much about learning disabilities so I can't make connections there. In session, if my counselor slowly spells "cat" and "book" to me, I laugh a lot consistently, and it seems to work.

So I guess I'd like to ask you about treating something as a physical disability even though it might not be. It seems to work, and it seems to be a more guilt-free viewpoint, and away from the survival aspects.

I'd appreciate hearing any experience you know of about the above, and people discharging their disabilities in a physical sense.

I have the feeling that if you say, "of course, it's possible," there might be a lot of poor doctors around; doctors practicing differently; and a very happy Co-Counseling class.

One thing I really enjoy about the class, in addition to its being a good support group for me, is the pushing on the frontier and seeking additional theoretical insights by thinking and by counseling practice both.

Thanks a lot.

Isabel Auerbach
San Francisco, California, USA

Dear Isabel,

It's sometimes very difficult to tell whether, on the one hand, a particular disability is a structural disability, that is, some component is missing or some nerves have been cut and not been able to grow back, or developed ineffectively, or whether, on the other hand, it's a patterned disability where a distress pattern simply interferes with function, as a lot of patterns do interfere. For example, mis-functioning immune systems leave us vulnerable to certain diseases and, in auto-immune diseases actually attack other parts of the body and cause them to misfunction. There are recorded illnesses which certainly feel like disabilities when the record is playing again. Colds are a familiar example of this. When a cold infection becomes recorded, you get all the symptoms back after restimulation and the ever-present viruses proliferate so that it's very difficult to tell it from a new infection except that it clears up with discharge.

The person himself or herself will have a pretty good intuitive sense of what is possible, but the block will likely be on his or her confidence. This usually has to be furnished by the counselor. If someone were to tell me that he or she wanted to regenerate an amputated arm, my attitude generally would be, "Well, fine, let's try it and see if it will work," and with my giving encouragement and confidence I am quite sure there would be a lot of discharge. The person would make his or her own judgment, after discharge, as to whether this was a fruitful avenue of work past a certain point. I can imagine the person deciding, "Well, more research has to be done to learn now to stimulate the growth of a new limb, (as the salamander grows a new tail).

I would be careful not to say, "I know you can do it." That means I would be very honest about the fact that I don't know what the research has not yet revealed in this area, but I would also be positive and say we regenerate lost skin very quickly and easily, and we do re-enervate areas where nerves have been cut (I would show the space on my foot which has been re-enervated.) and otherwise generally be positive.

Perhaps your "treating a disease recording as if it were a physical difficulty" is being positive in a kind of reverse way. I don't know; I think the bottom line is that you treat any condition, either an obvious physical impairment or an obvious distress recording, or a condition which you haven't any way of knowing is one or the other, or both as an "interesting condition." Assume that it is well worth examination, discharge, and re-evaluation and give it the best counseling you can give. Even a clearly *physical* impairment is going to be surrounded by a lot of emotional distress by now and will have been the focus of many oppressive attitudes from other people. Such work will always be helpful and you will learn a great deal in the process.

Harvey

What Is Reasonable and Possible?

Dear Harvey,

Over the centuries, as physicians have sought to monopolize the market for healing distress, the profession has salved its conscience by coming to believe in its own mystique. Many physicians are distressed that they do not have enough time or free attention to spend with all those who want them. Thanks to RC, persons can learn to give each other all the time and attention they need at little cost. I recently started a patient support group modeled on RC and I am pleased at how well it works for the patients. It also frees me up for the things I enjoy most. Your clear thinking about human relationships feels like a generous gift to me personally, and to posterity.

I continue to think about RC theory in relation to the cause and treatment of persons with allergies and other environmental sensitivities. An increasing number of scientific studies are confirming that distress suppresses parts of the immune system, and some affirm that reduction of distress improves immune parameters. In some instances, when clients experiencing allergic reactions discharge the distress around them, their symptoms improve. This has been my personal experience. If the client will accept a certain degree of allergic distress and discharge on it, instead of focusing on complete avoidance of incitants, there is also a chance for biological adaptation to occur. Of course, there are environmental conditions which should not be tolerated, particularly when economic incentives encourage the exposures of workers and others to dangerous levels of toxic and sensitizing chemicals. Your appreciation of these insights and support for my position is important to me.

There are other areas around environmental sensitivities which are less clear cut and I would value hearing your reflections about them. While the *failure to discharge distress could be the initial cause in environmental sensitivities, the resultant immuno-suppression may sometimes lead to chronic infections which, once established, may require anti-infective drugs or immuno-modulators. Infections of the intestinal mucous membrane may lead to malabsorption, and nutritional replacement of deficiencies may be necessary to re-establish health in these persons. In such instances, Co-Counseling alone would not seem to provide as rapid recovery as would a combination of approaches.*

What environmental measures are appropriate to enhance the effectiveness of discharge? Most counselors would list such supportive environmental measures as the absence of tobacco smoke, extreme temperatures, loud noise, filth, and other disconcerting stimuli. Many others would add fumigants, kerosene heaters, and cat and dog danders to the list. It is difficult to decide what is "too toxic." Chemically sensitive persons are sometimes like canaries in the coal mine, warning others of potential danger. Genetics research indicates that scientists can often find a biochemical basis for increased susceptibility to environmental pollutants. Regardless of variations in sensitivity, the client reacting to environmental incitants must have enough free attention for discharge and be able to counsel another person. A severe reaction that overwhelms the client with distress for a long period is not likely to be helpful.

We have agreed that when several especially sensitive persons who live close to one another are introduced to RC, they should find an RC teacher and form their own classes. But as their Co-Counseling skills advance, some are wanting access to workshops and making special requests. More commonly, the especially sensitive person who wants to learn RC is unable to form a class of persons with the same disability and asks to enter a local fundamentals class. These persons may ask for unexpected environmental conditions.

How far should the RC Community extend itself to prevent major difficulties for a small percentage of Co-Counselors? If the RC position encouraging wheelchair accessibility were used as a guide, we might consider some accommodation for sensitive persons. One important difference is that the special needs of a wheelchair Co-Counselor are somewhat apparent, and thus easier for the Community to accept. Attempts by the en-

vironmentally sensitive Co-Counselor to manipulate the environment may or may not be the dramatization of a distress pattern around the issue of control, which if present needs to be interrupted and discharged. Would you agree that when concern about this possibility arises, leaders at the Community level can judge specific requests and complaints about the environment?

As the profit incentive leads to larger amounts of new chemicals in the environment indoors, clear thinking around this issue will be needed. When a Co-Counselor requests controversial environmental changes, some factors which Communities need to consider are: (1) information indicating whether incitants may be dangerous; (2) the extent of the sensitive client's patterned distress around control; (3) the severity of his or her sensitivity reaction; (4) the willingness of the client to explore discharge as one way of managing the distress of environmental reactions; (5) the practical feasibility of achieving requested environmental changes; and (6) the interest of the Community in accommodating the request.

Harvey, in thinking about this issue, I have had to act outside my own pattern of wanting to ignore any issue which cannot easily be reduced to simplicity. My love for the Co-Counseling Community and for survivors of real environmental insults has led me to address this problem. I want us to work together to assist Communities in finding happy solutions to this recurrent problem. The consistent way in which you have held up the biggest picture of what is possible makes me optimistic that we will make progress.

Larry Plumlee, M.D.
McLean, Virginia, USA

Dear Larry,

Thank you very much for your letter. It is an excellent statement of the temporary quandary that I and some other RC leaders are finding ourselves in, in terms of requiring certain things of the workshop environment and of the other attendees, that are difficult for them to comply with, in order to create the safety which sensitive individuals feel is necessary for themselves.

THE LONGER VIEW

The general principles that "no oppression is too small to deserve attention and liberation support" and that "dramatizing is not the best way of communicating" are about as far as I have been able to communicate to people who get involved on both sides of this question. The question certainly should not be dismissed nor preparatory changes be made without understanding by Community leaders. But, there must be some way of working out the problem.

It is similar to the economic one where some people demand that the RC Community assume the cost of their attendance at classes and workshops permanently and the RC Community, in general, takes the position that it can invest "seed money" in helping people get started, but the people involved must, themselves, eventually solve the problem (even if it involves changing the entire society). I think, perhaps, support groups and discussions, as to what is a reasonable policy to put before the RC Community generally, are a necessary first step.

Harvey

"Criticism" of the Artist

Dear Harvey,

I'm back in Berlin. It was a wonderful October with very special light and often sunshine.

Co-Counseling in West Germany is going very well. C— is doing good work, decisive and clear.

There is something I want to ask you. In my theatre work, I am confronted with perpetual judgment of me and of my colleagues by friends, teachers, and "important" people like journalists. Also, I like to know if people liked our play or not.

I completely lose my clear thinking in this situation about having talent, about my teacher, and about acting. If you could tell me your thinking in this and if you know some good direction in getting independent of other people's opinions, I would like very much to know. At the moment I am very confused in this theatre atmosphere.

K—

Dear K—,

On the questions you raise about not being vulnerable to the patterns in the criticism of journalists, theatre-goers, and other people toward your art, it *is* difficult and all artists suffer from this difficulty. The artist's job is not only to create, but also to communicate what he or she has created to other minds. And whether you've communicated it well or not is in part evidenced by the kind of feedback comment you get from others.

Appeared in **Present Time** No. 67, January 1987.

So you do need to hear it, but it is difficult to be vulnerable to the patterned content which can also be in there. And of course this becomes internalized on artists and they are oppressive of each other by competing, invalidating each other, and so on.

If you have read my article, "The Good and the Great in Art," you will know what I have come up with in terms of one possible basis for making some judgment on art. (Many artists do not like this. They feel too afraid to risk any judgment at all.) I have said that one can feel accepting of the person who produces non-art simply to earn a living, that is, someone who simply copies other people's production and doesn't create anything herself, because often one has to do that to earn a living; that one cannot be satisfied with being a poor artist who presents painful emotion and distress as if it were the human; that one can be pleased and somewhat satisfied with being a good artist who presents distress in her work but makes it plain that the human being is distinct from the distress and makes that distinction; and one can be overjoyed at being a great artist who presents something new, something that is helpful to all human beings, that is outside of the distress.

Certainly the artist cannot stand to be submissive to the invalidation of others because it interferes with his or her essential role, that of creating. Also, it is no good being defensive. When one is relaxed enough that one can say to the invalidating critic with a warm voice, "Thank you for pointing that out to me. I don't know what I would have done without your help in seeing that," while at the same time not believing the invalidation one little bit, but only using the words to interrupt the dramatization of the critic, then I think one suffers very little.

Harvey

Stuttering

Dear Harvey,

I am a Co-Counselor from Virginia and a physically different woman who stutters.

I was told by S—, who is in my local RC Community, that people who stutter have been able to discharge almost completely their distress about stuttering. What do you know about this? If true, are there special methods or techniques which are effective in discharging about this particular distress? Do you know people who have been successful in this area?

I would appreciate any information you have on this subject, so I can continue my re-emergence in this area of my life.

P—

Dear P—,

Stuttering responds to good counseling very, very well. The problem is, it's difficult to find a counselor who is relaxed enough to play a good role. Stuttering is simply caused by anxiety that has been put on the person, usually very early. The thing that works is for the counselor to request of the stutterer one word which they never have trouble with, and then have them say the one word, not anything else, not anything additional, just stick with that one word while the counselor praises and enthuses and exclaims with delight about how the person pronounces it perfectly, over and over and over. The client then will laugh on and on and on and on, and shaking will follow the laughter; the stammering will begin to disappear. It's

Appeared in **Present Time** No. 66, January 1987.

simple. But in the wide world and unfortunately in counseling also, almost everyone who tries to be counselor gets tense and "expectant" which signals to the client that the counselor is anxious and restimulates the client's anxiety.

If you can ever get to a workshop of mine, I will be happy to show people how to do it and start you out, but show this letter to your counselors and remind them that just to have you pronounce the one word you never stutter on, over and over and over while they wildly enthuse and are pleased with you, will be enough to keep you laughing and eventually shaking right out of the stuttering.

Harvey

Bereavement

Dear Harvey,

At the moment I am grieving the cot death of my beautiful eleven-month-old grandson. This is a fact, a reality, a present-time occurrence. It is not an old distress; it is not restimulation.

With attention away from distress, I can say that his life was short and bright, that he was surrounded by love and delighted attention all his life. I can rejoice in the gentleness and strength displayed by my son, his father.

However, I cannot deny the event, that would be pretense—distress.

There have been some few Co-Counsellors who have given acknowledgement to the reality of this experience, but I have had from many, including some who counsel with me, an attitude that this is something to only be talked about in sessions. Some Co-Counsellors coming across me for the first time after the death have given no acknowledgement of my loss.

I believe this is incorrect and reinforces society's denial of death and bereavement. With people who give no acknowledgement outside of sessions, I no longer feel any safety to work on any matter.

I know that I am not the only Sydney Area Co-Counsellor suffering bereavement at this time, and I would like to see Co-Counsellors being human for each other at times of real loss.

Please tell me what you think.

J—

Appeared in **Present Time** No. 66, January 1987.

THE LONGER VIEW

Dear J—,

I agree with you completely that it is the Co-Counselors' fears that lead them to an incorrect attitude and incorrect theorizing about how to handle bereavements such as the death of your grandson. The present time needs to be a time of discharge in every way and for Co-Counselors to express their concern is simple politeness; to offer an opportunity for the bereaved to discharge should not at all be limited to formal sessions. The fact is that it is hard to face such a loss and to be encouraged from outside to weep is excellent. To allow you to talk about your wonderful grandson or to reminisce about the good times with him, as a contradiction to the grief that will allow the tears to flow, is simply elemental thoughtfulness. You have many goodbyes to say to him before the grief can all be gone and I send you all encouragement to say them well and thoroughly.

Harvey

What Are the Seattle "Intensives"?

Dear Harvey,

I have heard references made, and occasionally read some mention in letters in **Present Time**, *about "intensives" in Seattle. This has made me curious. Is this some form of super-charged Co-Counseling? Is it one-way counseling? Who is eligible to take advantage of it? Is there a cost? Who is involved?*

Could you clear this up for me and satisfy my curiosity?

A —

Dear A—,

No mystery was ever intended. I think those of us whose work base is at Personal Counselors in Seattle have probably not talked much about the intensive one-way counseling because we felt some vague embarrassed urge not to appear to be "soliciting business" or something like that. That is silly, once I look at it.

Personal Counselors, Inc. is the corporate framework of the original research and development group of Re-evaluation Counseling, that is, myself and my associates. It owns the service marks "Re-evaluation Counseling" and "Co-Counseling" and allows the RC Community to use them under the terms of the Community Guidelines. Personal Counselors has always taught classes and encouraged Co-Counseling but, early on, found it must do one-way counseling for a fee in order to support itself. This one-way counseling turned out to allow the in-

Appeared in **Present Time** No. 67, April 1987.

tensive research through which the foundations of Re-evaluation Counseling theory developed.

We soon found that it was in the interests of the paying client to make an initial commitment for a certain number of hours because otherwise the client wasted the counseling time worrying about whether to have another session or not. For a while, we required a commitment to thirty hours and then, as we became more skillful, reduced it to twenty hours. Twenty hours almost always either solves the initial problem or gives the client enough experience with the process to be realistic about his or her goals and how much work has to be done.

Experience with how absorbing and distracting people's distresses about financial relationships can be finally led us to require that all one-way counseling be paid for in advance on contract. The initial contract requires twenty hours. At present rates this costs $800 US.

As the RC Communities began, Personal Counselors, Inc. became largely transformed into a service organization for supporting the RC Communities. For several years it paid all the bills and performed most of the work of the International Community. It still makes enormous work and financial contributions to the Communities, although it is now assisted by grants from International Outreach and the General Funds of the Foundation. The income for it to do this comes largely from the one-way counseling.

Clients living in Seattle pay for twenty or more hours of counseling and schedule their sessions over a period of time, or intensively, as they prefer.

People living elsewhere in the world usually choose intensive counseling, for one week or several, with twenty hours in each week being about right. For this, paid reservations of the time must be made in advance. This $800-for-twenty-hours covers only the counseling time. People stay with Seattle friends, at convenient nearby bed-and-breakfast places, or, if that is their taste, at luxurious hotels.

Intensive counseling is not magic. If someone hopes for miracles without effort on their part, they will be disappointed. It is simply good, intensive one-way counseling by competent, supervised counselors who work and think together to assist the client's re-emergence. Almost always the results are very good, and people return regularly, as they can, for another "boost" to the Co-Counseling they do, or learn to do, in between times.

We have a policy of reserving time for, and giving priority to, leaders of the RC Communities whenever we can. Often, however, there is room for other Co-Counselors. By special arrangement family members and friends of Co-Counselors may come. We do not want "deeply distressed" individuals, we cannot furnish custodial care (the client must be able to show up for her or his sessions without the staff's help), and it is up to the client to keep busy or entertain herself or himself outside of session time. (Seattle is a wonderful city to visit.)

(It is a policy of the RC Communities that Outreach Funds may not be used for one-way paid counseling, for obvious reasons.)

For detailed information, or to schedule an intensive, you should write Personal Counselors, Inc. at 719 Second Avenue North, Seattle, Washington 98109, USA or telephone to 206-284-0311.

Harvey

How Does Oppression Start?

Dear Harvey,

In **The Upward Trend**, *you write, about oppression, "The principal individual means for the perpetuation of oppression is the feeling of wanting to switch roles in a distress recording of mistreatment, to accept the more 'comfortable' role, in a re-enactment of a mistreatment recording, of being the mistreator rather than being the mistreated, and to settle for cooperating in oppressing someone else rather than ending all oppression." I have heard you say similar things several times and have never felt really comfortable with that way of putting things. I don't disagree with what you say, but I want to put it in another way, and that leads to some interesting implications.*

You and others in RC have stated many times that all oppression starts with being oppressed yourself. This has been demonstrated over and over again in demonstrations in workshops and, of course, in individual sessions. But that still does not answer one important question: Why do human beings start to oppress other humans? Even if our intelligence were temporarily damaged, it seems strange that we would actively start oppressing others just because we got hurt or oppressed ourselves.

My hypothesis is that humans start oppressing because:

1. We are oppressed ourselves.

2. We are shown oppression of others.

3. We are told more or less directly, "If you don't take part in oppression we will oppress you in the same way." This scares us into taking part in, or at least not opposing, the oppression.

4. We try to get rid of our hurts in this area. Because we do not know how to do this, we instead act them out on the oppressed.

Appeared in **The RC Teacher** No. 22, 1987.

THE LONGER VIEW

We have found out that it is a bigger hurt not to be allowed to show your love than not to be loved. In analogy with that, I suspect that seeing the oppression of others (whether you belong to that group or not) is as hurtful as being oppressed yourself. Because of the hurts that we receive from being oppressed and seeing the oppression of others, it is possible to scare us with a threat of being oppressed again. If we hadn't been hurt in this way, we would probably just laugh at such a threat. But, as we are already hurt, we can be scared into taking part in the oppression. One example of this is that, when boys get to that age when they are conditioned to do oppressive things to girls, the worst insult from another boy is being called a "girl." The message is: "Do as the other boys do, or we will treat you in the same way as we treat the girls."

Still, I think that these threats are not the real driving force of active oppression. Because we have a strong, strong desire to get rid of all our distress, we try to work on our experiences of oppression. We very early acquire the habit of focusing our attention on the distress, for the obvious reason of not being listened to. Without the information about how distress, discharge, and re-evaluation work, we work on our distress in ways that are often oppressive. I think that the real motive behind any oppressive action is a misdirected attempt by a person to get rid of some distress around oppression.

If this thinking is correct, there should be a common fear of belonging to an oppressed group, for example, men being afraid of being a woman. A direction for a man of pronouncing loudly, "I am also a woman," should challenge that fear and bring discharge. Working on the feeling of seeing others being oppressed should also be possible. The first memory of seeing somebody else being oppressed should bring discharge if the story is told and the guilt contradicted.

I have applied these directions to myself as a client, and they work. As a counselor, I had hoped to be able to test my hypothesis, but (perhaps fortunately for my clients) I cannot design experiments the way I do in chemistry. I had hoped to gain more experience with time, but it just doesn't happen, so I decided to write about it anyway.

Elis Carlström
Göteborg, Sweden

Dear Elis,

I agree with much of your thinking about oppression, but perhaps not in every detail. First, there are many hurts besides the hurts of oppression, and though oppression only operates on the basis of a distress pattern, there are many distress patterns which are not in themselves oppression (we have defined oppression as "the systematic one-way mistreatment of a group of people with the mistreatment supported and enforced by the society"). Thus, I don't think that all oppression necessarily starts with the person being oppressed himself or herself but certainly starts with the person being hurt himself or herself, but not necessarily always oppressed, or oppression would never have gotten started in the first place.

When people have asked me how the suppression of discharge started, I have offered a fantasy of a tribal people hiding in the thicket during a raid by an enemy tribe and a baby being fiercely quieted when it begins to cry, for the safety of all the people who are in hiding. This would leave a recording which would lead the baby when grown up and a parent to shut off the discharge of his own child without any current reason except the restimulation. You can think of many other possible examples.

I agree that we are hurt not only by being oppressed ourselves but also by witnessing the oppression of others. It is almost a truism among experienced counselors that the person who is not beaten but had to passively observe the beating of others tends to be much more frightened than the person who was actually beaten.

I agree with you that the acting out of the oppression stems from the attempt of the original victim to discharge their own hurt. I think this is true of every dramatization or rehearsal. Unfortunately, however, understanding it does not by itself heal the distress. Discharge of the pattern is necessary, even though a decision not to rehearse the pattern can prevent the dramatization during the interim period when discharge is being achieved.

I think you are right that people tend to be afraid of belonging to any other group which they see being oppressed.

I look forward to hearing more from you.

Harvey Jackins

Comments and Questions
at the First International Mental Health System Survivors' Workshop

Sunday Morning

Question: What do we do at an RC workshop or in a class when someone is too disruptive for our current resources? My suggestion would be, have the person get the best, appropriate help needed, and be sure the person feels welcome to return.

Harvey: Well, I don't have much more to say than that. The "flip-out"-at-workshops phenomenon I interpret, after trying many other theories on it, as an unaware decision to try to force enough attention to get out all the person's distress right now, under the illusion that there's that much attention available because people are acting so well.

Once that mistaken decision is taken, the person gets lost in the distress that they dove into, and with the resource not available, the situation spirals down. I have learned, I think, that to pay *attention* to the person under these circumstances simply reinforces the mistake. I have learned, I think, that to get the person in contact with present-time reality, *not* being paid attention to, is the immediate emergency measure. Where I've succeeded in just grabbing the person, sending them back to town, and making them promise that they would go back to *work* on a job that required their attention, the pullout has been the quickest. Not all jobs are equally demanding of attention—a good mechanical, dishwashing, or gardening job, or running a lathe or something is the best.

Also, there's generally a sprinkling of psychiatrists around

Appeared in **Recovery and Re-emergence** No. 4, 1987.

who have gotten into RC, and used it for themselves and are committed against drugs and shock and lobotomy. They can sometimes, for pay, or as a donation of gratitude to the Community, work with such a person patiently and remotely, in the way that fits this particular circumstance.

X—: I still don't understand what you're talking about—what circumstance?

HJ: Where somebody splatters their distress all over a workshop.

X—: What does that mean?

HJ: Goes into completely irrational behavior and dramatizing and the more attention you pay to them, the more they do it. On a couple of occasions since I decided this was a correct policy, I have had to fight other RCers at the workshop. I've gotten a commitment from the person acting irrationally. I've said, "Go to *sleep,* and if you can't sleep, just *lay* there." Then I find that crews of people have been organized to sneak in to listen to the person, and they're very disappointed in me that I don't understand RC. (laughter) They feel that what the person needs is attention.

Y—: I'd like to share that I've done that same kind of thing with friends in the mental patients' liberation movement, and exactly what you're saying is the exact thing that worked.

HJ: Yes, they need to get their gardening fingers into soil or run and chase a rabbit, or something like that that pulls their attention out, because the basic decision to extort attention is irrational. Now, should people be blamed for it? No. God, they've been waiting all their lives. To make a miscalculation is the simplest thing. I sometimes get furious with them after the twentieth time, but that doesn't mean that I *should.*

To go back to where I was answering, when we have such a

psychiatrist, we get the person to him or her, and generally it takes only a little while. If they go into a hospital, if we've got an RC doctor around, we try to get that doctor to be their physician, so the doctor can protect them from the usual mistreatment. People come out of it, and some of them come out of it and resume leadership. We've got some very fine leaders right now who have done this sort of thing, so it isn't a permanent habit that they get into. Some of them have come back and joined the Community and have been "pills," but no greater proportion, on the average, than anybody else. The only distinctive thing that there seems to be about this kind of occurrence is that in the apparent presence of so many goodies, of an apparent warehouse full of attention, the mistaken decision is made to try to feast on it, and it doesn't work.

Z—: Yesterday you were talking about people taking on withdrawal from medication at a workshop. It's unpredictable in terms of how they're going to respond.

HJ: They are often extremely uncomfortable and discharging wildly. Most of withdrawal is discharge, if there's any attention available. It's usually so tough simply because you get locked away and don't get paid attention to. That isn't the same phenomenon. For somebody to discharge voluminously and need lots of attention, that's one situation. We know how to handle that, if we can drop other things and give them attention.

Question: The derogatory term "shrink" seems inappropriate and offensive from this group of aware, loving people. Any comment from you?

HJ: I guess my offhand response is that I thought it was a very neat, humorous invention to deal with an authority figure and cut him down to size a little bit. But if it is derogatory, then it shouldn't be used. The vicious malpractice carried on by psychiatrists is one thing; the psychiatrist is something else. The person should not be maligned or put down. They use the term proudly but perhaps defensively themselves. I don't know—I'd have to think about that a lot more.

THE LONGER VIEW

Comment: There's a psychiatrist who wrote a book called **Shrink**. *Maybe he was just trying to sell copies.*

HJ: I'll tell a little anecdote. There's a friend of mine, J—, whose patterns are difficult for me, who's a longshoreman on the waterfront. He's part of the crew that ties up and unties the big vessels when they come into the docks. I've never been able to work with him successfully, but he won't leave me alone, either. He says he hates my guts and writes me hateful letters, etc., but he won't go away.

He's acquired a considerable practice among distressed people that seek him out, and he works with them night and day and has many successes with them. But he says he despises me because I haven't been able to help *him.*

At a time when our relationship was a little more workable than it is now, he had told some people that he worked with that he was doing counseling. He's French. He was a commando for the French in Indo China. He can kill with one finger, and he's terribly afraid to use his strength for that reason. Word had got passed around, distorted, that he was "mentally ill." There's a system of seniority under the union agreement with the longshoremen's union where he would have become crew chief at a certain point, and when it came that time, they passed him over. When he asked why, the company told him that the word out was that he was "emotionally unstable" and they couldn't trust him in such a position of responsibility.

He was very upset, and he came and told me about it. I asked him to go and talk to the business agent of the longshoremen's union, which is a pretty good union. He did. I told him to tell the man he could call me. So the vice-president of the union called me and asked me what was this, and I explained. He said, "Is he *nuts?*" And I said, "Well, I wouldn't guarantee he is *completely* free from nuttiness, but no more than for you or me or the average person." Then he said, "Oh, well then, what's this business?" I said, "Well, he's studying to be a counselor." (Actually, he couldn't stand to stay in class, but he read all the literature.) I said, "To help *other* people." He said, "Oh, he's being penalized for trying to help *other* people, is he? Well, we'll see about *that.*"

Meanwhile, my friend J— was being heckled *unmercifully* by another member of his crew who'd got the word. He said, "Ah, J—, you go crazy today, huh? I think I gotta stay away from you, J—." And J—, because he feels that if he ever lets loose of his temper, there'll be dead bodies all around, was suffering acutely from all of this. The crew member rode him, and rode him, and rode him, and J— would come tell me about it; the man was just unmerciful in his heckling.

Then the union acted. At the shape-up, the company officials came out, called everybody into a meeting, and explained that they had acted on false information. They publicly apologized to J— and gave him his crew chiefdom, which was fairly satisfying. J— said that the next night, after he'd driven his car down on to the dock and was waiting for a ship to come in, the man who had ridden him so unmercifully came up, opened the door, got in, and sat down. He said, "Well, J—, as long as you're the head shrink on the waterfront (laughter), I'd like to tell you something. My life hasn't always been easy" and burst into heavy sobbing.

B—: *Harvey, could I add a piece of information?*

HJ: Sure.

B—: *A lot of the stigma that we ourselves have experienced as victims of the mental health system attaches to the psychiatric profession. It is the least respected among doctors of any of the medical professions.*

HJ: With good reason. (laughter)

B—: *A lot of psychiatrists do some of the things they do to prove how medical they are, that they can use drugs, too, that they can use surgery,* too, that they really are scientific. I think this stigmatization of mental health workers adds to the whole cycle of further oppression of the victims of the system who are labeled "patients." Psychiatrists are not an esteemed profession within the medical profession.

HJ: No, but I think for good reason, that there's a deep sense that they *don't* know what they're doing. And I wouldn't want to disturb that. (laughter) I wouldn't want to put respect on top of that. Respect for the individual, yes; for the profession, no.

X—: There really are some excellent psychiatrists. Thomas Szasz has done some brilliant thinking. He's shown that it is an important field. Cooper, and a few others, are also doing some fine things.

HJ: But they are rebels against the profession.

Y—: They almost got kicked out of APA meetings.

X—: *Just* forming a profession, perhaps.

HJ: Well, they hope to. But they're not in the *tradition* of psychiatry.

B—: I think the point is that we know that further stigmatizing any group doesn't make them more rational, and that our attempting to further stigmatize people who feel a stigma will not make them treat our fellow people who have gone through what we've gone through, better than the way we were treated. We don't want to give them respect for what they've done to us or other people, but that stigma is not the way of making them more rational.

HJ: Okay, how about this? Supposing we agree to attack psychiatry but not psychiatrists?

B—: That makes sense.

Question: It is not clear to me what the difference is between maintaining the balance of attention and what you were talking about this morning *about making the decision not to be weighed down by distress and to focus our attention outward.*

HJ: What we were seeking for when we said "the balance of attention," when we used that phrase, is the same thing that we're seeking when we say "contradict the distress" or when we say "take your attention *away* from past distresses." What we're seeking is a situation in which the distress turns to discharge.

All of them were and are understandable descriptions of it. But the "balance of attention" phrase is not as helpful practically as the newer formulations because it implied, or seems to imply to me, that sometimes you have to put more attention *on* the distress. We were led to that by the phenomenon of occlusion. But I think the reality is that the attention has always been in the distress, *locked* in it, and holding the distress up to awareness is quite a different process. So I think that in practice the words "contradicting the distress" imply a better picture of what needs to be done.

In my opinion, at least at this point, the distress *always* has more than enough attention on it, whether we're aware of it, or whether it's occluded; that our efforts need to be directed completely the other way to *attain* what we called a balance of attention. I don't intend to use the phrase "balance of attention" much anymore except in answering questions like this, because I think people understand and act much better on the notion of "contradicting sufficiently" or "pulling attention away from."

Question: What relationship makes sense between survivors and family members of survivors? Does it make sense to make distinctions sometimes? Should there be separate support groups or not? And what about mental health workers?

HJ: I assume this means in RC. Yes, separate, separate, separate, separate. The basic process of attaining unity, the big insight that RC achieved about attaining unity, is exactly this: separate first, unify later. Let me spell it out, and try to remember it and tell it to each other.

THE LONGER VIEW

The insight is that our yearning for immediate unity is undependable, should not be acted upon. It isn't workable. We've always had this yearning, and in the last millennium, it's been tried repeatedly; it does not work. The divisions caused by distress are too deep to be handled that way. The groups that merge into one loving mass never really merge; they cover themselves with pretense, or at best, they achieve some kind of an accommodation.

First the different groups need to separate, with expert help and leadership available to them; they need to meet in as small divisions as possible.

To set up Third World groups separate from whites allowed us to make some gain. Then we learned to to set up black groups. Later, at a workshop, we organized a U.S. black group, a West Indies black group, and an African black group. In these separate groups, with expert help, people work out excellent programs. Then they come together, report to each other, and work out the common parts of their programs easily.

This doesn't mean they can't use an expert from outside. A good RC leader can be helpful to whatever brand of Wygelians she meets with. Help from an outside person is fine, but each group needs to be separate.

Later temporary mergers, or coalitions, can take place. At Liberation I and II, the Africans, West Indians, and U.S. blacks got together after a day. On the next day, they were negotiating with the Latinos who had meanwhile fused with the Cubanos, the Chicanos, and the Puerto Ricans into a Latino/a group.

At present, the key organizational move in RC is the Wygelian leaders' groups. All my experience would say that the effective leader, the Regional Reference Person or whoever is going to do the job of being the support person for these groups, should call them together in the smallest divisions available. Even if you've only got one of each, meet separately with the plumber at a plumbers' leaders' meeting; meet separately with the machinists at a machinists' leaders' meeting. It will take time. It took eight months of meeting with the first working-class group in Seattle before they ever did a thing except come back for more counseling, but *eventually* it works; the process is workable.

Then, if the machinists and the ironworkers and the plumbers get together separately at first, they can later work out a coalition. Later still they will meet with the hospital workers and the office workers and the psychiatrists in a workable way.

This is basic. First the divisions. First the safety of *whatever* division you need. Working-class groups that at first brought together people presently working in blue-collar jobs, and people who are now social workers and professors but have a sentimental alliance with their past were ghastly. The present blue-collar workers felt completely unsafe and would have left completely except the theory was too good.

The basic principle is separation first for safety and working out a program, then unity on a coalition, equals basis, where the individual positions are taken into account and the joint positions are negotiated. Negotiations are similar to those that work between a man and a woman. Each should prepare their programs separately and then negotiate with each other on what they now agree on, what they will work to agree on, and what is forever banned.

Sunday Night
HJ: In thinking it over, it seemed to me that I had not communicated what the general thinking of the RC leadership is in this field. Maybe I had better try.

Much of this comes out of the work at Personal Counselors in the early years of RC, when most of what we learned was from working with one-way clients for a long period of time.

THE LONGER VIEW

There was a period of something over two years when I sought out and took as many "deeply distressed" people as I could, to find out, if possible, if there *were* two kinds of people in the world, which the prevailing opinion then was, and still is, to a great extent. I tried to find out whether there were the "sane" and the "insane."

I worked with these people under very difficult conditions and without adequate resource, but persisted long enough to settle the question very completely in my own mind. Based on that experience and the continuing one-way work, and interactions with many people both in the mental health system and those challenging it, I'd like to say what *my* opinion is at the present time.

First of all, there is only *one* kind of human. Second—and this will be rambling a little bit—the term "mental health" is a completely fraudulent and misleading term. It has nothing to do with "health." We need another term completely. I suggest "behavioral function," or something like that. In the mental health professionals' draft policy, I make the point that we have no definition of what is "mental health"; particularly in RC, we reject any definition of what is correct functioning; we see no limits to the functioning of human beings. This doesn't mean that we can't tell *mis*functioning, and I try to define in that policy what misfunction means.

The whole notion that there is such a thing as "mental health" which can be defined, is simply a spinoff of the basic attempts of the oppressive society to define roles for all people for the purposes of oppression. This makes no sense at all. We cannot define mental well-functioning because it's a continually burgeoning, ever-more creative process. We don't think that there are any limits to the excellent functioning of people. We'll continually function better and better and better.

But there is such a thing as misfunction. It is a problem that needs to be dealt with, but the term "mental health" misleads completely. It has nothing to do with "health" in the usual form.

There are misfunctions that arise from physical reasons. Certain dietary deficiencies, very basic ones, can make our central nervous system misfunction. That *practically* never happens. Almost always, if it does, it's an indirect result of some other part of our physical plant misfunctioning, from a dietary deficiency. But it *can* happen. The cases usually adduced as examples of this were almost certainly frauds or wild guesses. They had very little or nothing to do with the reality of it.

There are behavioral misfunctions arising from physical damage. Certainly the results of lobotomies are tremendous misfunctions. The destruction of a large part of the central nervous system leaves the person with just a faint, flickering part of their ability to be human. And it's amazing what *gallant* attempts these people make to function with the shreds left to them. In the period of which I spoke, I sought out work with victims of lobotomy and leucotomy to see for myself what the actual situation was. I found that they did respond to counseling, but very, very slightly, and with tremendous slowness, and were unable themselves to ever report any improvement. However, in both the cases that I worked with at length, they had not been able to find jobs before, and they both got jobs and held them after that. I comforted myself a little bit with that. In terms of their enjoyment of life, it was difficult to indicate anything. The equipment with which they could re-evaluate had been destroyed by surgery.

Mechanical damage to the central nervous system does cause misfunction, behavioral misfunction. The mechanical damage can be caused by injury, it can be caused by destruction of tissue by syphilitic lesions, for example. To what extent electric shock does it is not yet determined, and I'm not very anxious to find out. I think we need to hold out a hopeful future for all its victims in that regard.

And it is done by cancer. There was only one client I ever

had who did not respond to counseling in the predictable way. She discharged every session she came in, improved during the session, felt better at the end of it. She came back the next week having lost ground. I was beside myself, because it was apparent she had lost ground. She'd been under the care of a psychiatrist for a long time. Her husband was reluctant to have her have a physical exam because he felt sure the psychiatrist must have given her one. Finally I got her husband to take her to a good clinic and they discovered a brain tumor which was spreading rapidly. She died two weeks later. She could re-evaluate slightly, but there was too much misfunction caused by the destruction of the tissue by the cancer to allow for more re-evaluation.

So there are such things. We don't pretend mystically that the mind exists apart from the central nervous system, or anything like that. It's a function of the central nervous system. If the central nervous system is damaged, misfunction can occur.

But having said that, as a footnote, *almost* all behavioral misfunctioning is the result of the acquiring of distress patterns from incidents of hurt of one kind or another. Almost *entirely* the situation is the result of the familiar phenomenon of distress patterns, distress recordings. This is one of the central discoveries of RC, and a discovery which makes all other theories completely obsolete which do not deal with it. Once the explanation of the distress recording and the discharge and re-evaluation process are out in the light, then it doesn't matter how well-intentioned or humanistic Dr. Freud or others are, or what historical credit should be given to them; all theories that do not include this are completely obsolete at this point, and ridiculously so. The distress recording is the central, previously undiscovered factor that explains *everything,* if applied intelligently, and it leads to useful work. Current theories that do not include this are ridiculous, in the historical sense that they are completely out-of-date.

Besides what has been called "mental illness" for reasons of non-conformity (like political protests), what has been called "mental illness" is a kind of misfunction. With the tiny exceptions noted that actually are based in physical destruction of the central nervous system, it arises out of distress patterns. It would not be upsetting in most cases in a culture that was not already wound up in terror about this issue. There *are* cultures which have been explored in which the different behavior is regarded with respect. I don't know whether that helped a lot, or not. It did not lead to the *vicious* kind of destruction that we see going on today in this culture. There were cultures in which it was treated with even greater fear than ours, where the person who misfunctioned, in certain ways at least, was simply wiped out.

If the entire society, the entire population, were not so deeply wound up in misinformation and distress and in the coils of the operations of oppression, it's quite obvious that almost every, if not every, indication of so-called "mental illness" is exactly a very intelligent person holding out a distress pattern as a way of asking for help. In a population where intelligence was functioning, responding to that with resource and attention would accomplish very quickly, not only the alleviation, but the disappearance of the misfunction. Almost every misfunction would be correctly interpreted as the holding out of a distress, asking for help with it.

Probably the great bulk of the "symptomatic behavior" for which people get caught in this destructive setup, is simply discharge itself. What are the "symptoms" of a "nervous breakdown"? Crying, shaking, laughing wildly, "weird" yawns rolling off, over and over. Discharge, the healing process itself, has been identified as misfunction. Now, *we* know *one* thing; we know better than that. Also, we have learned in RC that any dramatization is a call for help. We tell people at our workshops that if a person comes up and says, "I don't like you, and I'm going to knock your block off" that if you keep your head and think, you'll be able to recognize that the person is *really* saying, "I have a problem here, a pattern that leads me to go around threatening people. It creates all kinds of difficulties; I wish I could tell you about it in mild language, but I can't, so here's a sample." (laughter) This is the *real* meaning. Any dramatization, including the ones you feel most justified in being upset about, *is* a cry for help.

Now I'm not saying here that you turn to the mugger or the rapist and say, "I understand you're just asking for help." (laughter) Call for a cop. There are all kinds of ways of handling the differently threatening situations.

Even if it's not clearly discharge that's regarded as the misfunction, which is *completely* wrong, we know that the rehearsal of a distress is in itself a call for help. Understood, all those situations that have led people into these *enormously, repetitively* destructive courses of action, could have been *completely* avoided. Now, does that help the person in the wide world, at this moment? You see, you don't need a psychiatrist, you don't need drugs, you don't need a doctor, you don't need an institution, you just need people to pay attention to you lovingly. That's valuable information, but you know what the person asks you. "Where the hell do you find people to pay attention to you lovingly?" (laughter) That's a good question.

Almost all the questions asked to me at workshops are asked in the role of client, "How can I cope?" Sometimes they say, "How could *someone* cope with this kind of condition?" Very thinly veiled; it means "How can I cope with this problem?" And the only *real* answer I can give to people is, "Get yourself a good counselor. A good counselor would have you discharging on that very quickly." Of course they ask me the question, "Where can I get a good counselor?" Sometimes I say, "Well, if you're well-heeled, come to Seattle. Give us plenty of time ahead of time to arrange an intensive for you, if you've got lots of money to spend." But almost always the person says, "Geez, I can't afford those prices," and I agree with her/him.

So I have to give another answer, which is what I give repeatedly: "You have to train counselors. You have to master the theory and train your Co-Counselor, and do it carefully." I'm offering this nice, rational solution, you see. "You should improve your environment," I say to the person who feels they're sitting on the nose of an express train with the brakes locked and it's heading for the edge of the abyss. Okay. But I don't know any better answers; and certainly other answers offered as a substitute are going the wrong way—those of the "mental health system" being expressions of a most destructive edge of the oppressive society, operating in order to force people to conform.

Now, should we be of poor cheer because of this? I don't think so. Here our point of view comes in. It's true that things are bad. My God, look at what the people in this room have endured, and how big the problem is, and how slender our resources, and how oppressive the societies are, and how many guns and atom bombs they have, and so on, and so on. But look at it the other way. Compared to any previous times, this time is filled with hope. This is the best time there ever was. We have connections, we have knowledge, we're in the process of making things work, we have allies outside, we're *enormously* fortunate to be living here, to have a chance to be a mental health system survivor's champion, to play a great role in overthrowing one of the nastiest expressions of a nasty society, to have a chance to play hero. What does anybody want out of life, outside of living forever, which we're working on? You want to have a meaningful life, a good life. What an opportunity we have!

In terms of the chemicals, my personal opinion, but a thought-out-one, is that all drugs used, all mood-altering drugs—including lithium, as a sample of a lot of things that are rationalized with the same excuses—are simply destructive. The human organism needs fresh air, good water, food, exercise, rest, and almost anything else you put into your physical plant is going to cause difficulties. Despite all the native home-remedies, all the herbal things that "must be good because they're natural," people get well only because their bodies recover. I'm not saying you shouldn't use antibiotics. Antibiotics are poisons, but they poison the bacteria more than they poison you. If you judge the dose right, that's a great help. There are other helpful things like that. You cut your finger and you paint it with mercurochrome. Well, mercurochrome kills about three million of your cells. But in the process, it kills off the bacteria so the infection won't get started, and the cells replenish themselves very quickly.

So you can be smart about it. Not everything we do is *absolutely* "upward trendy" because we evolved to live in a world of enormous, complex conflict. But anything that interferes with our essential us, such as our central nervous system's operation, is destructive. I don't think there's any question about it. Can you survive lots of it? Yes, we're very sturdy. We can recover from months after months of drugs. Is it going to be some extra work? Yup.

I thought J— made an important point in his talk at the mental health professionals' workshop. Somebody had said (I've heard the same arguments here), "But you *have* to use drugs because it's a better alternative. We don't have the resources; therefore, we *have* to use drugs." J— was very patient and dear with them. He said, "I understand how you feel about it. There are certainly some things you have to do. But do remember that the drugs you gave me to 'make it easier' for me represent many extra hours of counseling I have to do to get the results off."

You got all the drugs, and you'll recover from them, but you've got lots of discharging to do, lots of yawns, because they're all poisons. It's true that some have "weirder" effects than others, but they're all poisons. And what do you want to alter your mood for? Basically, the answer is, so you won't discharge. It's just about that simple. A drug is to interfere with your discharge. Now it's true that you can't discharge unless you've got enough support to contradict it out there, and it's true that we haven't totally solved that problem. So we don't run up to a psychiatrist and say, "You murderer, you, you poisoner of people, RC will take care of it," when we haven't got the slightest notion of how we're going to give them enough RC resource.

We don't have the alternatives yet, but that doesn't mean we buy into a wrong position simply because we haven't brought order out of this terrible mess that we've inherited; it doesn't mean that we don't know what a correct policy is.

Basically, the "flippiest" that any of us ever acted needed only some time and some reassurance, and we would have found the way to discharge, and we would have been *just fine,* long, long ago, had we not been hacked to pieces by the operation of the so-called "mental health system," which destroys people, does not recover people. I think we have to be flat about that.

Leadership

The Enjoyment of Leadership

The world of humans is currently in a critical and exciting place. On the one hand the present mastery of the environment and accumulation of knowledge has proceeded to the point where an Eden-like, exquisite future beckons and welcomes the entire human race if we simply apply what we have learned about good will and cooperation to our existence on our lovely planet. On the other hand the accumulation of human distresses, the inherent conflicts in the oppressive societies, and the emergence of enormously destructive weapons of war make it possible that the human race will not only wipe itself out but destroy all other complex forms of life in the process. This crisis is clearly seen by many people and awarely or dimly feared by all people. Yet a strange kind of paralysis seems to afflict the human race overall and keeps it from acting decisively for a favorable future instead of a destructive one.

This paralysis is caused in part by the absence of adequate leadership everywhere that humans live. The approximately five billion humans now existing are in the main leading lives of great hardship in the midst of potential plenty. Their moods are often of quiet despair simply because there do not seem to be adequate policies or leadership available to solve the problems that they face.

Without any such initial intention, those of us who have learned and practiced Re-evaluation Counseling and have associated ourselves together in the loose relationship that we call the Re-evaluation Counseling Communities have learned a great deal about leadership and the production of leaders. We

Appeared as a pamphlet **The Enjoyment of Leadership**.

THE LONGER VIEW

did this in order to solve certain problems involving our relationships with each other. After we had put this information to use, it became apparent that what we had learned are general principles that could be useful and valuable to all people.

LEADERSHIP IS NECESSARY

The first principle that became clear was that leadership is *necessary*. Many of the early recruits to RC, as the Communities developed away from Seattle, expressed a great deal of resistance to this. The people involved often felt hostile to the idea of "leaders." They had adopted certain "theories" of the human growth movements that "leadership was unnecessary"; that it was best that "everyone do their own thing"; that "planning" was too rigid; "intuition was enough," and so on. On counseling these people, these strong feelings against leadership turned out to be the results of experiences with oppressive leadership operating in their lifetimes in the oppressive* societies. Compromising with their feelings turned out only to create difficulties in the activities we were attempting. It became very clear that for human beings to work together as a group it is necessary that there be leadership. Claimed examples of success without such leadership, when examined, turned out to be situations where intuitive leadership, or low-profile leadership, had been operating. Individuals had taken leadership, but had not announced it, in the groups that were claimed to have worked well without leadership. *Leadership is necessary* for a group to function well.

(Where conditions permit, clear designation of who is the responsible leader for particular activities, including leadership titles and "holding office," is advantageous and desirable. There is an underlying reality, however, that you, the individ-

---

*All class societies are oppressive in that their central purpose is the economic exploitation of the majority of the population for the benefit of a minority. Thus, slave societies exploited the slaves for the economic benefit of the slave-owners and feudal societies exploited the serfs for the economic benefit of the barons or nobles. Present societies transfer much of the value produced by the working classes to the owning class minority which holds political and economic power. All class societies also develop auxiliary oppressions, such as racism, sexism, and adultism toward children in order to divide the working classes and keep them busy oppressing each other in order to prevent them from uniting against the economic oppression.

ual reader of this paragraph—first person singular from your viewpoint—need to keep in mind. This is that *you* are really in overall charge of everything in the universe that is centered on you and that, from this viewpoint, you can be very effective in quietly making sure that the designated leaders, the ones holding the titles, function well because of your encouragement, your listening to them and counseling them and your assistance.)

(Also, there are certain conditions where leadership, to be effective, must be undesignated or even concealed. Sometimes, very insecure patterns are in positions of great authority and repressive power and the real leadership has to take place quietly, by undeclared agreement, without the title-holding patterns becoming aware of it. Under conditions of repression, also, the concealment of leadership and protection of leaders is desirable and necessary.)

It is a corollary that, in the current world of humans at least, most unsolved problems require group activity. There are areas in human functioning which require individual initiative, individual creativity. Thinking is only done on an individual basis. An artist needs interaction with other artists and other people intermittently, but the act of creation, as well as the act of thinking, takes place individually and often best in solitude. For the most crucial problems facing humanity at the present time to be solved, however, it is necessary that a group act and act *as* a group. Individual actions are not sufficient. Not only is leadership necessary for group action, but, since group actions are necessary in most critical areas, leadership is necessary for handling the most challenging and interesting human problems of the present era.

EVERY PERSON CAN BECOME A LEADER

There is a widely-held supposition that only certain people are able to become leaders. Since we needed far more leaders for our planned activities than the numbers such supposedly "elect" people provided, we had to consider the possibility of making leaders out of the "non-elect." We came to the third important principle very quickly. This is that *every person is a potential leader*; that leadership is not an "elite" or "elect" characteristic. The potential of being a leader is an essential feature of any human intelligence.

We began to develop many leaders. We encouraged many persons into leadership. It soon became evident that there is a deep, intuitive (although usually repressed) feeling in every human, that she or he is capable of leadership. Apparently human intelligences will not have fully flowered until they have mastered the essential function of leadership, which is to organize other intelligences with one's own intelligence for the cooperative solving of problems and cooperative action.

Our experience is that many people, when first invited to become leaders, deny the possibility, reject the invitation, insist that this function is not within their grasp. Yet secretly they are thrilled at the prospect, wish with all their hearts that the inviter will insist on their being leaders, welcome such insistence and persistence when it is extended to them, and are pleased and triumphant when they discover that they can actually assume the functions of leadership. Every person *is* a potential leader and to achieve this potential is part of the complete development of the intelligence of every human.

WHAT DOES LEADERSHIP MEAN?

What does being a leader mean? In one way it means taking responsibility for the conduct of the universe which is centered upon oneself and providing guidance, organization, and inspiration for the other humans who fall within the scope of that universe.

The person who accepts the responsibility of being a *leader* of a group adopts a different point of view than that usually held by other *members* of the group. Because of the conditioning of the educational system and the experiences of living in an oppressive society, members of the group tend to think only of their individual role in the group. Leaders must transcend this point of view and think of the group as a whole. At least one person in a group must think of the group as a whole if that group is to function well. It is excellent and very workable if more than one does; it is splendid if *every* person in the group becomes able to think of the group as a whole; but *at least one person* must think of the group as a whole, not just of her or his individual role, for the group to function well.

(There is an insight from the general theory of RC that is helpful here. This is that *for every human being* it is *always possible, in any situation,* to adopt a new and different point of view than the person has held previously. In fact, it is probably possible to choose from an infinity of different points of view, but certainly it is possible to choose a different one than one has been operating on. This affords the opportunity, through adopting a new point of view, to take charge of any situation. The realization that at least one person (leader) can and must adopt the point of view of thinking of the group as a whole is a subset of this more general principle.)

It is not sufficient to think about the group as a whole in a *static* way, to think of it only as it is at present. To think well about the group means that one must think of the group as it is now, and *also* of its origins and past history, its goals, and its future. One must not only have a realistic picture of the group as it exists now, but also of its past and of where it's going. "Those who do not learn history are doomed to repeat it." "Know the past, but plan ahead."

This is not only true of the group as a group. A leader needs to think about the individuals in the group in the same way. A good leader thinks about them as far as her or his knowledge goes (and continually acquires additional knowledge) in terms of the past history of the individual, the individual's current status, and what the person's goals are or could become. Only with this multiple perspective can the elegant, helpful, cooperative relationship that is possible between a leader and other members of the group be attained.

For optimum results it's also necessary to think of the group and the individuals in it in terms of the difficulties (rigidities) of each and the *potentialities* of each.

Any group, for example, operates in a particular culture and any culture is composed not only of valuable lore but also of cultural patterns: rigid, nonsensical restrictions and/or assumptions. The group needs to be seen in terms of its rules, its by-laws, its constitutions, its guidelines, and its usual expectations, not only in terms of what is nonsensical or limited about these, but also in terms of how these can change, how the group can acquire loftier goals, a wider perspective, larger membership, and increased functions.

The members of the group carry distress patterns, as well as an enormous potential for creative, flexible goodness and achievement. The leader needs to think of the individual members in terms of their great creative potential, and also in terms of their patterned difficulties which they chronically endure.

USUAL OBJECTIONS ARE NOT VALID

Occasionally a Co-Counselor challenged to take leadership will object to taking on such leadership responsibilities, feeling they will slow down her or his re-emergence. One patterned description of leadership offered by the oppressive society is the leader as martyr, a taker-carer-of-others, a server of other people's needs at the expense of his or her own. (The other usual description is the dogmatic leader who leads *against* other people instead of *with* them.) This objection must be heard and answered. The reality of all our experience to date is that to correctly assume leadership, to work well at it, is to enhance the possibility and the rapidity of one's re-emergence. To lead is to refresh and repleasure one's life rather than to degrade or overburden it. When one really takes charge of things, one soon realizes that one can have one's life the way one wants it. One can delegate almost all necessary tasks to other people who are often thrilled at being asked to undertake them. Tasks need not be turned into drudgery for oneself. To undertake full leadership enables one's life to become less compelled, less drudging, less monotonous. One has more free time. Life is more challenging, more enjoyable.

The functions of correct *leadership* are on a higher level, and generally more enjoyable, than those of group *membership*. Thinking about the group as a whole is refreshing. People are generally eager to cooperate with someone who leads correctly. They appreciate someone who asks for help, instead of "ordering" it. They respond to a leader who explains clearly what needs to be done, who appreciates each person's efforts (not only to the person but publicly) and who encourages the person who does one job to do a more challenging one and so move farther into leadership. In general the fear of being overworked, bogged down, and "burnt out" turns out to be a phantom fear. One can, of course, get into these troubles by leading incorrectly or in a patterned way, but to lead correctly is to enhance one's living, enhance one's re-emergence, enhance one's enjoyment of life.

The means of leadership are probably infinite in number. Some of the main ones are initiating the creation of correct policy, modeling activity for the members of the group, providing clear information, and using counseling tools when rigidities are confronted.

ELICIT THE THINKING OF OTHERS

The leader thinks about the group as a whole, but this is not actually a complete statement of the task of the leader in this respect. We have realized that no leader can do all the thinking for the group. What a skillful leader does is elicit the thinking of all members of the group and listen well to all the suggestions.

The leader needs to understand that many of the people lis-

THE LONGER VIEW

tened to will spontaneously shift over to "trying to be client" (and occasionally discharge). They will often rehearse many of their distresses in an unaware, but desperate, attempt to ask for counseling help. So they will offer, along with their good thinking, a great deal of distressed "garbage." The understanding leader welcomes this flow of "garbage" but searches through it for the "diamonds" which are concealed beneath the old cabbage leaves as they go by.

Even the most distressed person, when listened to well, will offer ideas that will not be heard from anyone else. Listening well to the group members' thinking about the group, however distressed much of it is, will be very rewarding.

The leader elicits the best thinking of the members of the group about the group (when time and circumstances permit, this can be done in a group discussion, *but does not need to be*), separates the good ideas from the patterned dramatizing "calls for help," integrates this thinking into an overall plan, fills in the gaps with her own or his own thinking, and puts together an overall coherent policy.

This may be challenging and even difficult to do, but it is *possible*. To do the thinking *for* the group is not possible.

The leader then has the task of communicating this coherent and correct overall policy back to the members of the group well enough that they can hear it and accept it. This, too, is not necessarily easy, but is possible.

Often when such a policy is communicated well and accepted, it may seem that the group gives no credit to the leader for the leader's contribution to the process. Rather than be disappointed, the leader should be pleased that the members of the group, having adopted the policy, now feel it is their own and "forget" to give the leader any credit.

MODELING

From another point of view, the functions of the leader are to *inspire*, to *lead*, and to *organize*.

Inspiration can come from a leader's communication. There is an advantage in being able to give a good talk in a confident tone of voice with a bright, cheerful expression. More profoundly, however, the inspiration will come from the leader's modeling. An old Quaker saying puts it: "What you do speaks so loudly to me that I cannot hear what you say." The enduring channel for the inspiration by the leader will be the leader's modeling.

This is sometimes a hard lesson to learn. The quick applause for an inspirational speech is misleading. The apparent enthusiasm for one's leadership from a group to whom one is a relative stranger, as contrasted with the way one's family and neighbors and long-time associates respond to one, is also confusing, especially if we feel starved for appreciation and applause. Over a period of time, however, the modeling carries a far more solid and enduring content of inspiration than the applauded speech or the easy impression of strangers.

(The solid response to one's modeling may not always take the form of appreciation. Some of the best responses I have ever experienced to my modeling have begun with, "Well, if someone as stupid as you can do it, then I ought to be able to. I'll give it a try.")

Modeling, particularly in beginning a project, will often require showing that a job *can* be done and actually *doing* some of the work. To move the group into action it works better if you say, "Well, let's go, people," then pick up your shovel and set off first down the road to the hard labor. This is better than trying to dispatch people in the way that the army often does: "You men go out and do your duty."

In the western United States where I grew up, it was an

often-stated principle by calm and effective leaders that "I won't ask anyone to do anything I won't do." If trees had to be climbed and topped, the leader of the group climbed and topped the first tree and showed himself or herself willing to take the risks and the discomfort before expecting other people to do so.

DESIRABLE CHARACTERISTICS

Some of the desirable characteristics for a leader to display and model are: integrity, correctness, commitment, decisiveness, bravery, endurance, responsibility, ability to innovate, flexibility, and the ability to encourage and develop other leaders.

In my opinion, *integrity* is crucial. If a leader does not demonstrate integrity I will follow him or her only with great caution, ready to detach myself from his or her leadership at any moment. Under integrity I would include honesty, a commitment to doing what's right, the keeping of agreements and promises, refusal to exploit one person for the advantage of another or for oneself, furnishing accurate information to one's associates, and not indulging in pretense.

Correctness comes second. It's possible to be honestly wrong; in fact, all of us do indulge in this to a certain amount when we make mistakes. It is possible, it's understandable, but it's *not* virtuous. There is no virtue in being incorrect. It's quite important to be correct.

This does not mean that a leader will not make mistakes or should not be expected to make mistakes. Leading, in part, means moving into new situations, and in new situations data are never complete enough to guarantee against the possibility of mistakes. The making of mistakes is an inherent and essential part of the learning process. One should plan to make as few as possible, to choose the soundest assumptions one can when moving into a new situation, but mistakes will occur. What is important is that mistakes be admitted to be mistakes when they are so revealed. They should not be concealed or defended by the leader, but seen as mistakes, admitted as mistakes, and corrected as quickly as possible. A mistake is not necessarily serious, unless it is concealed, defended, or persisted in.

The leader needs to be *committed* to the goals of the group. If you're attempting to lead others in a certain direction, the people who follow you need to be able to count on this being your direction, at least up to the point that you have stated or they have assumed to be your common goal. It's possible to lead people up to a certain point whose ultimate goals are different than yours, but you need to make plain to them that you are not committed in their direction past this point. It is good to be clear that past this point your goals differ from theirs or may even be in conflict with theirs — but to whatever point you are leading them they need to feel you are committed. Nothing is more disheartening to a group than to be abandoned by its leaders. It leaves the group in complete dismay and disarray.

The leader needs to be decisive and *act decisively*. There's a time for debating policy. There's a time for deciding on a direction. There's a time for eliciting the best thinking of the members of the group as to which is the best policy in a given situation. This time may not be very long, it may even be zero on some occasions. In the middle of conflict there's sometimes not time for consultation and the leader must decide alone, but to the extent that consultation is possible, it should take place.

However, once a policy is decided upon, the leader must be decisive in carrying it out. Indecisiveness is an invitation to all the distresses of the members of the group to come to the surface and rehearse and take over. There is a principle, usually uttered on behalf of an oppressive action in the English and U.S. law courts but, nevertheless, a crucial and valuable principle. The judge of the court says it this way: "The court may be in error but not in doubt." This is true also for the individual leader once the goals and plans of the group are decided upon. You, as leader, must act decisively. If your decision turns out to be mistaken, you must act decisively in changing it; but to vacillate, become wishy-washy, indecisive, or confused is to disarm the entire group.

A generation or two ago, some individuals in our societies, particularly men, were encouraged to model bravery, to act bravely. That was expected of them. It was often expected of them in imperialist or oppressive causes, but it at least was expected in these sections of the population. In the last generation or two, with the decay and collapse of the society, this has changed. Hardly anyone is currently educated or conditioned or encouraged to be brave. Instead, there's encouragement to conformity, to "staying out of trouble." There is persistent encouragement to act on one's own fears or timidities, or those installed in one's group.

Since the actual survival of humankind depends at this point on challenging the destructive tendencies which the installed timidity was designed to tolerate, a leader in almost any group on almost any issue will need to be brave, to make a display of courage, to loan courage and model courage for the members of the group. At first, a leader may have to be alone in his or her bravery but the modeling will be responded to and will be copied by an increasing number of members of the group. As others are encouraged to step outside of their timidity patterns, the job will become easier. A leader who starts as the only brave one in the group will soon find others becoming confident also.

Bravery does not necessarily mean concealing one's fear. On some occasions it may mean that, but on other occasions the members of the group will get a much better picture of what courage is by watching the leader go ahead while openly afraid and shaking violently as the fear discharges. I've been inspired recently by a quote from Georgia O'Keefe, the great woman painter. She told an interviewer, in the last days of her life, "I have been absolutely terrified every moment of my life and it has never kept me from doing a single thing that I wanted to do."

A leader will also have to model endurance. This means not just physical endurance, but endurance against the pull of the patterns, against the lure of giving up, of being "comfortable" by slipping back into an addictive or patterned way of behavior. "...you can make your heart and nerve and sinew to serve your turn long after they are gone, and so hold on when there is nothing in you except the will that says to them 'hold on.'" (Kipling) This endurance can be, of course, from a combination of clarity of purpose, an intelligent view of the situation, commitment, and "guts."

Responsibility is inherent in every person and, if irresponsibility patterns conceal it, effective counseling of the person will exhume it. Innovative ability and flexibility likewise tend to appear with a person's general re-emergence. Facing the unworkability of a rigidity can be helped along with humor. "I cut it off six times and it's still too short."

The development of new leaders will be discussed farther along.

INDIVIDUAL LEADERSHIP

Often a timid leader will feel pulled to deal with his or her timidity by "co-leading," by getting others to agree that two or more people will "lead together." A frequent excuse for this is that this is "more democratic," that "individual leadership is oppressive and undemocratic" and that "if a group leads, better leadership will result."

There are some examples where groups of leaders have seemed to lead well. Detailed observation of how they functioned, however, always indicates that they have divided up the leadership and each of them functioned *as an individual leader* in each one's own separate area of responsibility and that there was one individual who led overall in every case.

We have had much experience with this in the Re-evaluation

Counseling Communities. (Early on, most new teachers wanted to "co-teach." New Area Reference Persons wanted to "team up" with the Alternate ARP instead of using him or her as the "spare part" or the "emergency substitute" that the role is defined to be.) It doesn't work. All of our experience indicates that *leadership is individual.* It is fine if other people are able to step in as replacements. It is fine if people take particular areas for leadership, but leadership, like thinking, is always done on an individual basis if it's done well.

The lure of "co-leading," of having "collective leadership" is basically a yearning to have an excuse for failure or for irresponsibility, to have someone, at least in one's own mind, to "blame" for difficulties, so that one doesn't have to quite face up to solving the difficulties oneself as one's own individual responsibility. This, of course, does not mean that the individual leader will not request and assign many more people to assume leadership in certain areas. It does not at all mean that the individual will not seek to train her or his replacement as rapidly as possible. These tasks are crucial. The leading itself, however, is done individually. It needs to be very clear at any given time who is responsible for a particular area of leadership. It needs to be clear, of course, to the individual who is assuming it as well as to the people in the group.

In the Re-evaluation Counseling Communities' Areas, there is *one* Area Reference Person, not a committee of leaders, and the Area Reference Committee is for consultation, usually as individuals, not as a "collective leadership." There is *one* Alternate Area Reference Person. When the Area Reference Person has to step aside through promotion, illness, accident, retirement, or whatever, there's no question exactly who is responsible for stepping in and taking charge of the situation. This is true on the level of the International Community as well.

A teacher usually has assistant teachers and the assistant teachers can be delegated as much responsibility as the teacher and the assistants agree upon, but *the teacher* is in charge of the class. The teacher sets the fee, chooses the agenda, is responsible for the class. To have it otherwise would not be training the assistant teacher to be a good teacher, but modeling how to be a sloppy one. The assistant can learn with delegated responsibility as fast as she or he wants to, and the teacher can delegate it as fast as the assistant can learn, but the assistant will learn to be a good, responsible teacher much better if the teacher she or he is assisting models complete individual responsibility.

BREAK WITH THE PAST

The Re-evaluation Counseling Communities created new leadership posts with new titles and, in general, new definitions of job responsibilities in an attempt to break with the traditions of the oppressive society around us. This has worked well wherever it has been carried out. Unfortunately, the addictive pull of the patterns to revert to functioning in the old ways of the society and its organizations has often slowed our progress and interfered with the functioning of the Communities and their leaders in many ways.

Even so, we have produced leaders at a far faster rate, in greater numbers, and to a much higher level of quality than any organization that we have ever heard of before. If we did not need so many more of them, we could be quite satisfied with our speed of production and the number of leaders that we have produced. Realistically, however, the need for leaders within the Co-Counseling Community and in the wide world is much greater than the numbers we have produced so far, so that we are continuing to study, expedite, and evolve a better theory and program of leadership development all the time.

Incidentally or accidentally, we have produced within the Re-evaluation Counseling Communities a remarkably benign environment for the emergence of people into leadership. There is safety to practice leading, to be surrounded by good models, to take one small step at a time, to have a chance to counsel on and discharge any difficulty that shows up in one's

THE LONGER VIEW

pursuit of leadership. Friendly supervision of one's leadership takes place in classes and workshops. The aware, deliberate attention paid to the evolution of a theory of leadership within the RC Communities has made it astonishingly easy to become a leader within RC as compared to the usual situation in the oppressive society.

(In the society, in the "business world," the person challenged to leadership is generally mistreated, forced to fight for the information necessary to do the job, and threatened with punishment if she or he fails to conform. This is usual even though the highest rewards of leadership in the oppressive society [money! power!] are saved for those who successfully evade the rules and win "over" the competition. One may become a department head by conforming but to be president requires finding clever ways to "break" the rules.)

A person challenged to lead a support group at an RC workshop, for example, is already interested in the topic of the support group or he or she would not have chosen to be in the group. The support group leader is encouraged to choose an assistant to consult with immediately. Usually people are available and eager to be such an assistant as the first step toward leadership themselves. The leader is encouraged to take a turn before the group to discharge any discomfort or difficulty he or she is feeling about taking leadership. The leader meets with other support group leaders, usually at breakfast, under the guidance of the overall leader of the workshop. Here the group leader can report on what went well, be appreciated, and receive suggestions on whatever was difficult or unsolved. If a difficulty turns out to be rooted in the individual leader's own distress, he or she can have a short demonstration session to discharge the distress enough to make it easier to lead.

This production of leaders turned out to be not only for the work within the Community but for the wide world as well. It is one of our proudest satisfactions at the moment that many people who've learned to lead within Re-evaluation Counseling are achieving astonishing success as leaders of organizations in the wider society. They are doing this, not by conniving with the oppression, but by holding to rational principles in a flexible way and winning support from the people they lead. Often the organizations they lead that were formerly ineffective or even oppressive, are becoming effective and liberating.

USE OF COUNSELING SKILLS

RC leaders, or leaders who have learned to use RC, have one decisive advantage over leaders who do not have these skills as yet. Any leader will meet situations where difficulties arise because of some patterned intransigence of the individuals involved. This has often defeated or demolished organizations. It can lead to the abandonment of a group's program or to its defeat or failure in the wide world. The leader who is equipped with RC skills can and often does apply them to counseling the individuals who are caught up in the intransigence. Success with this leads to a greater flexibility on the part of the person who was "stuck." On occasion, it can lead to their agreeing to or becoming enthusiastic about the project which they had objected to, "now that they understand it." At the least, it makes it possible to renegotiate and agree upon another project or another form of the project which will be satisfactory to all the people concerned, rather than remaining frozen in conflict. This is a powerful advantage to any leader, obviously.

The leader can also find herself or himself caught in intransigence. Taking such a situation to one's sessions as a client is very helpful in deciding whether one is "standing up for an important principle" or "being pig-headed."

PRODUCING OTHER LEADERS

A key function of being a leader is the production of other leaders, the training of other leaders, the "cloning of oneself." Given rational goals, there are never enough leaders. Every group of people is held back or slowed by lack of enough leadership. If we could produce a million leaders overnight there would be tasks for them. There are leadership roles that need filling in every direction. In a sense, the most important job before us, in surviving the nuclear threat or creating an Eden-like earth is exactly the production of more leaders.

We begin this by asking other people to help us. If we ask in a rational, friendly way, to be asked to help is almost irresistible. (In counseling theory we list it as one of the most powerful techniques for reaching even the deeply distressed person.) People's built-in natures are eager to respond to a rational request for help. One can enhance the request with a validation. "I hear you're very good at this. I wonder if you could show me how you do this and give me a hand." The accomplishing of the task should bring thanks, a word of appreciation from the leader to the person who did the task. This should include validation of the person, not just of the completion of the task, but of the person. Then, at some time, there should be a request for help in handling another, *more challenging* task. Notice, public notice, notice in front of others, should be taken of the willingness, the good intent, the talent, the skills, the creative thinking, the determination, or whatever other qualities the person puts to doing the task. If the person succeeds in the accomplishment of the task, she or he should be appreciated in front of other people. This is highly rewarding. It is very, very scarce within the oppressive society which usually invalidates people at every step. Such sincere public appreciation and recognition will thaw out the individual and her or his willingness and eagerness to become a leader.

Giving individualized challenges to individual leaders and celebrating their achievements in meeting these challenges is "frosting," but the basic satisfaction of doing a job well is basic.

We can also help the upcoming leader to notice that the job itself can be a reward.

There may sometimes be an appearance of "too many" leaders in an existing organization. There are many jokes about "too many chiefs and not enough Indians." This is not actually a surplus of leaders. Sometimes this appearance is caused by a tangle of distress patterns, of competition between leaders, of jealousy, envy, of trying to succeed at the expense of someone else. Where this is not the case and there is still the appearance within an organization of too many leaders, the goals of the organization are too limited, too narrow for the situation. If the goals are expanded, if the full capacity or the full possibility of the situation before the organization and before the people in it are clarified, then, very quickly, the reality of the actual situation will be revealed to be a shortage of leaders. One will be motivated to challenge, train, and produce new leaders with great vigor.

FURNISH CONFIDENCE

Part of the perspective which the leader must hold up to the group is that situations *can* be improved. No difficulty is unsolvable. "There is at least one elegant solution for any real problem."

This perspective must be offered in the broadest, no-limit context because otherwise the attempt at solving the limited goals of an organization are likely to bring it up against the crunching reality of the existence of an oppressive society. A leader must learn and dare to make clear to the members of the organization that a rational, good-for-everyone, non-oppressive society *is possible*.

Currently it is becoming almost impossible to solve the smallest general problem in this society without a change in the society itself. Crime is apparently not removable from the streets. Violence in the schools is apparently not possible to be solved. Drug addiction is moving to younger and younger sections of the populations and cannot seem to be halted. Clean air appears beyond our reach. Pure water in sufficient quantity appears to be a thing of the past. Even the repair of potholes in the roads and streets is becoming more and more difficult and

THE LONGER VIEW

"close to impossible" without a complete reform of the entire society.

Even though one wishes to lead only on a limited scale, even though one's own goals start out to be modest, even though one wants only to be a leader on one's own block, the logic of the situation will require that one must inspire, must inform, must reassure people that it is possible to change the whole society.

BE CLEAR ABOUT THE SOCIETY

There is nothing holding the present society in place except misinformation, the existence of distress patterns on individuals within the society, and the distress patterns' inertia within the society. There is nothing standing in the way of complete transformation of the society except distress patterns which can be challenged and discharged. The leader must communicate this, not only about the limited situation of the group, but about the society as a whole, or the group's momentum for action will, at some time, tend to be lost. The group members will not usually have this perspective to begin with and the leader is the one who must furnish it. Offered this perspective, people will tend to learn quickly through their own experience of discharge and change, and through observing the changes discharge makes in others.

As each group moves on to the path of its liberation (and each group will of necessity move into liberation activities because otherwise the collapsing society will make its members' lives unbearable), the nature of the oppressive society and its oppressions must be looked at and faced. To be a good leader of even a small association in a small village one will need, for best functioning, to have some knowledge that our current societies are based on economic oppression. The leader needs to know and be able to explain that the sole goal of the society itself is the economic exploitation of the people who work, by the people who own. He or she needs to understand that all the other oppressions in their many vicious forms, the oppressions of sexism, of adultism toward children, of racism, and so on (including the oppression of the members of the group) are all divisions and diversions that were invented originally and are maintained in order to divide the economically oppressed and exploited from each other. All other oppressions exist to divide the members of the working classes and pit them against each other so that they cannot resist and undo the system of economic exploitation.

The liberation of people from the oppressive society will come about through the initiative, building, growth, and mutual cooperation of and between many, many, many individual liberation movements. The best activity for general liberation will be a logical consequence of the activities of the individual liberation movements.

Any particular liberation movement, any particular group of people who are seeking liberation, may accomplish its goals through four steps. First, seeing accurately the reality of the present situation — getting a realistic appraisal of the situation and the functioning of the oppressed group. (The use of counseling tools, of discharge and re-evaluation to eliminate rigidities in people's thinking will be desirable at this and at every other step.) Second, the creation of a rational liberation policy for that group. Third, the uniting of the members of that group around this policy. These two steps can profitably be taken together. The drawing up of a liberation policy will involve a first draft (which may with profit be written by someone outside the oppression who is thereby able to have a clearer view of it) and its discussion and amendment in a continual, never-ending, ever-improving way (at every step the policy is a *draft* policy, to be periodically improved) with the participation of the people in the group in drawing up the liberation policy. This in itself tends to unite the people around the policy. It is theirs. They participated in it. They drew it up. So the two steps can well be taken together.

The fourth step is crucial but seldom recognized in wide

world liberation movements. This is *the winning of allies* for that particular liberation group. Most oppressed groups are very much minorities in the society in which they function. Even when the people they represent are majorities, the aware sections that can be expected to engage in active liberation activities prior to the change of the society are minorities. Even the women's movement, which speaks for a majority of the population, or the working-class movement, which speaks for a vast majority of the population, function as minorities. The winning of allies is crucial for their full strength to be felt. It is an elegant, effective way of working as well.

It will be important for a leader to iterate and reiterate one reality which we have been conditioned to deny and which so much of our experience in the oppressive society seems to contradict. This is that there is no *inherent* conflict of interest between any individual human beings, nor, rationally, between any groups of people or nations of people. All rational human goals are far better served by cooperation between people than by conflict. A leader will need to explain and re-explain that the omnipresent current conflicts are artificially engendered, automatically by the operation, contagion, and rehearsal of distress patterns, and also by the oppressive society. This society functions at all only on the basis of conditioning individuals to continual competition and conflict, requiring groups to battle each other for fragmentary or illusory rewards, while the exploitation and robbery built into the society go on.

LEADERS WITHIN EACH GROUP

It is essential that each group be able to put forward its own leaders. Women can have excellent male allies, but women must lead women. Whites cannot be *the* leaders of blacks although they can be excellent allies to them. To develop enough leadership to preserve the world safely will require developing leaders in every group of the oppressed.

This will not always be easy. The heavier the oppression, the more layers of oppression any one individual has suffered from and internalized, the more these patterns will interfere with the person's confidence to take leadership, the harder it will be for her or him to respond to the challenge. If one is counseling someone who has endured multi-layered oppression, for example, one must furnish a great deal of confidence and expectation that the person will become a leader, as well as furnish the other contradictions that will allow the person to discharge the fears and discouragements.

(In the past, some individuals have spontaneously *decided* to lead, in spite of the heaviest oppression, and have done so. We have much to learn from this of the power of decision. Yet, in three thousand years of such spontaneous process, China produced *one* Mao Tse-Tung. With the use of our counseling knowledge and skills we should be able to produce *thousands* of such capable leaders.)

There will be real difficulties to be overcome in creating leaders for every section of the population. Oppressed people will find great subjective difficulty in responding to the challenge to become leaders, because of the internalized oppression. They will need consistent challenge, much sincere validation, and confident expectation for them to move against the internalized oppression, to follow a confident, powerful model.

As a leader developing additional leaders, trying to bring members of particular oppressed groups into leadership, you can be most effective by helping them move out of their internalized oppression. You are outside of that oppression (usually). You can see how wrong it is that they have been hurt and forced to accept the oppression's negative judgments of them and their abilities. You can remember our basic theory that *every* person is enormously intelligent, able to be completely aware, completely free to decide anything she wants to, any way she wants to, any time she wants to, and completely powerful. You can firmly not buy into the internalized oppression judgment of himself or herself on the part of the person, no

THE LONGER VIEW

matter how persistent or insistent they seem to be in accepting this attitude.

Because the internalized oppression which you do not share seems so ridiculous, you will be pulled to treat it lightly. Instead, you need to remember how insistent it is, how sticky and clinging. You need to write yourself memos, that in all your relations with this person that you are bringing into leadership you express pride and affection in the fact that this person is a Wygelian ("Wygelian" standing for whatever kind of group the person is a member of). You make it clear always that you love these persons because they are human, because they are smart, because they are attractive, because they have such great potential, but also that you love them *because they are Wygelians.*

At the same time, your underlying attitude needs to be based on the fact that all humans are 99.99% *similar.* The differences, even between genders, let alone races and ages and classes, are very, very surfacy and minimal. These differences need to be paid attention to because they have received so much attention, because they have had so much distress stuck to them by the operations of the racist, sexist, in-every-way-oppressive society, but, basically, "all men are sisters." With this as your fundamental knowledge, you will treat each person's culture with respect, but you will not buy into the cultural *patterns*, nor the individual patterns, nor, particularly, the patterns of internalized oppression.

One will need to check that associates and other leaders are reminded to express respect and delight in each person's Wygelianism. Otherwise the operation of the oppression of racism, for example, will go on unawarely and persistently. The group which should be a support and inspiration for the person will instead become oppressive. Great difficulty is created simply by unaware ignoring of a black person by whites, or persistent condescension or uneasiness patterns of which the carriers may not even themselves be aware. Aware expression of appreciation, love, and delight to an oppressed person makes it almost impossible to unawarely be oppressive to him or her at the same time.

People from groups that have been made to play an oppressor role (such people have always been oppressed too, of course) will often "seem" to be more ready for leadership. Men, on the average, will "seem" to be bolder about taking initiative, about being courageous, about working on their own, than women, on the average, will seem to be. Owning-class people "expect to be in charge of everything" in a rigid way which may seem a relief to a leader after experience in trying to push working-class people to take initiative. Remember that these people who have been made to operate in oppressor roles have great hurts binding them into these roles. Their motivations are numbed. They will often have difficulty with policy. They're likely unawarely to act as if "what's good for the oppressor is good for everybody." You must be kind and understanding of their difficulties, but nevertheless aware and firm that these dramatizations are not allowed to discolor their leadership.

YOU MUST RE-EMERGE YOURSELF

As you begin to function as a leader of leaders and take wider responsibilities, you will be moving beyond the "comfortable" zone of your own re-emergence. You will be putting your own chronic patterns under attack. If you are chronically timid, you will find yourself having to act bold. This means that you create many more opportunities for yourself to discharge, but in between discharge times you will not necessarily be "comfortable." You will find yourself pulled to resort to certain patterns that are rigidly parallel to what would be a rational attitude in the particular area. Where you have no re-emerged courage yet, you may find you have a kind of despair which can lead you to charge against the enemy. With certain precautions, such as armor and bullet-proof spectacles, it is quite all right, where you are not yet able to be rational, to "ride a pattern into battle." You and the people whom you expect to support you need to remember, however, that the pattern is there. The

THE LONGER VIEW

group should not simply cheer your patterned leadership but also remember to help you out of the pattern.

I referred earlier to the "necessity," almost, of making mistakes. If one is going to do original or important work or make important decisions, the future is basically somewhat unpredictable, so that it will be necessary, on occasion, to risk making mistakes. Correct policies cannot always be exactly determined ahead of time.

In fact, all *important* decisions are like this. If you know for sure ahead of time what is the right thing to do, it is not, in one sense, an *important* decision. The making of a mistake is not a sin, is not an occasion for reproaches. One minimizes the uncertainties as much as possible, one makes the best judgment one can, but then one goes ahead and risks making mistakes.

What is critically important is that one not persist in a mistake once it is revealed as a mistake. One needs to keep one's eyes open as one starts to implement a policy that one cannot be certain is correct ahead of time. As soon as it's clear that a mistake has been made one must take, as rapidly as possible, whatever measures are necessary to change it. One must not persist with it just because it is "our policy." One will be tempted to defend it against the criticisms and the questions, which will often seem like attacks. It works best to just agree that it was a mistake and say, "Thanks for pointing it out" as you rush to make the correction.

Do not become afraid of making mistakes. That's the biggest mistake of all, to be afraid to take action.

THE PROBLEM OF PATTERNED MOTIVATIONS

As you invite people to become leaders, most of their patterns will tend to hold them back, but some will furnish irrational motivations *towards* taking leadership. People will agree to try to become leaders so they can feel they "belong," because they've always wanted the prestige of being a leader, as an excuse to get attention for themselves, or even to extort additional counseling from you. They will seek to become leaders so that they can feel important, so they can boast to others, so they can display their prestige. They will seek to become leaders so they can associate with other leaders (which *is*, or can be, a real satisfaction and pleasure), in the hopes of making money out of it, because they've always wanted to feel worthwhile, because their folks were disappointed in them and they hope that you will be pleased with them, and for all kinds of patterned considerations. To ride these patterned motivations into the beginning of leadership activity is understandable and not necessarily to be avoided. All of us start deep in feelings of powerlessness and distress and anything at all that we can do to get started is fine. These are not, however, sufficient motivations to take one all the way into being a good leader, and they are not good motivations for leaders to operate on. The oppressive society operates on these kinds of motivations and in fact installs them regularly. We cannot compromise with that.

The only really satisfactory, long-range motivation that will stand up under all conditions, is the inherent (however covered over and concealed) motivation in the humanness of every human being, *the deep desire to have things right.* This is the motivation to have change proceed in the upward-trend direction, to have human beings flourish, to have the world the way it should be. To operate on this motivation yourself, to hold it out before others and to endlessly encourage and explain the reasons for replacing the patterned motivations with this, will determine to a great extent how sound a core of leaders you develop.

YOU CAN LEAD EVERYBODY

Because one is outside of the oppression of a particular group, does not mean that one cannot furnish *general* leadership to that group. Your ultimate goal in your development of yourself as a leader is to be a good influence on everyone, to lead everyone. You *are* a member of the biggest group of all. You *are* a human and all the humans that exist are members of this same group. For you to aspire to generally lead every human is perfectly reasonable, perfectly feasible.

You can also be helpful to members of the groups of which you are not a member in certain specific ways. You will find it much easier to counsel them well out of their internalized oppression than the members of the group themselves will, at least to begin with. If you are a member of a group that's been assigned an oppressive role by the society, you can be particularly effective with the members of groups that have been assigned an oppressed role with relation to yours.

White persons, for example, are often held back by fear from taking the initiative in friendliness and support to members of non-white or "Third World" groups. They know concretely, or intuitively sense, that white persons have been oppressive, have been the agents of oppression against the non-white people, and they fear that the non-white person will actively resent their approach and will reject or attack them immediately. They are afraid that it is not proper for them to be aggressively friendly or seek contact with, friendship with, and the role of ally with, such a non-white person.

It is true, of course, that the white individual may meet an unfriendly response from any particular individual Third Worlder. The individual the white person approaches may be filled with resentment and ready to dramatize it (in an attempt to discharge it) by attacking the approaching white. It will seem safer to do this to a "friendly" member of the oppressor group than to the habitually-threatening white people that he or she has been used to.

A moment's thought, however, should make anyone realize that of necessity a person subject to mistreatment from whites all of his or her life has wanted and will eventually be glad to accept as an ally (no matter what dramatizing takes place to begin with) a white person who can be depended on to act decently. Such a white ally will be a tremendous relief. It makes the world make sense. To have an ally among whites is a very real advantage. You as a white simply need to persist.

If you are a man, you need to persist in demonstrating that you are a dependable ally for women. If you are white, you need to demonstrate in action, in attitude, and speech that you are a dependable ally of non-white people in every way. If you are an adult, you need to persist in repressing the adultist way of acting that you learned from your parents' patterns and instead treat young persons with complete respect and as complete equals.

FIRST DRAFT OF POLICY STATEMENTS

You will also find that it is much easier for you, given the same level of writing skills and same familiarity with the material to write the *first draft* of a liberation policy for members of an oppressed group of which you are *not* a member. You can see the oppression from outside much more clearly. You are not inhibited by the internalized oppression feelings that "nothing can be done about it," or that "there is no way to liberation," and so on. You can be very free in offering to write first drafts and, as things progress, later versions of new drafts as well. Of course the members of the oppressed group must go over the draft, criticize it, and re-write it. It must be their own before it is circulated. You, outside the oppression, cannot write the final draft. You simply are not knowledgeable enough, are not aware enough of the fine points of the oppression, to do that. But a preliminary draft, a first draft, at any stage of re-drafting, will tend to be easier for you, and a helpful contribution for you to make in your role of ally.

STREAMLINED ORGANIZATION OF LEADERS

The "Wygelian" leaders' group organizational form makes the relationship between leaders simpler, more productive, and much less laborious than previous forms. "Wygelian" here simply means "commonality" and is a common term to represent all specific commonalities such as "women," "men," "blacks," "young people," elders," and so on. Such a women's leaders' group, for example, does not meet regularly, but is only convened when "there is something to meet about."

One member of the group serves as Convenor. The best leader and counselor available, whether a member of the group or not, is called in to act as Consultant. The Consultant serves as chairperson on the first three points of the agenda and serves as counselor on the fourth point.

On the first point each leader reports on how she has been leading women (assuming it is a women's leaders' group) in the recent period. Each is listened to *without discussion*. On the second point each leader shares opinion and information on the reality of the situation confronting women, world-wide down to family. Again, each person is listened to without discussion or argument, although questions may be asked. On the third point each leader announces *her* plans for leading women in the future and is listened to without discussion. On the fourth point the Consultant, now a Counselor, counsels each leader as well as possible on whatever is interfering with her effective leadership. Since time for each leader is limited, commitments by other members to continue with effective directions later are often made. Then the closing circle allows each leader to state what she liked best about the meeting and they adjourn.

The Wygelian leaders' group does *not* develop a coordinated program to which everyone is committed, does *not* provide for "checking up" to see that programs are carried out, does *not* provide for monitoring whatever contacts or information the individual leaders make or arrange with each other between meetings of the group. It does *not* meet regularly, but only when someone feels there is something to meet about.

These functions which the Wygelian leaders' groups do *not* do are usually taken for granted as necessary in the wide world, and still may "seem" to be desirable at first consideration. In actual practice, however, they have always interfered with good leadership and inhibited the release of individual initiative and the rapid development of good leaders.

The Wygelian leaders' group *does* meet the four fundamental needs, in their relationship with each other, of leaders who share a commonality. It provides aware, informed attention for a review of past work, the sharing of pertinent information and opinion, goal setting with informed attention, and assistance in moving out of inhibiting distress.

The Wygelian leaders' groups can release great individual initiative. They can provide a nourishing, free environment for rapid growth into leadership.

RESISTANCE TO, AND ATTACKS ON, LEADERS

Resistance to your leadership from the people you are trying to lead will usually come from their accumulated distresses arising out of their experiences with oppressive leadership in the wide world. Leadership has often been used to exploit people, to rip them off, to take advantage of them, to dramatize patterns at them. You are likely to have to weather a considerable amount of suspicion and hostility until such distress from the past is discharged and re-evaluated.

You will often meet attacks, or the appearance of attacks, on at least four levels. The first level is that you will be criticized if you make a mistake. The best way to handle this is to admit the mistake, promise to not repeat it, and listen the criticism out. This will enhance the confidence the group has in you.

Leaders who fear to admit a mistake because they fear such an admission will make the group "lose confidence in them" are deceiving themselves. The group will always come to know the mistake has been made, and the group will have far more respect for the person who admits and corrects the mistake than for a person who denies and conceals it.

THE LONGER VIEW

The second level is attacking and criticizing you as a "test" to see if you can handle attacks from outside and stick to your program. The more relaxedly and confidently you can hear these, without being tense or defensive, the shorter this period will be.

Some of this will arise from the internalized oppression, as in the "trashing" of women leaders by members of the women's liberation movements. In these cases an explanation of the phenomenon of internalized oppression will prove helpful in ending the practice.

The third level of attacks will come from individuals, not necessarily from within your group, who are locked into patterns of seeking revenge or "hurting somebody back" from the vicious mistreatment endured in their childhoods. These are the "pickers of fights," the muggers, the assassins, the rapists. These patterns may be drawn to attack you because they will identify your having a caring, rational program with your being a "timid idealist," a naive "do-gooder," an "easy mark." On the organizational level these patterns seek to disrupt and sometimes "plunder" organizations. From these you need to organize protection, shed any naive patterns of your own, learn self-defense. Do not assume "permissive" counseling will reach the humans inside these patterns.

The fourth kind of attacks will be inspired by the repressive agencies of the society, by the Ku Klux Klan members holding local offices, by the national security agencies, the FBIs, the CIAs, the secret police, or whoever they secure to act as their agents. These attacks are a tribute to your having achieved significant influence.

For these you need to anticipate the possibility and to prepare your group members to counter-attack without hesitation, unitedly, and with indignation when such attacks occur. The slanders voiced against you are best undebated and even undenied until after the counter-attacks have defeated the attacks. The group members should have agreed ahead of time to not discuss or argue the assertions but only counter-attack indignantly until the attacks have been defeated. Any mistakes or weaknesses of yours that are offered as excuses for the attacks can be dealt with if necessary, but only within the group privately and *only after* the attacks have been defeated.

To understand and be prepared to handle all these difficulties is part of being an effective leader and all leaders you produce need this knowledge and preparation. Once prepared, however, these possibilities need not preoccupy your attention. Doing a good job of leading reduces the frequency of their occurrence and knowing what to do when they do occur limits the time and energy that will have to be spent on them.

ON OUR WAY AND MOVING FORWARD

This is a summary of some of the important things we have learned and are learning about leadership and leading. We will go on learning more and more as we lead more widely and more boldly and will try to bring that additional knowledge into print periodically.

I would like to remind you, the individual who reads this, that you are the possessor of a vast intelligence, of complete freedom of choice, of unlimited power. You have been lied to about this, have been mistreated and discouraged, and invalidated. Some of the discouragement and invalidation has probably become internalized and you have come to "believe" these discouragements and limitations.

You do not need to go on believing these negative attitudes. They can be discharged and thrown off and taking leadership is an important channel for organizing and accelerating this re-emergence.

Become a leader. Reach for your full functioning. Join those of us who are already committed and active.

Leadership can be enjoyable.

Commitments

Commitments Refreshed and Up-Dated

TO BE YOUR OWN ELEGANT, WISE, AND POWERFUL SELF

From this moment on, the *real* (your own name)! This will mean _____.

AGAINST PRETENSE

I am obviously completely incompetent and completely inadaquate to handle the challenges which reality places before me.

However, (fortunately or unfortunately), I happen to be the best person available.

TO RECLAIM POWER

From now on I will see to it that everything I am in contact with works well, and I will not limit or pull back on my contacts.

AGAINST IDENTIFYING ONSELF WITH PATTERNS

Recordings of past distress experiences have no power of their own at all.

They only have the appearance of power and influence to the extent that I slavishly submit to letting them use my power and my influence.

(If I think of them as pieces of recorded tape, they have, at most, a trifling historical significance, *unless* I insert them

Appeared in **Present Time** No. 67, April 1987.

in the tape recorder that is myself and allow them to play me, an action which I am free to decide to do or not to do.)

Therefore, I now decide to deny past distress any credibility in the present, any influence, or any operation in my life.

And I will repeat this decision as often as necessary to free my life completely from the influence of past distress.

TO UNITY OF ALL HUMAN ASPIRATIONS
From now on I will inspire, lead, and organize all people to eliminate every form of humans' harming humans.

WOMEN
I SOLEMNLY (FIERCELY, CHEERFULLY) PROMISE THAT, FROM THIS MOMENT ON, I WILL NEVER AGAIN SETTLE FOR ANYTHING LESS THAN ABSOLUTELY *everything*. THIS MEANS THAT _____.

ELDERS
I promise that I will never die, that I will never slow down, and that I will have more fun than ever.

PARENTS
I promise to remember always that I am a *good* parent, that I always have done the best I could, that I have passed on to my children as few of the hurts that I endured as a child as I could possibly manage.

MEN
I PROMISE THAT, FROM THIS MOMENT ON, I WILL BE PROUD TO BE MALE, AND WILL SEEK CLOSENESS AND BROTHERHOOD WITH EVERY OTHER MAN OF EVERY AGE, RACE, NATION, AND CLASS.

I WILL PERMIT NO SLANDERING OR DISRESPECT OR BLAMING

OF ANY MAN FOR THE HURTS WHICH HAVE BEEN PLACED UPON HIM AND I WILL SEEK TO RESTORE SAFETY TO ALL MEN TO DISCHARGE THESE CRUEL HURTS.

I WILL FIGHT TO END AND ELIMINATE THE BURDENING OF MEN WITH OVER-FATIGUE, OVER-RESPONSIBILITY, AND COERCION INTO ARMED SERVICE IN WHICH WE HAVE BEEN BRUTALIZED, AND FORCED TO KILL OR BE KILLED.

I WILL CHERISH MY BIRTHRIGHT OF BEING A GOOD, INTELLIGENT, COURAGEOUS, AND POWERFUL MALE HUMAN.

YOUNG PEOPLE

I solemnly promise that, from this moment on, I will never again treat any young person, including myself, with anything less than complete respect. This will mean that _____.

WORKING CLASS

I solemnly promise that, from this moment on, I will take pride in the intelligence, strength, endurance, and goodness of working-class people everywhere.

I will remember to be proud that we do the world's work, that we produce the world's wealth, that we belong to the only class with a future, that our class will end all oppression.

I will unite with all my fellow workers everywhere around the world to lead all people to a rational, peaceful society.

I am a worker, proud to be a worker, and the future is in my hands.

WORLD CHANGERS

I have chosen the responsibility to change society, but I also choose to be intelligent in the way I do it.

The future needs *me*, well-rested, well-nourished, and well-exercised.

THE LONGER VIEW

The past is useful as information, but never as a substitute for my own fresh thinking. Mao respected Marx, but did his own fresh thinking. I will respect all past thinkers but my thinking will necessarily be more brilliant than theirs because I stand on their shoulders.

If I am not enjoying what I am doing, then there is something wrong with how I am doing it and I will correct it.

TO END PREOCCUPATION WITH DISTRESS
It is logically possible and certainly desirable to end the ancient habit of paying attention to past distress and replace it by a new attitude or posture of paying attention to interesting and rewarding concerns, including the present-time situation, and so I now decide to do this and will repeatedly so decide until the ancient habit is broken.

RC LEADERS
I PROMISE THAT, FROM THIS MOMENT ON, I AM IN COMPLETE CHARGE OF *absolutely everything*, INCLUDING THE ENTIRE RC COMMUNITY. HA! HA! HA! HA! (IN TONES OF TRIUMPH, SATISFACTION, AND POWER.) THIS MEANS THAT _____.

BLACK PERSONS
For the complete liberation of my beautiful, wise, strong, and courageous black people, I solemnly promise I will always remember our/my own goodness and strength. I will fight against every division that tends to separate us from each other and from other people. I will settle for nothing less than complete liberation, complete equality, complete opportunity, and complete respect for everyone.

JEWISH
For the long-range survival of my people, I solemnly promise that, from this moment on, I will treat every person I meet as if she or he were eager to be my warm, close, dependable friend and ally, under all conditions. This will mean that _____.

CHICANO/A

IN RESPECT FOR MY BEAUTIFUL LAND AND THE ENDURING AND PROUD PEOPLE THAT INHABIT IT, I PROMISE THAT I SHALL CHERISH MY CULTURE AND LANGUAGE, UNITE MY PEOPLE, AND IN ALLIANCE WITH ALL PEOPLES OF THE WORLD, SEE THAT ALL OPPRESSIONS ARE ENDED.

IRISH

For the long-range encouragement of my brave and noble people, I joyfully promise that, from this moment on, I will never again demean myself, or permit myself to be demeaned, nor permit any Irish person to be demeaned by anyone, including the person herself or himself, but shall stand as a proud example of the beauty, nobility, and wisdom of my wonderful people.

ISRAELI

From now on I will see to it that everything I am in contact with works well. However, remembering that the person and the pattern are completely different and separate, and that the pattern is reinforced and the person is hurt by criticism, I promise that from now on I will never again speak or act critically to, or about, another person, including myself, but instead in every contact with every person I will find and express some appreciation of that person and of myself.

(in Hebrew)

מתחה והלאה אראג לכך שכל דבר שאני במגע איתו יעבוד היטב. עם
זאת, בזכרי שהאדם והדפוס נפרדים ושונים זה מזה לגמרי, ושהדפוס
מחוזר על ידי ביקורת בעוד האדם נפגע ממנה, אני מבטיח/ה שמעתה
והלאה לעולם לא אדבר או אפעל בביקורתיות כלפי או אודות אדם
אחר, כולל עצמי. במקום זאת, בכל מגע עם כל איש אישה אמצא ואבטא
הערכה כלשהיא לאיש/ה זו ולעצמי.

CANADIAN

I promise to always treasure our beautiful land and waters and our vast spaces and thriving cities, and to love every Canadian, celebrating our diversity, our Native hosts, and our anglophone, francophone, and other guests, and remembering our stamina and boldness now and throughout our history.

The True North, Strong and Free!

ARAB

In total respect for the beauty and wisdom of my people, I cheerfully promise that I will cherish my culture and language, and remember how delightful and important we are to all human beings.

DISABLED PERSONS

I CHEERFULLY PROMISE THAT FROM NOW ON I WILL ALWAYS REMEMBER THAT MY BODY IS WONDERFUL AND THAT I AM FULLY HUMAN, THAT I AM TOTALLY ADMIRABLE AND LOVELY TO BE CLOSE TO, AND I WILL CONFIDENTLY EXPECT TO BE CHERISHED EXACTLY AS I AM BY ALL HUMAN BEINGS.

JAPANESE-AMERICAN

With all my honor, I solemnly promise that from this moment on I will never again be less than fully visible as a proud, strong, beautiful, and dignified Japanese-American — Hi!

MIDDLE CLASS

I cheerfully promise from now on to stand proudly visible, to be my true self without caution or pretense, to work for the unity and liberation of all working people, and never to be quiet again.

OWNING CLASS

I PROMISE THAT, FROM THIS MOMENT ON, I WILL REFUSE TO FEEL GUILTY OR ACCEPT BLAME OR ISOLATION FOR THE CLASS POSITION IN WHICH MY BIRTH OR OTHER EVENTS PLACED ME, BUT WILL INSTEAD TAKE FULL PRIDE IN MY COMPLETE HUMANNESS. I WILL RECOGNIZE AND REMEMBER MY CLOSE TIES TO ALL OTHER

HUMAN BEINGS. I WILL TREASURE AND APPRECIATE THE FAVORABLE FACTORS IN MY BACKGROUND WHICH ALLOWED ME TO KEEP MUCH OF MY HUMANNESS AND ABILITIES INTACT AND FUNCTIONING. I PLEDGE THAT THIS HUMANNESS AND THESE ABILITIES AND ADVANTAGES WILL BE USED, WITH ZEST AND JOY, FOR THE COMPLETE LIBERATION OF EVERY HUMAN BEING FROM EVERY OPPRESSION.

LES QUÉBÉCOIS

Pour moi, pour mon peuple, et pour mon beau pays je permets solennelement de toujours être fier(ère) de ma langue, de ma culture and de mon héritage, et d'exprimer cette fierté en tout temps.

D'éliminer tous les effets de l'oppression intériorisée sur moi-même et sur les autres québécois.

De travailler sans relâche à construire l'unité entre les québécois and à établir le respect et l'amitié entre tous les peuples d'Amérique du Nord. Je me souviens!

Vive le Québec libre!

QUÉBÉCOIS

For my own sake, and for the sake of my beautiful country and people, I solemnly promise that I will forever express pride in my heritage, my language, my culture, and my nation.

I will resist and eliminate all the effects of internalized oppression, upon myself and upon other Quebecois and shall work unceasingly for unity among us and for respect and friendship between all the peoples of North America. I will remember!

We will be free!

LES ACADIENS

Sous le joug de l'éxil and de l'oppression, avec un coeur plein de confiance, d'espoir and de détermination, je promets de toujours chérir mon héritage et ma culture. De toujours être fier d'être acadien(enne) et toujours être de tous les Acadiens où qu'ils soient. D'éxige le respect pour tous les Acadiens de tous les autres peuples et d'offrir le respect en retour à tous les autres peuples, de favoriser la sororité entre tous les francophones du monde. Pour l'unité entre nous où que nous soyons!

Pour la fin de l'éxil!

Pour une Acadie libre!

ACADIANS
Out of exile and oppression with a heart full of faith, hope, and determination, I promise that I will forever cherish my heritage, my language, and my culture, that I will forever be proud that I am an Acadian and forever be proud of all Acadians everywhere, that I shall require respect for Acadians from all other peoples and shall offer respect to all other peoples in return. That I shall advance the sisterhood and alliance of all French-speaking people in the world.

For unity among us wherever we are!

For an end to exile! For a free Acadie!

CATHOLIC
I pledge to never again demean or apologize for myself, my family, or my church for being Catholic, but to esteem them all as beloveds of God and all the universe.

AGAINST RACISM
I resent and will fiercely oppose racism's crippling limits to the progress of my beloved human race. Always keeping in mind my proud heritage of fighting oppression, and wanting to enrich my present and future, I will engage and join with others to smash racism so that we all may live in a free world.

CLASSROOM TEACHERS

As a proud worker in the liberation of all human intelligence, I cheerfully promise that I will always treat every learner and every teacher, including myself, with complete respect.

ARTISTS

I PROMISE TO ALWAYS REMEMBER MY POWER, LOVE, AND INTELLIGENCE AS AN ARITST, AND THE VITAL ROLE THAT ARTISTS HAVE PLAYED IN EVERY CULTURE AND TIME, I WILL NEVER AGAIN INVALIDATE ANY ARTIST, INCLUDING MYSELF, OR ANY WORK OF ART, BUT RATHER ALLY MYSELF WITH ALL ARTISTS TO END OUR ECONOMIC OPPRESSION, AND ENTHUSIASTICALLY ENCOURAGE THE CREATIVITY OF EVERY HUMAN.

LESBIANS

BECAUSE I AM GOOD, AND BELONG, LIKE EVERY OTHER WOMAN, AT THE CENTER OF ALL MATTERS, I PROMISE NEVER AGAIN TO ACCEPT ANY LIMITS ON MY LOVING, MY RELATIONSHIPS, OR MY ABILITIES. I AM COMPLETELY GOOD, I AM FULLY FEMININE, I AM A LESBIAN.

GAY MEN

Beloved brothers, because of our supreme importance to the world now and forever, I promise to always remember that my love is good and my manhood is complete and without limits.

COLLEAGUES

As a full-fledged human being, I promise to think and to respect thinking, to allow no invalidation of any scholar or teacher, including myself, to refuse to be isolated from my colleagues or to act as an agent of oppression, and to boldly apply my full knowledge and power to the creation of a just world.

UNITED STATESER

For the survival and cleansing and long-range flourishing of my beloved United States, I promise that, from this moment on, I will speak out and act against every injustice, no matter how long-established. I will insist that the ideals and goals which inspired the founding of our country and for which our people have repeatedly striven and fought and sacrificed, shall be lived up to.

The United States is my country. I shall forever claim her with pride in her every good quality and with determination to correct any of her past, present, or future wrongs. My United States! With freedom and justice for all!

SOUTHERN UNITED STATESER

I SINCERELY PROMISE THAT, FROM THIS MOMENT ON, I WILL NEVER FALTER IN MY PRIDE IN BEING A SOUTHERNER, IN MY LOVE FOR THE BEAUTIFUL SOUTHERN LAND, FOR THE THOUGHTFUL COURTESY AND CARING OF ITS PEOPLE, FOR THEIR OFTEN-OBSCURED BUT ALWAYS-PERSISTING RESISTANCE TO OPPRESSION, FOR ALL OUR PROUD HERITAGE AND OUR BRILLIANT FUTURE. I SHALL NEVER LOSE SIGHT OF THE FACT THAT *all* PEOPLE OF THE SOUTH ARE MY SISTERS AND BROTHERS, NOR ALLOW ANY SLIGHT AGAINST ANY SOUTHERN PERSON TO GO UNCORRECTED, NOT EVEN IF VOICED BY SOUTHERNERS THEMSELVES. THE *real* SOUTH WILL RISE AGAIN!

The 1985
World Conference

The World Conference

The 1985 World Conference of the Re-evaluation Counseling Communities met at John Abbott College, in Ste. Anne de Bellevue, a suburb of Montreal, Quebec, from July 27th to August 3rd. The Regional Reference Persons met for two days preceding the main Conference.

One hundred and fifty-five delegates attended from twenty-seven countries and forty nations. Forty-four Regions were represented by Regional Reference Persons or elected delegates. Seventeen International Liberation Reference Persons were present, as were eighteen editors of RC journals.

Very few changes were made in the Guidelines at this Conference. The new, revised Guidelines were printed in **Present Time** No. 61 and are available as a separate pamphlet.

The following texts are the outlines of the class lectures of the first five classes as delivered at the Conference. These outlines appeared in the delegates' workbooks. Following them is the transcript of the lecture on Friday, August 2nd.

Appeared in **Present Time** No. 61, October 1985.

Outline: State of the World Report
The 1985 World Conference

The present situation is one of great dangers and great opportunities.

There is an upward trend in the Universe, a trend toward complexity, order, freedom, independence, and initiative.

This trend has led to the emergence of life on at least one planet and, in the evolution of life, to central nervous systems of such complexity as to permit the emergence of intelligence and certain other capacities for their possessors.

This intelligence, in the case of our species, has been vulnerable from the beginning to the imposition of distress patterns, which represent devastating regressions to a more primitive level of interacting with the environment.

Although natural processes for the elimination of distress patterns have also been available, these processes have been interfered with in various ways by interactions with other distress patterns, cultures, and oppressive societies. Thus the essential nature of human beings has largely been obscured for most observers.

Distress-pattern-laden human beings, at critical points in their histories, submitted to being organized into oppressive class societies, in which one small group of individuals exploited the rest of the population economically, robbing them "legally" (by the laws of the society) of the value produced by their labor. The pretext for such exploitation was the organization

Appeared in **Present Time** No. 61, October 1985.

which accompanied it, which made possible a better mastery of the environment and allowed greater population growth.

Such oppressive societies were able to function at all only on the basis of the distress patterns of the people, since no undistressed human would submit to being oppressed (nor would an undistressed human accept or continue in the role of an oppressor). It then became crucial for each oppressive society to install and maintain certain sets of distress patterns within the population in order for the society to operate. Such patterns were and are installed by violence, invalidation, misinformation, and punishment. Principal vehicles for such installation of patterns are the adultist mistreatment of children, "educational" systems, military training and combat, and control of the sources of public information.

To maintain the economic oppression (classism) the oppressive societies have developed and installed the auxiliary oppressions of sexism, racism, adultism, imperialism, and many other oppressions in order to divide the economically-oppressed against each other and secure their help in oppressing each other while submitting to the economic exploitation. These auxiliary oppressions also continue only on the mechanism of distress-pattern installation.

Each such oppressive society contained certain internal contradictions which eventually led to its collapse and violent replacement by another society. Slave societies were replaced by feudal societies. The change involved great violence and loss of lives. Feudal societies were replaced with owning-class/working-class societies (usually called capitalist societies), again with great violence and bloodshed. The present societies are in the final stages of collapse and much violence and loss of life has been involved in their attempts to prevent replacement by a classless non-oppressive society (the Paris Commune, the 1917 October Revolution in Russia, the Liberation of China in 1949). (So far, the persistence of patterns of oppression within the new leadership has restored oppression after each such attempt.)

The tendency of a collapsing society to resort to war and mass destruction of people is at present everywhere evident.

The present collapsing societies possess atomic weapons which, if used, will destroy all humans and all forms of life more complex than bacteria. On the other hand, present knowledge and technology make quickly possible the creation of a veritable Eden on earth, free from want, drudgery, or oppression.

The present situation is one of great opportunities and great dangers.

Knowledge of the existence, nature, and remedy for human distress patterns is only thirty-five years old. During these thirty-five years our preoccupations have moved from "feeling better," to thinking better, to counseling others better, to eliminating oppression, to taking charge of everything, to reclaiming our full power, to seeing that everything goes right. The rate of progress for experienced Co-Counselors is obviously accelerating.

We have great opportunities and can assume great responsibilities in the present situation.

What shall we do, as individuals and as a Community?

Taking Our Bearings

There is a universe. At least one universe exists. Science fiction writers have speculated that there are or can be a number of universes, but certain logicians are confident that it is proven that there is only one. We can be quite contented that there is at least one and we are in it.

We assume along with physical scientists and logicians in general that the universe is real—that it exists independently of our observation of it, though there are certain mental exercises that can be performed by assuming that we are projecting its existence mentally from our minds, or that God is projecting it from her mind or something like that. In practical terms almost all the effective results in what human beings cherish as progress have stemmed from the viewpoint that the universe is real and exists and we observe it.

The universe is dynamic; it is moving steadily. We are able to distinguish two general trends within its movement. One is a trend of which entropy is a part, which we in RC have called the downward trend—a trend towards disorder, towards uninteresting characteristics, towards a leveling out, towards uniformity. On the other hand there is a trend toward integration, toward meaning, toward the relative independence of certain entities within the universe, toward complexity, toward interesting characteristics.

This trend has produced, in at least one galaxy, in at least one solar system, on at least one planet, a level of complexity, of complex interrelationships, that we've called life. Life has

First report to the World Conference, July 1985. Appeared in **Present Time** No. 64, July 1986.

emerged on at least one planet. People who deal with the figures and the probabilities of astrophysics are pretty well convinced that it must have appeared in many, many other places. I've heard that they suspect that in our local galaxy, the Milky Way, there are probably twenty billion planets that do support, or will eventually support life, but we have no direct knowledge of this. We only have the direct knowledge that on one planet at least, the complex upward trend has produced complexity of the level of life.

Life is very much dependent on the environment, but also has attained a remarkable degree of independence from the environment in some ways. Within this complexity of life, once it appears, the upward trend continues in the medium of evolution. On this one planet of ours, this beautiful planet of ours, it has produced central nervous systems that enable their possessors to function in a completely different way than simpler forms of life have done.

EVOLVED TO INTELLIGENCE

It has produced intelligence, which we in RC have redefined as the ability to construct a brand new successful response to the environment at every new instant.

We think that this is a general trend, at least on this planet, and at least within this complex of life, because as we've examined the behavior of some of our closer relatives, the orangutan, the chimpanzee, and the gorilla, it is evident that at least the beginnings of intelligence exist there. Now that chimpanzees and gorillas have been taught sign language in order to bypass their lack of vocal cords, they've shown themselves able to communicate with at least the beginnings of intelligence.

Some of our more remote relatives among the mollusks, some of the larger squid and octopi, are also suspected of having the beginnings of this ability to construct fresh responses. People who observe the little squares and triangles that the octopus lays out around his burrow from pieces of aluminum foil and white shells are struck with the beginnings of a geometric sense there, in this not-such-a-close relative.

Apparently we are not such a freak accident. There is a general trend in the universe moving in the direction of entities like ourselves. Probably as we become able to reach out, communicate and travel more widely in this universe, we will find that we need not be lonely, that there are other intelligences. I personally hope that older and more experienced brothers and sisters will arrive someday, take our hands, and help us over some of the rockier roads that we face that we seem to be stumbling around on. In any case intelligence appeared on this one planet, among our forebears and more recently, in the last one, two or three million years, within our species and closely related species, of which we are the only survivors.

NOT ONLY INTELLIGENCE

The complexity of the central nervous systems which allowed the development of intelligence has also produced certain other capacities in us, which have been largely hidden from us during our lives so far. We have had glimpses of a super-capacity which we've called "awareness," but we find this very difficult to think about, apparently because it's right at the edge of our complexity. I have tried to make a working definition of it by calling awareness "thinking about thinking while thinking," but I'm not sure that I'm doing anything more than playing with words there.

More recently we've become aware that this complexity has also given us an inherent sense of **complete power**, a sense which has been concealed from us almost all the way through our existence. This complexity has also conferred upon us an **absolute freedom of decision**. These interest us greatly at this point in our re-emergence, both the power and the freedom of decision. They seem to be tools that will fill in a gap in expediting our re-emergence that we have felt for some time.

VULNERABILITY TO DISTRESS CONDITIONING

From the very beginning of the complexity which allowed intelligence, intelligence has been parasitized upon by the **distress pattern phenomenon**. The fact is that when a possessor of intelligence moves into a condition of stress, this intelligence tends to suspend and the person regresses to a more primitive form of behavior. This more primitive form of behavior is familiar to us in the functioning of other mammals. We use it in domesticating other mammals, for example, and other animals as well. We use this phenomenon to train our horses and our dogs to behave in the ways we wish them to relate to us, in the ways that are convenient for us.

With the horse or the dog the use of this **stress pattern conditioning** in training confers no degradation of behavior. The acquired behavior is not necessarily on a lower level than the instinctive behavior which it replaces. When the same phenomenon impinges upon us human beings, it imposes a great degradation of function. At the very least it leaves us confused and dull, and at the worst it turns us into monsters who occupy the headlines of the newspapers with the tales of the forty murders they've committed and buried the bodies under their front porches. It produces phenomena such as mass murderers, promoters of wars, oppressors, and all kinds of other vicious things.

The distress pattern phenomenon has been really examined only within the context of RC and only in the last thirty-five years, but we've learned a great deal. We've grasped the fact that, in effect, a recording is made of what goes on during a period of stress. That fact has begun to answer many riddles about human activity. The notion of the **distress recording** is very fundamental to all our RC knowledge, all of our RC development, all our progress in re-emergence.

It is plain that all humanity has been victimized by the distress pattern, the distress recording phenomenon, ever since we first became human, ever since we first acquired intelligence and these other high-level characteristics. The essential nature of human beings has been largely obscured ever since those beginnings because of the imposition of distress patterns and because of their perpetuation through accident, contagion, and organized oppression.

Humans have not appeared to be enormously intelligent in the mass. They have not appeared to be possessed, inherently, of tremendous individual power. They have not always appeared to be good, benign, cooperative, and loving. They have not always appeared to be caring of all other humans. They have not always appeared to be supportive of the freedom and well being of their fellow humans. The explanation for this great obscuring fog of not-upward-trend characteristics seems to lie solely within the operation of distress recordings.

An intelligent human being entering a situation of stress is likely to have the intelligence function suspended, is likely to operate on a more primitive level and endure a distress recording during that time. If kept from recovering from that distress recording a human being becomes vulnerable to the triggering of the recording as a reversion to the more primitive behavior. If this is experienced enough times, the human tends to be caught chronically within the repetition of the distress recording as the human's usual behavior. This behavior is total. It includes the recorded distress feelings. It includes the pseudo-thoughts that seem to go through our minds. It includes the posture, the tone of voice. It includes the facial expression.

OUR REAL NATURES OBSCURED

The distress recordings have accumulated since human beings first became intelligent. The excellent characteristics of vast intelligence, good character, power, freedom of decision, cooperativeness, and all the rest have been largely obscured for humans in the mass, so that we have tended to regard people who show these characteristics as elegant accidents. We speak of "geniuses." We say this individual is a genius because he thought the way through to a general theory of relativity. This human being was a genius because he painted a beautiful painting. This human being was a genius because she unravelled the secrets of radioactivity. Our cultures have offered us this kind of picture of humans instead of having the picture as we in RC now have it, that these are characteristics of all of us and that every human being has all these capacities and would exhibit all these capacities if they were not obscured by the accumulation of distress patterns.

ACCIDENT, CONTAGION, AND OPPRESSION

Distress patterns can not only be imposed by accident, they can be imposed by contagion. Observably, the victim of a distress pattern, once it is restimulated, whether by accident or decision (and we are leaning more and more to the notion that there is always a decision involved in restimulation and have now explained why we make that decision), and enduring the restimulation of the distress recording, is pulled, is lured, to endure the restimulation in a more comfortable role than he or she occupied in the original hurtful experience. Taking this other more "comfortable" role (I put the word "comfortable" in quotes because it is not rational comfort but rather a sort of numbness or dullness that passes for comfort in our cultures) the person then acts out the distress recording at the expense of another individual. The person who was beaten as a child tends to become a grown-up possessing a distress recording from the beating, and restimulated in the presence of his or her own child, tends to slip into the beater's role, and beats his or her own child. Thus, by contagion, distress patterns are spread on and on and on through the population.

Distress patterns are acquired by accident. They are acquired by contagion. At some time in history, most human beings were maneuvered into accepting being organized into oppressive societies. (We have with us a very few representatives of tribal peoples who did not, as peoples, go through this kind of decision, but have suffered from it because they have been imposed upon by other people who did.) In every case the first oppressive society was a slave society.

HOW IT POSSIBLY HAPPENED

Though the organization into oppressive societies was imposed by violence, threats of death, withholding of food, and enforcement of many sorts, the rationalization which undoubtedly helped persuade our ancestors who agreed to be slaves was that the organization which accompanied the oppressive society made possible the survival of more humans to maturity. Through most of our history human beings have been preoccupied with the survival of our species against the dangers in the environment, a preoccupation which we share with every form of life. Every species of which we have any knowledge puts the survival of the species right up at the top of their agenda of priorities. Because we share this preoccupation with survival the oppressive society could claim credit (which actually belonged only to the organization which accompanied the society), for more people survived if organized into an oppressive society than when operating on a tribal level. These claims must have been persuasive to our ancestors. That rationalization must have had a good deal to do with the fact that almost all our ancestors agreed at some point to accept being slaves.

A very few of our ancestors agreed to accept being slaveowners, and became human beings who acted viciously (to the great detriment of their central humanness, just as the majority's acceptance of acting submissively was to the great detriment of their humanness).

FLEETING PHENOMENA, IN THE LONG VIEW

There is a widespread impression, the result of misinformation imposed on all of us, that the present society and the present social relationships, whatever they are (and there is some variation around the world, not fundamental differences at this point, but some variation.), are eternal and installed by God,

THE LONGER VIEW

that this society which we grew up in is the only possible kind of world and that it could never be changed. The phrases that are used to persuade us to this, differ from country to country. In the leading imperialist power we hear different phrases than in the one which is a satellite, but all of us receive this message.

The actual reality is, of course, that the organization of class societies is a very recent phenomenon. We have been our present species or something closely related to it for somewhere between one and three million years. Oppressive societies have existed for at the most ten thousand years, probably about six thousand.

The slave societies replaced the free associations almost everywhere. Only our Aboriginal sister and some of the Native Americans of those who are with us here escaped going through this organization into a class society. Of course many Native Americans did not escape it. There were many slave societies organized in the Americas before the Europeans' impingement. These slave societies all carried within them certain internal contradictions, inherent in them, and these contradictions worked their way out until the slave societies collapsed and were replaced by a different kind of class society. Slave societies lasted, probably, about three to five thousand years.

They were replaced everywhere by feudal societies, where the principle classes were the feudal baron and the serf. The economic relation was a slightly different one. These societies carried within them certain internal contradictions, and as these contradictions worked their way out, the feudal societies lasted about one thousand years, and then collapsed and were replaced by a new kind of class society.

We've started calling this society the owning-class-working-class society, but it is mostly called the capitalist society. Here the principle classes are the group of people who own the means of economic production, the owning class, and the group of people who do not own the means of economic production, the working class, who sell their labor to the ones who do.

These societies have lasted about three hundred and fifty years. They carry within them certain inherent contradictions which have been working their way out and these societies are in a state of collapse, actually in the final stages of collapse. They are not the Eternal Verities which we must conform to or God will be angry with us. They are just a fleeting historical phenomenon, which humanity has endured, probably for understandable reasons.

Perhaps all this was necessary. The past is determined; it happened. I like to speculate, however, on the possibility that perhaps when the first tribal peoples were being coerced to organize themselves into slave societies, a flying saucer could have landed from one of our older brothers' and sisters' populations out somewhere in the galaxy and they had rushed out and said, "Stop! Stop! It isn't necessary to oppress each other. You can organize yourselves and develop technology without that." Wouldn't that have been wonderful? It didn't happen, but perhaps it is about to happen.

PRESENT SOCIETIES COLLAPSING

The present societies are everywhere in the last stages of collapse. You need only look at any peripheral phenomena of the current advanced societies to see how absolutely untenable their continued operation has become. Armaments, exploitation, oppression, overpopulation, pollution, crime, and environmental destruction are all out of control.

The replacement of these societies has been attempted in a number of places. The Paris Commune is venerated by those of us who believe in social change. It lasted about three months, but human genius flared and showed itself brilliantly in those three months. The October Revolution in Russia in 1917 went forward a long ways before the continuing patterns of the oppressive society penetrating the leadership of the new society took it back toward the same kind of class relationships that existed before. The liberation of China in 1949 and the period that followed that was a golden epoch taking people far forward in rational relationships until the same kind of patterned regression took place after Mao's death and is tending to push China back into the same kind of oppressive class relationships as before 1949.

Not all gains have been lost. I'm sure that Marie could tell us that the workers of Paris still remember the lessons of the Commune — not well enough, but to some extent. I'm sure that the people in the Soviet Union cherish and exhibit in many ways the gains which were once made. I'm told on authority that I believe, that both in Russia and China, children are still held in such high regard and are given such priority to resources, that it makes the treatment of children in the western countries appear shameful to those who have seen both at close hand. Not all the gains have been lost.

The big breakthrough to a rational society has not yet come. At the present moment it is still not certain that it **will** come, because the total destruction of nuclear holocaust threatens to intervene.

UNCARING OF INDIVIDUALS

Each past class society in its collapse has cared not a whit how many of its members were destroyed in its efforts to preserve itself. The great slave empires, when they collapsed, destroyed millions of people. Wars ravaged the ancient world at this great change-over. Much of the population was destroyed. Much of the accumulated wealth was wasted in this violent change-over to the new society. When the capitalist societies replaced the feudal societies the feudal societies cared not a whit how much of the population they destroyed in their efforts to preserve themselves. Many of the countries of Europe lost as much as eighty percent of their populations in these turnovers to capitalism which were called the Thirty Years

War, the Hundred Years War, the Great Black Plagues, and the other uncherished titles.

There is no indication that the present societies which dominate the world and which place profit, and if possible quick profit, ahead of all other considerations including the health and welfare of the people are any different in this regard. These societies show no hesitation over burning women and children to death with napalm if it will guarantee that more Coca Cola can be sold in the future. There is no indication that these capitalist societies care more about their human members than the slave societies or the feudal societies did.

These blind, destructive, oppressive societies have in their possession enormous numbers of atomic missiles, such enormous numbers that if even a small portion of them were fired and exploded the ensuing radiation would destroy not only all human beings, but all forms of complex life. The evolution of life would have to begin over again from creatures on the level of bacteria.

We have no way of knowing the future. The future is always unpredictable. (Thank goodness. Otherwise we would be bored to death.) The past is determined. The future is continually free choice. There is no present guarantee that we are going to surmount *this* crisis. People are concerned. It is easy to become very frightened and paralyzed by the thought of atomic weapons.

CHOOSING THE BEST ASSUMPTION

Scientists who are aware of the great listening antennas that we have set up to detect any intelligent communication from outside our solar system are concerned that we have so far not received any. It is true that our listening equipment is still primitive. It is true that it has not been in operation for a very long time yet. It is true that stellar distances are very, very vast. Yet some of the scientists feel a little concerned that no coherent message has been received. As yet there has been no

THE LONGER VIEW

indication of intelligence out there in the universe reaching us. They wonder, they speculate, is it possible that there is a built-in difficulty in intelligence? Is it possible that it can never survive past achieving a certain level of technology, that at that point it must always destroy itself?

That is an unproductive speculation. We have learned that when we cannot be sure ahead of time which of two assumptions is correct that it makes sense to choose the one that leads to the most interesting results. So we deliberately choose the assumption that intelligence can survive past its development of this much technology, because the other assumption doesn't lead to anything very interesting for us. A future as a bunch of cinders or radioactive garbage is not exciting. So we assume that we have a future. I think it would be well to note here that some of our new insights in RC make a fine case for not being dismayed or demoralized by the possibility of atomic holocaust.

We have recovered awareness of our complete freedom of decision, the reality that we are free to make any kind of decision that we want to, any time, under any circumstances. This seemed difficult to believe at first hearing because all of us had been told something like thirty billion times during our lives that we have no freedom of decision, we must decide as we are told is proper or expected. This mass of suggestion and dictation has necessarily left a certain residue of rigid distress patterns upon us. We are now quite clear, among the theoreticians in RC, that every human being has, inherently, a complete freedom of choice. We are free to make a good decision and we are also free to make a bad decision. That may not, at first hearing, seem encouraging, but I would urge you to think about it and accept it because it seems necessary to take the step of reclaiming our complete power.

BY-PASSING DESPAIR

As part of the freedom of decision, we have the freedom to choose any viewpoint which we wish. Using this, I would like to offer you a comfortable viewpoint about the possibility of atomic holocaust.

I begin by offering you a comfortable viewpoint about your own death. Would you care to have a comfortable viewpoint about that? Let's consider me. I have promised that I will not die. I made this promise to my youngest son many years ago in order to solve a counseling problem. I was not dishonest with him. I told him that I did not know how I would keep that promise but I did tell him that I would keep that promise, and so far I've kept it. Nevertheless it is possible that something might happen so that I should die. I ride these jet planes all the time and those things are notoriously not well-maintained any more. As the society collapses it neglects the maintenance on its jet planes. (Enjoy yourselves flying.) So it's possible that one of these planes may go down with me on it. Now if anyone manages to reach me in some mythical hereafter and charge me with having died when I promised not to, I have my answer ready. I will say, "I didn't die, I was killed." I can conceive of being killed, but I still promise you that I will never die. You can count on it.

If it happens that I am killed, will this be very important? I don't think so. The fact that I have been killed, if it happens, will not be very important. What will be very important and significant, at least to me, is the fact that **I will have lived**. The fact that I lived is very important, very significant. The fact that I may be killed is relatively unimportant. I have lived. That is exciting. (I, in my case, have really lived. It happened late in life, but I have done some real living. I did some important things earlier, but I was too distressed to appreciate it at the time.)

What is very significant is the fact that a person has lived, *not* that the person may die or be killed.

For all of us, if the very worst that we can conceive of happens, if the stupid patterns in charge of the red buttons let loose the missiles and we all die and temporarily remain as a few rows of blackened cinders, **this will not really be important**. The fact that we have lived and advanced to this point, that humanity stormed the heavens thus far, **that will be significant**. If there are celestial chronicals kept somewhere that will be noted in the books in letters of gold. The fact that we stumbled and destroyed ourselves in atomic holocaust will be a minor footnote.

We have reached this far. We have been ourselves and if the holocaust should happen before we get any further out, at least there will have been a Re-evaluation Counseling Community that was almost world-wide, where people had pooled their highest aspirations and their most productive tools and were heading up the ladder toward even greater heights of complexity and meaning and achievement.

THE WORST POSSIBILITY DOESN'T JUSTIFY DESPAIR

Of course the factory will start over again. You cannot keep life from evolving. The surviving single cells will start clustering together and become complex creatures which will evolve and evolve and evolve and evolve and evolve and eventually intelligence will appear again on the surface of our earth and, looking at the traces of the mistakes that we made, they undoubtedly will be able to avoid them and go on to a brilliant future. If we don't make it somebody will. Some relative of ours (because the bacteria are closely related to us) will eventually make it all the way. That will be splendid.

It's possible to stop and say, "Wouldn't it be nice, maybe a little better, if we didn't waste these three billion years of evolution? That we just go on all the way ourselves?" I heartily agree. I have every intention of trying to see that that happens. That is a major reason why I'm talking this morning, that we do plan to skip this danger and go all the way.

At the present time the human species (actually the human

subspecies since all of us around the world are closely related, we're all members of the same subspecies *Homo sapiens sapiens*) is no longer in danger of being wiped out by weather and disease. The only danger to our existence as a species is our own foolishness, embodied in the operation of distress patterns individually and in the oppressive society organizationally. We have acquired our knowledge the hard way inside the trammels of the oppressive society, but we have acquired knowledge of the environment around us such that we are able easily to master it. We have a tremendous amount of knowledge and, except in the fields of economics, government, and human relationships, our knowledge is increasing exponentially at the present time. What is being learned in physics, in mathematics, in chemistry, in the biological sciences, in technology, is increasing at a great rate. We are piling up enormous amounts of knowledge. Our knowledge will certainly soon be at the point that we can terraform other worlds, that we can begin our great trek out into the galaxy, out into the universe, and spread out from our lovely home planet while preserving it lovingly and exquisitely as a home base. Our technology has reached the point that there is hardly a problem that we cannot master quickly. Many, many inventions are gathering dust in corporate safes because they do not promise a quick profit even though they would bring ease and well-being to large populations. We have everything we need to make this planet a veritable Eden, where there is no drudgery, no oppression, where everyone lives a life of well-being and contentment. This is one side of the picture. We've reached a point where everything that we've ever dreamed of is within our grasp.

The other side of the picture is that we are on the brink of destroying ourselves with atomic holocaust, with pollution, with war, with oppression. Millions of people are still starving.

The oppressive societies have never been able to function except on the basis of distress patterns. The distress patterns were already there or oppression would never have worked. We have seen enough of people emerging from distress to say with complete confidence that no human being would ever accept being oppressed, would ever submit to oppression, except through the installation of patterns of oppression upon him or upon her. We have seen enough to say clearly that no human being would ever accept functioning in any oppressor role, without first having patterns of oppression installed upon that person and then being manipulated into the oppressor end of the pattern.

NO HUMAN ENEMIES

For a long time in the past, we activists assumed that greed is what makes oppressors function. It certainly has something to do with it. Theories that some of you have been coming up with that assume that if we were just nice enough to the oppressors that would end oppression, do not appear realistic to me, because the oppressor patterns do function on the basis of greed. But it's also plain that no human being would ever agree to be an oppressor had he or she not first been oppressed and then manipulated into the other end of the pattern.

England has been a great window for the rest of us. It's always easier to see the picture outside your own culture. There the first ruling class topic group reported at an Arundel workshop. They told how as small children they had been taken from their families and sent to special schools where they were brutalized for a year to two, brutalized, beaten, degraded, treated just rotten in every respect, and then after a year or two forced to turn around and do the same thing to the younger children who came in, as preparation for being effective representatives of the British Empire. The picture was laid bare for us.

We can now see in every culture that the person who agrees to function as an oppressor has first been terribly oppressed. The pattern is installed, then they are manipulated into the other end of the pattern. We have enough owning-class, ruling-class people in RC now, that we can see that they have their own set of problems, that they need special help. We see very plainly that as human beings they have always hated having to play the oppressor role. Their great exaltation at being able to leave this role is just as great as yours or mine is at being able to leave the oppressed role.

I cherish the story of the last emperor of China, Henry Pu Yi, who was overthrown by the Nationalist Revolution led by Dr. Sun Yet Sen in 1912, but lived on for a long time. When Japanese imperialism invaded China, and set up a puppet empire in Manchuria, which they called Manchukuo, they resurrected the old emperor and put him on the puppet throne. He was still there when liberation came, but the very brave and keen man who was leading this particular revolution said that life should never be taken if it could be spared. So instead of his suffering the fate of the czars, Henry Pu Yi was asked what he would like to do. He said that the only thing he'd ever had much chance to learn anything about was gardening. So the old emperor was put to work as a gardener. In his greenhouses, foreign visitors used to come and talk to him and they reported that they would ask him, "Don't you miss the splendor of the imperial court?" and he would say, "Oh no, that was infinitely boring, but now I am serving the people. I am raising plants. I am doing something useful." They said that the old man seemed really happy for the first time in his life. That's a little fragment of reality that I cherish. It is a mark of confirmation of something that is very reassuring to us all, which is that **we have no human enemies**. We have only human fellow victims, some of whom get manipulated into the role of acting as our enemies and oppressors and all of whom will welcome liberation, if we become good enough counselors that we can pull them out.

TIME TO ACT DECISIVELY

Nevertheless the distress patterns continue to be imposed. Oppression continues to take place. The very existence of complex life is threatened. "Somebody ought to do something." On the one hand, we have the vista of a delicious world where everyone is nice and everyone is safe, and everyone is well fed and eager, and learning is progressing and exciting. On the other hand, there is the vista of a burned-up wasteland of a planet. Someone ought to make the decision to go the right way. I invite this quite marvelous collection of people that are assembled here in this World Conference to make that decision. I do not ask you to do it as a group. That is awkward and cumbersome and unworkable. I invite *each one* of you to decide to be the one that sees that humanity takes this road. We have ample theoretical reasons to think that this is possible. We have reached this clarity about our freedom of decision. Where this has been applied counseling begins to walk on tall legs. Counseling and re-emergence begin to work very well. The advanced theoretical insights we have about our total freedom of decision can be applied eagerly. The slow process of re-emergence, which for many of us has gone on for years, talking about our distresses until somehow we could cry a little bit about them while the great pile was slowly dissipated, can be turned into a wholesale, rapid onslaught.

It apparently is possible for any one of us, and theoretically for any one of the 4.8 billion people that are estimated to be alive, to make a decision to move, to end this sorry state of danger and put this world on the right track. We have reason to be confident that if one such human being did, there would be ample support for her. If just one of us reclaimed her power, used our present theoretical clarity, and *moved*, that one would be enough to guarantee the future of the world.

These are strong words, are they not? These may seem a little overwhelming at first, since some of us have at least been feeling we are having a little trouble tying both shoe laces at once. I think that at least these strong words need to be said, and then explored. I am quite confident that I am speaking sooth, that I am telling the truth.

This capacity of any one of us to make a bold-enough move to galvanize increasing numbers of the rest of humanity around her and accomplish what we all desire, is an immediate practical possibility.

We haven't done it so far, so there's no use feeling complacent in any lazy sense. We can feel complacent in a good sense because we *have* done quite a few good things. Considering how much confusion we started out in, we're remarkably unconfused, aren't we? Compared with what is possible for us, I think we're just standing on the shore of a vast sea. Enormous possibilities lie ahead of us.

EACH ONE AS AN INDIVIDUAL

Our Communities certainly have a role to play in the future. In talking about our Communities and what will happen, I urge that we not think of ourselves as a group, but as a set of individuals who can think for ourselves as individuals. I propose each one of us think of himself or herself as *the* seed which is going to grow the plant that will seed the rest of the world. There's a little weakness in thinking of ourselves as a "group." We have certain strengths as a group. We have certain advantages. We will explore in our discussions how to use our relationship in the RC Communities to the best advantage, but there tends to be a hangover from the oppressive use of groups in the oppressive society into a kind of helpless huddling if we think "group." If we start thinking "*we* are going to do this," the next step is often to think, "I will do this if you will do this first" or "She didn't do that, I don't see why she should expect me to do it," and other various disheartening notions tend to creep in from the patterns, so I would urge you to think of yourselves as "I," rather than part of a "we."

This flies in the face of many progressives' notions because progressives and even revolutionaries have, in the past, tried to gain enough confidence for themselves by thinking, "we, we, we, we, we," otherwise it seemed too frightening. This will possibly feel like a frightening idea, but I would like to place each one of you (and I give you power to do this to other people, to pass it on) in full individual charge of this universe of ours. If this universe doesn't work well, you know who I am going to hold responsible. *You*, individually. It will take some time to get used to this idea. We will explore this the last day of this conference, around the article "You Can Start Your Own World Community, Now." As the sub-title says, "Full Permission Freely Given, Precise Instructions Included."

We have a lovely world. Using one of our newer techniques, taking attention completely away from distress, we've found that just the realization of the reality of the universe and the world we are in, is enough to provide *massive* discharge without the slightest suffering. We don't have to take any time to get our attention out after the discharge, because it's been out all the time. This is nice!

We didn't set out in counseling to be the custodians of the universe or even of the planet. Almost all of us set out in this effort that we call Re-evaluation Counseling to *feel* a little better, didn't we? That carried us a short distance. Then we acquired a new goal, or clarified a new goal, of *thinking* better, and that has stood us in good stead. The results of the activity that we call Re-evaluation Counseling have certainly been for all of us to *think* better. This has been a consistent goal for us. We have all found that we think better with the use of counseling or not one of us would be in this room.

The motivation to think better has remained consistent. We now have other motivations. We want to be able to care better, we want to be able to relate better; we have learned to progress from one goal to another. Some of us have for some time been yearning to reclaim our complete power. Some of us have been using our freedom of decision more and more, in ways we didn't ever think of using it before, including expediting our own discharge. Now we're proposing that we move, *en masse* but as individuals, to the motivation of being in complete charge of absolutely everything and seeing that everything goes right. You individually. Not us as a group, but me individually and you individually. I propose that we leave here at least a hundred and fifty-five *individuals*, each one of whom will straighten out the world by herself or himself, even if the rest of us should fall in a swamp on the way home.

Outline: Organizational Report
The 1985 World Conference

Re-evaluation Counseling is thirty-five years old. It began as a research and development group, working through Personal Counselors, Inc., teaching classes and doing one-way counseling for a fee. Personal Counselors, Inc. is still in existence and owns the terms "Re-evaluation Counseling" and "Co-Counseling" which it permits the Community the use of under the terms of the Guidelines. Personal Counselors, Inc. still does one-way counseling for a fee, principally in the form of "intensives" for members of the Community, but it, together with Rational Island Publishers, Inc., mainly serves as a service agency for the support of the Communities.

The Re-evaluation Counseling Communities have been in existence for fifteen years and have operated under some form of the Guidelines for fourteen years. In this time participation in Re-evaluation Counseling has spread from the one city of Seattle to approximately four hundred other cities, and to forty-eight states of the United States, ten provinces of Canada, and to thirty-eight other countries. Re-evaluation Co-Counselors are active on six of the seven continents.

Besides the International Reference Person and the Alternate International Reference Person, there are at present forty-two Regional Reference Persons, nineteen International Liberation Reference Persons, one hundred and fifty-two Area Reference Persons and an equal number of Alternate Area Reference Persons, one thousand six hundred and forty-six certified Teachers of Re-evaluation Counseling, approximately an equal number of assistant Teachers, one hundred eleven Infor-

Appeared in **Present Time** No. 61, October 1985.

mation Coordinators, an estimated five hundred Support Group leaders, twenty-four Editors of international level journals, and an estimated two hundred Editors of local or Area newsletters.

It is estimated that approximately nine hundred thousand people have received elementary instruction in Re-evaluation Counseling theory and/or Co-Counseling practice in the last fifteen years. Most of these constitute a reserve of supportive allies but about ten or fifteen percent are in active contact with the Community and participate in Community affairs.

We have published twelve principal books on theoretical developments in Re-evaluation Counseling and a thirteenth, **The Rest of Our Lives**, is about to appear. We have issued, and continue to issue, twenty-seven journals for special interests of Co-Counselors. Some of the literature has been translated into twenty-one languages.

We have spent several hundred thousand dollars in assisting new populations to have an introductory participation in RC classes or workshops. Almost every bit of these funds came from the Outreach portions of class fees or the net from workshops. We have been almost totally independent or self-sufficient to date in financing our activities.

It is estimated that at least three-quarters of the leaders of the RC Communities are also leaders in wide-world organizations at the present time—a decisive change since our last World Conference.

The Guidelines of the Re-evaluation Counseling Communities were first written in 1971 and were heavily revised and rewritten in the Area Reference Persons' Workshops of the next few years (which served as the World Conferences of that period). Fewer and fewer revisions have been found to be needed in the last few World Conferences. Very few suggestions for revision were received in the preparatory period for this World

Conference and most of those did not meet the deadline that had been set. However, all of them have been considered and a very few proposals are made to the Conference for changes. The committee charged with making such recommendations by the 1984 meeting of the Regional Reference Persons was myself, Ann Steele, and Katie Kauffman. On Katie's resignation, Rachel Noble was added to the committee.

(Then followed the proposed changes in the Guidelines.)

(Then followed a report on finances compiled by the Foundation on the International Outreach Fund and by Rational Island Publishers on the Publications Fund.)

Outline: The Clarification and Generalization of the Fundamentals of Co-Counseling
The 1985 World Conference

A remarkable clarification of the fundamentals of Re-evaluation Counseling has taken place since the last World Conference.

Co-Counseling can now be clearly seen as a completely natural, spontaneous process which each human being is ready to use and, in fact, has been intuitively trying to use all of her or his life, frustrated only by certain identifiable factors in the nature of distress patterns themselves and in the functioning of oppressive cultures and societies. Observably, all human beings, in the presence of other human beings and not occupied with work or other attention-demanding activities, strive continually to have another person listen to them and pay attention to them. With rare exceptions, adult human beings do not pay attention to each other or really listen to each other.

We can now state what may be called the *Fundamental Theorem of Re-evaluation Counseling*:

What every human being intuitively attempts to do in the presence of another human being, that is, be paid attention to and listened to in the expectation that discharge will occur and the human will become free from distress, will work, *if the humans will just take turns.*

Why do not human beings spontaneously take turns so that the intuitive process can work?

Appeared in **Present Time** No. 61, October 1985.

In October of 1982 we assembled a special workshop of experienced Co-Counselors which we called a "Counseling With Supervision" Workshop. Our goal was to attempt to determine why the usual level of counseling, even of experienced Co-Counselors, was so far below the level of the theory and of the occasional brilliant, very effective session sometimes seen in demonstrations at workshops. With the use of video cameras we examined in detail how the persons in the counselors' roles performed.

We discovered the universal existence, in every counselor, of an "ancient habit-pattern" of keeping attention on his or her own distresses *all the time*, even when he or she had overtly promised to give attention to the client and the client's distresses instead. The habit had apparently begun in an attempt to have the distresses ready to be recounted if a second person ever listened and had become a pattern through the accumulation of frustration and other distress over the failure of other people to respond with the needed attention.

This explained why people, in the ordinary course of their lives, rarely if ever pay attention to or listen well to another person and why the spontaneous recovery process is everywhere frustrated. It also explained why the level of counseling in the RC Communities had remained so low, since the Counselor, in the grip of the "ancient habit" had often or usually (and unawarely) kept his or her attention on his or her own distresses even though he or she had committed himself or herself to putting his or her attention on the client.

Having located the source of the problem, the next step was to find a remedy. We have, so far, found one technique that works, however slowly and ponderously.

This is to decide, over and over again, to end the "ancient habit" and to replace it with an attitude or

posture of keeping one's attention on interesting and profitable matters including the present scene and, when a counselor, on the client and the client's distresses and the client's re-emergence. Such iteration and re-iteration, such deciding and re-deciding, seems to work well, producing discharge and changes in counseling effectiveness, whether done as client in a session, while having a turn in a group, or even when done by oneself.

The revelation of the "ancient habit-pattern" has also helped us come to grips with another puzzling phenomenon. This was the annoying tendency of many members of the RC Communities to claim the role of "client" without agreement from the people around them and to rehearse their distresses or even begin to discharge in many inappropriate circumstances. These bad manners can now be seen to spring from a combination of the "ancient habit-pattern" and a certain confused permissiveness we had introduced into our Communities in an effort to provide safety for people to recover their abilities to discharge and make a start on re-emergence.

The solution is to require that one receives permission from someone who is willing to act as a counselor at that time *before one assumes the role of a client, either as dramatizer or discharger.* **If we can make this the standard of good manners within the RC Communities I think the problem will begin to disappear.**

Help in discharging is not everything that the client needs from the counselor. There are situations in which the client needs other kinds of intervention, other kinds of thinking. Ninety-five percent of what the client needs from the counselor, however, is exactly assistance in discharging.

We are now able to say, with great clarity and conciseness, exactly what the counselor (the second person) needs to do in order for the client (the first person) to be able to discharge.

The counselor needs to do three things:

1. Pay enough attention to the client to see *clearly* what the distresses are.

2. *Think* **of all possible ways of contradicting that distress.**

3. Contradict the distress *sufficiently*. **The client will always discharge.**

These three are easy to read but have proven in practice to be difficult for a counselor to remember, possibly because of their anti-pattern content. They need to be memorized by rote so that they can be repeated accurately in the midst of any restimulation or confusion.

Effective contradiction of the client's distress almost always will require more than contradictory words. A good counselor will need to recover his or her flexibility in the use of tone of voice, facial expression, and posture.

As a general ambience, contradictory to almost every distress, the effective counselor will tend to turn toward every client attitudes of *appreciation, delight, high expectations, commitment, confidence, respect,* **and** *love.* **With these as a background, the specific contradiction of the specific distress will tend to be even more effective.**

We now have a conjecture, and some confirmation, that the most effective contradiction to any distress is to take attention completely away from it. This will be discussed with the "frontier" questions of our theory.

Outline: The Frontiers of Re-evaluation Counseling Theory
The 1985 World Conference

The most advanced concepts in counseling spring directly from the clarification of the fundamentals concepts. They also spring from the major philosophical contributions which RC has furnished over the last three decades. Among these are: the absolute distinction between the past and the future (the past is completely determined, the future is free choice); the fundamentally benign nature of reality; the absolute freedom of choice available to an intelligence in any situation; and the estimation of distress as a temporary aberration in the ongoing development of the upward trend in the Universe.

Other useful concepts have been regarding intelligence as being covered or occluded by distress rather than as being destroyed or replaced by it; love as simply being the way in which humans inherently feel about and regard each other; and zest and cooperativeness as being innate qualities of humans.

We have concluded that the development of our central nervous systems to the size and complexity which they have attained has not only brought us flexible intelligence as a qualitatively higher level of behavior than any life on Earth had previously attained, has not only brought us the super-function of awareness, but has also bestowed upon us an inherent sense of complete power and a complete freedom of decision independent of any other factors in any situation.

(These inherent characteristics are obscured, of course, in all or nearly all humans at the present by the accumulated distress patterns which have hidden this underlying reality from us previously.)

Appeared in **Present Time** No. 61, October 1985.

A crucial development in the recent period was the re-definition of "restimulation." Restimulation had originally been defined as "the *involuntary* association of past distress with some similarity in the present," and this definition had seemed useful to many of us in contradicting the guilt and blame turned on us by others for "being upset." As experiences accumulated, many developments put this definition into question and restimulation was eventually re-defined as "the usually unaware but nevertheless intentional bringing up of past distress with the excuse of some similarity in the present in the hopes of receiving attention from some other person and securing discharge of the past distress." In the usual language of Co-Counselors we now recognized that "we had to *decide* to be restimulated."

This opened the door to a much fuller responsibility on the part of Co-Counselors while in the role of client and clarified the reclaiming of power and the possibility of keeping our attention away from distress.

Distress discharges whenever contradicted *sufficiently*. Examination of the counseling of many of our best counselors revealed that they were usually directing the attention of their clients *away* from the distress while securing copious discharge. The conjecture followed that perhaps the best contradiction to any distress was to pay no attention to it, rather than putting attention to it and then contradicting it. Attempting this has worked well with experienced Co-Counselors and often with inexperienced Co-Counselors as well. When it has not succeeded, it seems likely that it was error on the part of the counselor rather than any inherent limitation of the process.

The use of directions, commitments, "Frameworks," "Synopses," and "attention away from distress" has extended the range of the effectiveness of a session far beyond the time of the session itself. A determined client can deny the old distress any influence on his or her behavior and feelings for a long (perhaps indefinitely long) period by holding to the purposeful thought and actions planned in a session. There is little or no "suffering" while discharging with attention away from distress and there is no problem getting attention to the present after such discharge. The attention has been in the present all along. The client "cries with joy," "shakes with excitement," "laughs with merriment," and yawns relaxedly in ways which are familiar in our cultures but whose importance or function have not previously been recognized.

The possibility arises that, having assimilated these theoretical developments thoroughly, one can put one's attention completely away from distress, take charge of the environment completely, act always in an optimum way, live every moment well, and continue to discharge profusely *as one lives well*, as long as there is any distress remaining to discharge. In other words, the distinction between a session and ordinary living, which we made in the beginning in order to provide safety for the discharge process to be recovered and protected from the usual invalidation and interference from the culture, may now be eliminated. We may now be able to re-emerge more rapidly than ever with no postponement of the rewards of re-emergence.

Each new moment presents us with the beginning of a brand-new future which we do not need to allow the distresses of the past to contaminate at all. Even if we slip at first and allow such contamination to take place in our awkwardness at mastering this new skill, we need not despair. The next new moment presents us with the beginning of another fresh, uncontaminated future and the one after that with another. With decision and practice our skill will improve sufficiently.

Our use of the "Golden Ring" marked the beginning of the end of the period of tolerance for thoughtless, unaware counseling and improvements have continued steadily since then. "Coached counseling," in which a coach supports an insecure counselor to gain confidence, was followed by "Counseling with Supervision" in which a competent counselor supervises another counselor as she or he counsels, critiquing and discuss-

THE LONGER VIEW

ing the work as it progresses. "Training One's Own Counselor" is Supervised Counseling in which the Supervisor is both client *and* Supervisor.

The techniques of decisive counseling and the role of leadership will be examined in the next section.

Outline: Decisive Counseling and Leadership
The 1985 World Conference

1. DECISIVE COUNSELING

Although the client armed with advanced theory can plan her or his own session, can remember and keep directions and commitments, can act against identified distresses in ordinary living, and can take responsibility for training her or his own counselor, we have basically been correct all along in assuming that each of us is already and at all times a perfect client, fully committed to making a total effort towards re-emergence, and that any appearance to the contrary is in fact the distress itself being presented for the counselor's attention, understanding, and contradiction.

Every one of the 4.8 billion people presently alive has been waiting, since first being hurt, for a second human to pay enough attention to him or her to see clearly what the distresses are (including *asking* him or *asking* her), think of all possible ways to contradict that distress, and contradict it sufficiently. Each one of the 4.8 billion would then immediately discharge, without having to have ever heard the words "Re-evaluation Counseling" or even the word "discharge."

It is as counselors that we have needed to improve. Through no fault of ours we have been conditioned to *not* do well or consistently the things which the client needs us to do. We have, understandably, become so preoccupied with our need to be someone's client that we unawarely slip into that attitude when we have agreed to be counselor. What are the elements that we

Appeared in **Present Time** No. 61, October 1985.

can well keep in mind in order to be excellent, decisive counselors for our clients?

First, join in a compact with all our fellow Co-Counselors to give up our preoccupation with *getting* good counseling and instead join in a compact to be preoccupied with *giving* good counseling. (This may well be the only practical road to *getting* good counseling.)

Second, give up forever the practice of being a lazy counselor. It is true that the client does ninety percent of the work of a session, but to do the counselor's ten percent well enough will require one's persistent, aware application. If one has contradicted one's client's distress well enough that the client has begun to discharge, it is still time to stay on the job, to think and plan and act on contradicting it even more and producing even more profound discharge. To sacrifice one's chronic tone of voice, chronic facial expression, and chronic posture in order to model for the client how he or she can step outside of his or her own distress has excellent results for both client and counselor.

Third, examine and clean up one's motivations. If one is counseling only to "get a session back" or some other low-level reason, it is time to take stock. The only adequate motivation for a counselor is the burning desire to assist that client to re-emerge into full humanness. That is thrillingly rewarding in itself.

Fourth, *really* pay attention to the client. Notice not only "what's on top" or what about the client's distresses bothers the counselor, but look for the client's deep chronic hurts of which he or she may no longer even be aware and plan the massive contradictions that will move him or her forward decisively. Think about one's client between sessions.

Fifth, keep up with and use the up-to-date tools of RC. Any of the commitments against the various internalized oppressions, if supported and persisted in vigorously by the counselor, will have decisive effects for the client in a fairly brief period of time. The general individual commitment—"From now on the *real* (Jenny Jensen)!"—*used persistently* will clarify goals and bring up important material for discharge for any client.

Sixth, it is important for the counselor to realize how important her or his own role is in the process. The counselor is the immediate source of effective contradiction to the client's distress. Persistently correct attitudes toward the client (see "The Counselor as Bagpiper") have tremendously good effects upon the client. The counselor needs to be prepared to function as an object of trust and an object of love for the client if that is what the client needs.

2. LEADERSHIP

Every person is capable of leadership. Every person is eager to become a leader whether able to admit this eagerness or not. The peoples of the world are suffering intense hardship, privation, and frustration for lack of effective leadership. Enormous amounts of invalidation have been placed upon people by the oppressive societies in order to conceal this universal capacity for leadership.

The Re-evaluation Counseling Communities have proven to be a remarkable training ground for leadership, in part because of the opportunities to discharge the interfering invalidations and in part because of the supportive safety for a person to learn to lead which the Communities afford.

There is much theory about the art and practice of leadership in the existing RC literature. Three recent developments are summarized here:

1. An aware return to the always-existing reality of the complete in-chargeness of everyone. This has been implemented with what has been called "The Leaders' Commitment," *"From*

now on I am in complete charge of absolutely everything, including the entire RC Community, and this means _____."

2. Direct attack on whatever distress keeps leaders from being completely close to each other and completely open with each other. "What would get in the way of you being completely close to me and completely open with me? First thought?" (Then proceed to counsel on what comes up, repeating the questions at intervals.)

3. Standing guard as a counselor for a definite period of time so that the overtired leader can discharge and rest. (This works like a charm and seems a sure cure for inability to rest, overfatigue and "burn-out.")

(Then followed a reprint from **Present Time** No. 54 and No. 55 of two articles on the Wygelian RC Communities. See **The Rest of Our Lives**, pp. 137-146 for these.)

Graduation Day
The 1985 World Conference

All these developments, the clarification of the fundamental concepts of Co-Counseling, the advanced breakthroughs, the maturing of our Community, the fact that we have proven in practice that it's possible to transcend any racial, language, geographical, or cultural barrier (however small the progress we have made in the field, we have surmounted every barrier we have challenged), all these factors come together to put us in a completely new place as far as the job which reality has apparently assigned us is concerned.

Most of us began RC in an attempt to *feel* better. Then we discovered that we could *think* better and this became our goal. We have advanced to the goals of taking charge of things, of living our lives the way we've wanted to live them, of examining, facing, and resisting oppression and then of undoing oppression. Now we are planning on taking power, of acting always on the basis of decision. Step by step we have moved towards more independence, towards more self-determinism, towards more initiative. We have reclaimed our lives step by step, often not really noticing how far we've come, because through a great part of our history, our attention has remained upon our distresses. We have, in a way, backed into the future, scraping away at our pile of distresses as we did so.

THE GRAND VIEW

Now we have reached this point. I don't think it's possible to attend this conference without having and keeping, at least for a while, the grand view of what reality is all about. How ex-

Talk to the 1985 World Conference, August 2nd, 1985. Appeared in **Present Time** No. 61, October 1985.

tremely fortunate we are to be in this universe, to exist at all, to be alive, to be alive on a lovely, nurturing, nourishing planet such as ours. How sublimely lucky to be intelligent, however much this intelligence has been held back, until now, by the distress pattern phenomenon. How fortunate to be a part of a species that can act despicably in the grip of patterns but when its heads are out of the patterns creates beauty and art and is noble and caring. How satisfying to be part of the proud, wonderful, human species which has used its intelligence to persist into every corner of the globe.

I hope you have seen the movie "The Gods Must Be Crazy" to get a glimpse into the marvelous culture of the Bushmen, to see the tremendous understanding and respectful handling of the environment which brings them such happy lives except where the European cultures have intruded upon them. We can thrill with our kinship to the masterful Inuit hunter who goes out in a little skin boat in icy waters with great confidence to tackle a whale several hundred times his size and with our kinship to the genius of a virtuoso violinist who picks up his hollow piece of spruce and maple and his horse-hair bow and creates sounds that thrill millions of people over and over again, sounds that will be pleasing to the heart of the galaxy if they ever reach there. We are learning to treasure the tremendous opportunity we have to be alive and intelligent, to be sometimes aware, to begin to grasp the reality of our power, of our absolute freedom of decision, to realize that our lives can be just the way we want them. We are learning to take pride in the community which we have created, the fellowship and sisterhood of being together while dealing with the most crucial issues facing humankind.

The struggles for liberation are not always comforting or reassuring to be in. B- of Nicaragua knows first-hand what it is like to try to care for people when the patterns of imperialism drop bombs on peaceful people, and destroy and ruin the food that they have gathered together. Those of us who have attempted to support this liberation from other countries have a little bit of a glimpse. The issues of liberation are very much the issues of re-emergence. Liberation, no matter how brilliantly fought for, how passionately sacrificed for, has always failed or gone backwards where irrationality had been allowed to intrude into the liberation effort itself. So that even though we sit here in relative comfort, in these excellently designed buildings, in this beautiful land of Quebec, we are battling, too, in an important way that will mean something to every freedom fighter alone in the jungle with only a mosquito net and a hammock to support him or support her.

"The seekers of the light are one." A U.S. poet said that a hundred and fifty years ago. What we are doing with our yawns and our tears and our hand-clasps and our laughter is very much a part of the struggle of humanity everywhere. We look forward to a time when the struggle won't have to be against irrationality but even then in the finest sense our struggle will continue. Our path to the stars (and I am confident that humanity will move out to the stars in coruscating swirls of light and that our descendants will find themselves at home on strange planets under strange suns) is being moved ahead by what we're doing here today. We have accumulated the resources of knowledge, a cooperative-enough community, an informed and aware enough sisterhood, an advanced and clear enough theory, a body of practice that works well enough. We're ready for a great giant step. I propose that we take this giant step.

WE HAVE PERSISTED

Our Community has done well. Sometimes it seems to fall on its face. Many organized Areas have dissolved for a while. Leaders change. People drift out of classes. Co-Counselors join weird movements because they want faster results than they've gotten from sloppy Co-Counseling. I have helped dissolve a score of Areas, have helped officially undo the organization. At the end of the year, I sometimes have a vague impression that behind me must be chaos and destruction and that I have participated in bringing it about. But I turn around and look back and the Community's twice the size it was when I began dissolving and disorganizing. We have usually disorganized wisely. We have thus provided an escape route from certain sticky patterns some Communities get caught in. Then Co-Counseling can revive and go on again.

It is a truism that no person who has had one *good* session can ever forget that glimpse of the possibilities of re-emergence. In the early years in Seattle, I sometimes made mistakes with my clients. I often didn't know how to handle them. Some of them left cursing me loudly and slandering me. I felt bad. I knew I must have failed in some way. I was very vulnerable to being disliked. But I learned as the years went by to be somewhat confident, because after a few years the person who hated me so loudly, and told awful lies about me, would reappear. A stranger would show up for an interview and ask about the use of counseling and then say, "So-and-So sent me in." I would work with the new person and the new person would have some success. Then one day this new client would say, "So-and-So is going to be in town and wonders if you have time to talk?" and the previous client would come in and say, "I don't suppose you ever thought you would see me again, but I've got a problem I can't solve any other way" (laughter) and we would resume counseling. No one who has had one good session has ever been able to forget it. I could tell you many anecdotes about this.

Our organizational forms and knowledge are important. We've learned that every gathering together of people should function like a support group, because that's what people gather together to seek, but without your intervention they won't know how to achieve it. The support group content is important. The Wygelian leaders' group content is tremendously important. Our classes, our gather-ins, our workshops, all these forms are valuable. All our publications are important.

THE COMMUNITY IS PEOPLE

But what our Community really consists of is the Re-evaluation Co-Counselors who act so well that other people trust them and listen to what they have to say and give them assistance in what they're trying to do. These other people who also do this, you and you, constitute the real Community. This is what it's all about. You who have some notion of what you're doing and sometimes do it, *and* the people who trust you and follow you (your followership, if you want to call it that), the people whom you inspire and lead in whatever subtle ways, whether they ever come to your class or not, these are the people who constitute the Community.

The last time I was in Israel, Avi took a day or two off from work and drove me around. I am a great admirer of stonemasons' work and the Arab stone-masons in Palestine are marvelous craftspeople. What they do with that lovely limestone can be admired forever. He took me out to one workshop and I watched how these skilled craftsmen carved the limestone. Then we drove to the West Bank and visited a few places. He said, "I want to show you a village where the Bedouins have settled into stone houses." We went to a Bedouin home where Avi was obviously welcome. I sat and watched. Bedouin Palestinians have a thousand reasons to fear and hate and distrust Israeli Jews. Terrible things have been done by this pocket-sized imperialism at United States' imperialism's urging, because the Israeli government has been a puppet of the United States government and its agent in most respects. But these Bedouins obviously liked and trusted and possibly loved Avi. I was welcomed because I was his friend. They turned warmth to me, and I know the difference between being accepted warmly and not. The only possible reason they would have for accepting me warmly was because they trusted Avi.

The people who feel like this about you, all of you Avis and Ullas and Kathys and Jokes and Tims and Marie-Claudes, the people who trust you, they are what constitute our Community.

You do not build a Community by setting up an Area Reference Person and an Area Reference Committee and an organizational structure like a box and then trying to lure people into

THE LONGER VIEW

that box. That is not the way you build the Re-evaluation Counseling Community. You build the Re-evaluation Counseling Community by being, in practice, the type of person that everybody is inspired by, likes to be with, trusts and hopes to learn from.

DO IT YOURSELF

This is exactly what I propose this morning. The title of the article in **Present Time** No. 60 is "You Can Start Your Own World Community Now—(Full permission freely given, precise instructions included)." This morning, I want to offer the precise instructions for you, as individuals, to do this. I'm not talking about you, plural, doing it as a group. Group intelligence does not exist. The notion of group intelligence is an excuse for an irresponsibility pattern to hide behind. Relying on "group intelligence" does not work well for the same reason that co-teaching did not, in general, work well. A teacher can use an assistant, yes; but *one* person has to be ultimately responsible, one person has to be sure to think. We have no indication that thinking is ever anything but an individual matter. It's true we check with each other. We learn from each other. That's a different process. Thinking is an individual matter. So I speak to you as individuals. I give each of you full permission. I will give you encouragement. I will give you whatever help I can give you, counseling or otherwise, to build your own world-wide Community but you will be the center, the inspirer.

How can you do this? It sounds quite challenging, doesn't it? I am quite sure, however, that you can very quickly build such a world-wide Community. You can permeate the population that lives around you now with such a delightful impact, with such influence that they will follow you on everything. If you teach them well what you already have available to teach them, they will teach others and very soon you will be the center of a World Community. This is not any longer just a speculation. It's not like proposing that you can go to heaven when you die. Remember the song "everybody wants to go to heaven but nobody wants to die"? We correctly view the proposal that we're going to be happy after we die, with a little bit of a raised eyebrow; but *this* proposal is practical, is possible.

Is it possible for one individual to build a world-sized Community of people who follow her and her ideas? Yes! I have no hesitation in saying yes! Of course! Someone did it already. One person did it. This person did it with great awkwardness, with considerable slowness, but you don't have to buy the awkwardness or the slowness. You don't have to be awkward. You don't have to be slow. You don't have to make all that person's mistakes over again. You can do it gracefully, efficiently. It is possible to establish a Community of world-wide influence stemming directly from you. That's not speculation any more. It's been done. Actually there are one hundred or more such Communities already spreading widely from specific individuals, many of whom are in this Conference. Many of you know that you're people of great influence. You haven't always known quite what to do with it or how to use it rapidly. This morning I will tell you exactly. I can tell you exactly how to do it so that your world Community will grow rapidly. In your case it will not take thirty-five years. I don't know exactly how long it will take. Six months? Well, a year perhaps; but do not delay.

We do not know how fast the crisis is approaching. On the great graph of events there is a line coming down the chart, moving from the left plotted against time, like this. This is the line of the downward trend, the danger and threat of nuclear holocaust, moving toward disaster. This trend is real. Read any speech by any United States President. The trend is very real. There is another line, perhaps in brighter colors, moving up from the left of the chart like this. This is the line or graph of human confidence, responsibility, and rationality. Humans are becoming more aware, more informed, more independent. You, as a group of humans and the people with whom you are coming in contact, are moving very fast in this period, for certain accidental reasons and because of your efforts. We can be pleased that we are living and participating in these times when these things are happening. This graph is rising. The whole question is, will this rising graph of human confidence and rationality rise fast enough to intercept this falling graph of the downward trend and threatened disaster before the point of final disaster for our species and other complex forms of life. I think so, but I would not recommend wasting any time. It doesn't seem sensible to fool around and delay under these conditions when we have no guarantees as yet of what turn the future will take.

BE SMART, NOT TIRED

How will you build your Community? Not with great extra effort. I'm not proposing that you go to an eighteen-hour day. I don't think so. I often work a sixteen-hour day and that's too much. It's not healthy. I'm going to cut down. I'm not proposing you put in extra hours. I'm not proposing that you run faster, unless you're taking it too easy on your exercise, in which case do that, but for fun. I'm not proposing that you worry more, I'm not proposing that you put any extra burden of any kind on yourself at all. I'm simply proposing that you take the knowledge and resources that you now have and, by decision, *live every moment well.*

No one of us can do any more. It's impossible for us to do more than live every moment well. You have a certain supply of moments. Each day you have twenty-four hours worth of moments. If you live every one of them well, in an aware sense, you will have done the ultimate. You can do no more. Will that have been enough? Yes. It has to have been.

What do you want to do with your moments? Do you have any desire to live them poorly? To waste them? There's an old Victorian saying, "Count that day lost whose low descending sun sees from thy hand no worthy action done." A little stodgy but they were trying to say something. You would not want to waste one of your precious moments. You would not want to live it poorly. It's all in your own interest to live it well and you need do no more than that.

If we are living well, we are aware of all issues. We are aware not only of the itch that needs to be scratched right now or the next mouthful of food that we hunger for, but we are aware also of B-'s compatriots in Nicaragua fighting for their independence. We are aware also of the machinations of the imperialist puppets' patterns that play their silly games across the checkerboard of power politics. We are conscious of the great untapped resources of the people and we know what we can do and we do what we can.

We will learn to eliminate nuclear armaments while we eat our breakfast and chat with our friends. That's all that we will have to do.

How will we relate to the people around us? (From this morning on, I trust.) We will have attention for the people that we meet, the people that we spend time with. We don't have to rush out and seek a new population. We already spend time with people; with our children, with our families, with our neighbors, with our co-workers, with our fellow bus-riders. Whatever the contact is, we turn toward that person an interested, positive, aware, attention-paying attitude.

Have we always done this? No. People in this group have done it sometimes, I think. Probably everyone here does it part of the time. But we haven't always done it. What have we been in the habit of doing instead? Shall I say the revolting truth? We've been trying to be clients, unawarely, unhappily, trying to be clients with unaware people who aren't going to be our counselors.

I ask, of course, that you give up forever this attempt to get counseling from the untrained, unaware population. It hasn't worked yet. It's never going to work. It has spoiled our precious moments. It has wasted our moments and it has spoiled our relationships with people.

Are people ready to love you and be cooperative and supportive and enjoy you and like you if you are always positive and attentive and helpful? If we treat each person with attention, with assistance in keeping their attention away from past distresses and model for them by keeping our own attention away from our own past distresses, each such person will be pleased with us.

We will be delighted with all persons. We will have high expectations of them. We will be confident for them. We will be supportive to them over a great range, a spectrum of supportiveness.

WIDE RANGE OF INVESTMENT

In talking to other workshops about this range, I have used two examples as endpoints. Once I got a glimpse of how willing G- was to do whatever was necessary to re-emerge I decided that I would be at her disposal no matter what I had to do, whenever it was at all possible. I've carried that out pretty well. G- and I have had some mammoth sessions. She's the best client I've ever seen. If I can figure out a direction that will take her out of her material she will look at me through heavy discharge and ask the question, "Are you supporting me through this?" and I say, "Yes!" and she lowers her head and butts down the brick walls. She has done marvelous work and I've given her full support and for the rest of my life, if G- ever wants anything from me, she has only to crook her little finger. I've made that full commitment, wisely I think. I will do something similar for as many of the rest of you as I can.

The other end-point is someone with whom I could spend only a few seconds. The first time I did a workshop at Newcastle-Upon-Tyne I walked toward the meeting room one morning, and passed an old gardener, gnarled and bent, taking care of beautiful beds of roses outside the building. I stopped for a moment and told the old man, "You bring great pleasure to all of us with those lovely flowers. Thank you." He looked startled and mumbled something and I went on. I had only that second to spend with him; but every morning of the workshop after that he was out there waiting for a good word. In the two seconds of time available, I was able to express a correct attitude toward a fellow human.

In between the end-points of G- and the gardener there's a vast spectrum of opportunities to be with people in a good way. I propose we take whatever opportunity there is. Whatever time and resource we have to give when we are with that person, we spend it liking them, encouraging them, appreciating them, exhibiting confidence for them, helping direct their attention away from past distress, and modeling for them how a human being can really function.

If you do this for a few days what's going to happen to the people around you? They're going to drift over to you. They're going to want to be with you. They're going to say to each other, "That's an unusual person with an unusual attitude. I thought at first she was going to try to sell me insurance, but apparently she's just nice." People will be rewarded by their contact with you. They will seek the contact with you.

This doesn't mean you have to spend all your time listening to them. You're in charge of your life. You can lock the door. You can excuse yourself and go to the toilet. You can say, "I have something I have to do right now." There are a thousand ways of managing your time in the face of the great urge of people to claim and use your attention.

All around you will be a growing group of people who look to you for modeling and example. It won't be all smooth and easy, of course. Your new constituency will test you. If they are going to believe in you, they have to know that you have some constancy. So, if you come into the office or shop all cheerful and bubbling about three days in a row, the fourth day someone's going to drift over and say, "What are you so blankety-blank happy about?" If you forget your own role, you can wilt and think, "I'm not going to do this anymore." But of course, the person is only testing you. "Have you really got the stamina to back up this positive attitude" is his question.

If you say, "Oh, a whole number of things. Meeting you, Mr. K., is one of them" (laughter), the river will continue to flow.

AN UNINTERRUPTED TURN

When you are with two or more people, you will arrange time (using your counseling skills), so that each of them gets a turn being listened to without interruption. If you're in a carpool on the way to work, when the fourth person in the carpool arrives you say, "Did you have any dreams last night, Ann?" She may say, "That's strange you should ask," and begin to tell. If Tony in the front seat interrupts and says something sarcastic, you say, "Shush, Tony, I want to hear this." You move to see that she gets attention without interruption. As she tells her dream, Tony may come up with three more interruptions, and you may have to say, "Keep quiet, my friend. I want to hear this. You'll get your turn," or whatever is appropriate to say to Tony. When Ann is through, you say, "All right, Tony, what was your dream?" He may not tell a dream, but he'll hand out something that he wants to be listened to about.

After three or four times like this your intervention will not be necessary. They will have experienced the tremendous worth of being listened to without interruption and they will enforce it themselves; but you will have to start.

Whenever you're with a person, you will be fully human, will be interested in the person, act as a model, and give the person attention to the extent that the situation permits.

Whenever you're with two or more people and you're not having to keep an assembly line at Chrysler going or something preoccupying like that, you will be organizing a support-group atmosphere. You will do this at the coffee break, in the carpool, on any social occasion. Why do people go out on a social occasion? In the extreme hope that somebody will organize a situation where they can be paid attention without interruption. That's what it's all about. If you'll manage things so this happens a few times, it will become their own precious procedure.

START TWO-WAYING EARLY

Among all the people you pay attention to, someone will seem a little more bright-eyed than the rest, a litte more understanding, a little more appreciative. At an appropriate point, you say to this person, "George, could you listen to me for a couple of minutes? There's something I need to think about out loud, so I can think well. It helps if you listen to me. You don't need to say anything or do anything. Just listen to me. Okay?" If he says yes, or at least if he doesn't say no, you go ahead. For two minutes you talk about an interesting problem, something real but not necessarily hugely important. Do not plunge into heavy discharge or dramatizing because if you do, when you open your eyes, he may have disappeared over the nearest hill. Do not frighten people in an effort to impress them. Let them learn a step at a time.

Talk interestingly for two minutes and when the two minutes is up, no matter how tempted you are to keep going, say, "Thank you. That helped. I can think better when someone listens to me. May I listen to you for two minutes?"

If George says, "Yes" then you listen to him for two minutes. If George says, "No, no, I don't need to be listened to," you listen to him for two minutes. He may explain for two minutes why he doesn't need to be listened to but he will drift into talking about the things that he needs to talk about.

Such a person will one day tell you, "You know, I enjoy this taking turns listening we've been doing. It makes a real difference in the day. I wonder why people don't always do this."

Around you will grow a group of people who are learning to Co-Counsel in this simple, easy way.

Even at this stage you must be prepared to take credit yourself for the ideas which you are using. If you give in to your embarrassment and academic conditioning and say, "It's something I belong to" or "Heh-heh, it's something that this fellow in Seattle thought up," you will put a block in the way of the person hearing you which will not be there if he can *consider* these things to be *your* ideas. Later, when they have become *his* ideas, it won't matter. He will be eager to learn more from any source.

INTRODUCE THE LITERATURE WISELY

At some point the requests for information will become so frequent that you can offer one of the eager people a carefully chosen piece of literature. Say, "These people seem to be trying to do some of the things we are doing. Will you take a look at it and see if you think we can learn anything from them?" If the response is, "No. I think we do things much better than these RC people," you have passed your first test of being the superior leader of a new world movement.

Then offer the literature to someone else. Somewhere along the line our excellent literature (and our literature is excellent) will set fire to their imaginations. Somewhere along the line people will want to read more and more and more.

Our literature is the sum of thousands of people's most excellent thinking. Even the part that bears my name as author, I gleaned from your brains, in thousands of sessions, hundreds of classes and hundreds of workshops and topic group reports. This is the best thinking of many people put together in a way that has never occurred before. The great thinkers of the past, Lao Tse, Moses (or J., the author who actually wrote the first four books of Moses), Marx, Mao, Einstein often did much of their work in great isolation. Modern scientists often know enough to communicate with each other. They organize congresses where they can talk to their peers about their research. They are unanimous in their opinion that the money spent in sending them to international congresses is well-spent in that it enhances their thinking.

We have our literature in which we found a way to bring together the elegant thinking of thousands and thousands of us from every walk of life, from every corner of every culture. Somewhere along the line your people are going to become excited about the literature.

STILL AN RCER

As I've talked with some of you about the building of your own communities, you have said, "But I want these people to be connected with RC. RC is very dear to me and I want them to share it." I agree. RC is a good deal. I think it's just excellent. And your people will become RCers, the ones who are ready for it.

Many of you, who have stepped out into the wide world and attempted leadership, have found that people are ready to elect you chairperson of the wide-world organization very quickly because you can do things there that you've taken for granted in RC. Just so, the Community that you build around yourself, your own world community, spreading, spreading, spreading across the world will look to you for leadership, and you will train many additional leaders and the most alert, more aware, most eager of them will come into our present RC Community.

Our present RC Community is going to change its nature. It's already changed its nature several times, but it's going to go on changing its nature as each of you begins leading your own World Community that will number ten members next month and one thousand next year, and a million two years after that. (Whatever your rate of growth is, and you'll each have different rates, of course.) As each of you lead your own world community, your association with each other in this existing community, the one that I started, will become more precious to you.

Hasn't the experience of being with each other at this World Conference been beyond price? You couldn't buy this experience for ten billion dollars, because you had to do your work of becoming a leader to be here in the first place. A lot of effort had to precede our gathering people from all these countries and dozens of races and scores of cultures, and being able to be together and relate in the way we do. This fellowship and sisterhood which we share here will remain very precious to us and many more people will be joining us.

In the future we will not be coming together as one general, a bunch of colonels and captains, and a few privates. We'll be coming together as a conference of generals of armies, Armies of the Smart and Good, Armies of the Light. We'll be coming together, each representing our own world communities. They may not all be world-sized at any particular step but will be heading in that direction.

DISTORTIONS CAN BE UNDONE

One factor might discourage you, if I do not warn you about it beforehand, if you believe everything I say and go try it. This factor is that the important ideas you have to communicate can get distorted in the process of communication. You will have said that two plus two equals four. You will have said it very clearly. Then you may find that some person to whom you said this, is teaching that two plus two equals four point three. Then you may hear that some of that person's disciples are saying that two plus two is an indeterminate, indecipherable entity. There's no occasion for despair. As long as patterns exist (maybe even after they quit existing), communication will become contaminated. I have heard myself quoted, over and over again, to the exact opposite of what I said. People have attacked me, some with fanatic righteousness, charging me with having said the exact opposite of what I did say. Patterns have that effect. Do not be too discouraged.

There is a science called information theory. It's not a very old science. Claude Shannon at the Bell Laboratories did the first work on it back in about the 1930's, I think, when I was already a young man. But it's a good science and it has a lot to do with our having good long-distance telephone service and good electronics. When this work began, it seemed that information, in being transmitted, would necessarily become degraded, would acquire "noise." Information does become contaminated in communication. It was accepted at first that this was an inevitable, irreversible process, that the more you communicate, the less clear your communication's going to be. An example is the old game of gossip, where people sit in a circle and whisper a message from one person in the circle all around the circle and then the last person who hears it says what he or she heard out loud. It's a funny game because what comes out at the end often has little to do with what went in at the beginning. This was regarded as a model of what had to happen in communication.

As information theorists began working carefully, however, they found there was no necessity for contamination of correct information to proceed unchecked. They found that it was perfectly possible to recover correct information from contaminated information. It's perfectly possible to take the "noise" out. Long-distance telephoning, for example, uses one solution to this, with certain circuits at least. Every message is sent several times at great speed and then all the versions are compared and any elements that are not in common to all the messages are filtered out and you have your original communication back, because the random contamination is gone.

As the information theorists worked on this, they began to realize that in human-to-human communication not only is information recovered, not only is the correct information recovered from the confused information, but sometimes the information is even enhanced. It's even more informative when it comes out than when it went in. Human intelligence has added to, and clarified, the original message.

THE LONGER VIEW

We can see this in a simple example. Someone is standing beside me for a demonstration and I say, "What's your problem?" and the person says, "I have no confidence." So I say, perhaps, choosing to contradict with my tone of voice, "That's nice. Tell me, happily, that you have no confidence at all." And they say (gloomily), "I have no confidence at all."

I say, "Try it this way, 'I have no confidence at all (gaily),'" offering the filter of my tone of voice, and they say (trying to sound happy), "I have no confidence at all...well, that's not quite true. I know how to make a sponge cake real good." I say, "That's fine, tell me, 'I'm a good sponge cake maker.'" And the person says, "I'm a good sponge cake maker, ha-ha-ha (or whatever the discharge is)." Then he or she says, "But I have no confidence at all, except with sponge cakes." And I say, "Fine, tell me happily, 'I have no confidence at all except with sponge cakes.'" (The client tries to repeat this and discharges.) Then the client says, "That's not true. I keep a clean house. I am a good housekeeper. I really am." We continue, and soon he or she says, "Well, more correctly, I have had the *feeling* that I didn't have any confidence." (Laughter) If I am on top of my job, I ask her or him to say, "I *used* to have the feeling that I didn't have any confidence at all," and the person says, "Well, I guess that's true, I do feel I have some confidence now." The reality has been retrieved from the patterns. The "noise" has been eliminated.

Occasionally an Area Reference person or a teacher in a growing Community has certain patterned behavior that upsets other people. So the Community, instead of growing, becomes absorbed with "What's wrong with the Area Reference Person?" Much talk. Much gossip. Another pattern leads the attack. The Community takes sides. They are handling momentous questions, they tell me. "We're really dealing with things here. We're going to get to the bottom of this." ("This" seems to be the question: Who's the worse clunk—the Area Reference Person or the leader of the opposition?) It seems very absorbing to the participants in the patterned way that much of the wide world spends its time. Sometimes I go to the Area and I try to adjudicate. I give both the combatants sessions. If that doesn't work I dissolve the Area, saying, "You're all teachers Outside of Organized Areas. Leave each other alone and we'll see who can teach a good class. Don't you dare talk to each other." I try other different things. It is an important phenomenon to notice — that everybody in the Community can get caught up in factionalism, can get obsessed with what's wrong with whom, who's got the wrongest set of patterns. If, however, in the Region where that Area is floundering, I can find someone to be Regional Reference Person who is rational enough that people can respect her, then people in the floundering Area start looking past the distress about the Area Reference Person and the leader of the opposition and see this person functioning well. They say to me, "I think we kind of lost track of some things. Could we have her come in and do a workshop, because I want to get back to learning RC?" If the new Regional leader comes and does a pretty good workshop, Co-Counseling begins again. They stop thinking in terms of battle and begin asking each other "What can we do to counsel these two people and get them out of this obviously irrational preoccupation with competing?" This has happened. I won't mention names.

If you have one roughly accurate model of how people ought to relate to each other, the correct policy begins to work in all kinds of ways. So, the contamination of our theory and policy as it spreads out from you into your own world community can be continually corrected.

LEARN FROM MISTAKES

Will you make mistakes? Of course you will. No one does anything meaningful without making mistakes, because the detailed future is unpredictable. Thank God, the future's unpredictable. If we could predict it totally, our lives would be endless boredom. "I know which tunafish sandwich I'm going to take how many bites out of at next Thursday's lunch." You see?

The future is inherently unpredictable in detail and this suits our nature well, because we love new things. We love to find out new things. I remember the farmers and mechanics with whom I spent my youth. Over and over I would hear one of them say, "I learned something new today," with a tone of great satisfaction. "I learned something new today." Maybe the farmer had been to town and he heard some screwball come up with a screwball idea. But at least it was something new. It was better than the same bunch of brush and thistle in front of his doorstep growing the same way every year.

We'll make lots of mistakes. The more we accomplish, the more mistakes we'll make. At this point I proudly confess, before I do self-estimation tonight, that I think I make more mistakes than anybody else in the Community. You will make mistakes and you will learn from them.

STAY INDIVIDUALLY IN CHARGE

At this point I charge you, individually, to not go home and become an interdependent group of leaders. Meet as chieftains, each with your own clan. Use the Wygelian form inside RC. Don't get together as a supervisor and Area Reference Person meeting with supervised teachers. We use the word "supervising" for counseling training but that is a completely different activity. Do not go home and get back into that. Meet as free chieftains in a Wygelian-type leaders' meeting, each with your own clan behind you. If your own clan consists of only you the first time you meet, well, listening to the others talking about their armies will motivate you to go out and scrape up a recruit or two very soon. If, by the next leaders' meeting, you only have two recruits, there's no basis for being ashamed or backward, as I think you could see in the Wygelian demonstration last night. You simply work well with two. So Diane works with thousands. So what?

You are each in charge of the entire universe. To live every moment well, to live the way you want to, you will need a world community. No one else is equipped to be the leader of that particular world community except you. If you thought I was the leader of your world community, it's time for an update. In a sense, of course, I have been the leader of my world community and you're all very welcome to remain in it, too, or to come back to it for rest and recreation. (Laughter) It's true. (Laughter) I hereby free you from any feeling that you have to help me build *my* Community instead of building *your* world community. Behave yourself when you're in my Community for rest and recreation or for a meeting, give me a hand with the housekeeping, and so on, but be sure to build your own. This Community of mine, since it was first, is going to be transformed into a gathering of eagles. Each of you will be coming here as a proud chieftain of your own clan, sharing information, offering mutual nurturance, on this level, but also an independent leader in your own right.

I think this World Conference will have failed if you do not hear and take seriously what I am saying this morning. All the rest of what we've done leads to this. (This includes the accidental beginning of counseling when exactly the correctly balanced desperate client fell into my lap and insisted on doing the right thing no matter how many times I tried to help him do the wrong thing, until I finally caught on a little bit.) All that has happened in Re-evaluation Counseling, all the mistakes and all the breakthroughs and all the brilliant insights and all the warm sisterhood and brotherhood we've had has been preparation for this step.

GRADUATION CUM LAUDE

You have been good children. You're now grown up. From this moment on, I not only permit you, not only free you, but I charge you and demand of you as intelligent entities that you each build a world class Community around you. If you forget the steps I've outlined for doing it, read the article in **Present Time** again. If you lost your article in **Present Time**, call me. If you are trying to build your world community in good faith and sincerity and intelligence, I will even take a phone call from you, from anywhere in the world. I won't take a lot of them if it turns out to be a bad habit and a pattern of yours, but I will take some. I will share with you everything that I know; but you are on your own, now. Welcome back into consultation with the general staff anytime. You always have been my peers, of course, but I now publicly declare you my equals. You are not only my equals in effort and opportunity but you will be my equals in prestige and glory if we ever get any of that. You are, from now on, my equals in responsibility. Let's go do it.

Gentiles and Jewish Liberation

How Can We Develop More Jewish Leaders?

Dialogue between M— and Harvey Jackins

M—: *I have learned that I can go into an organization and by being myself, making friends, and being helpful I can develop a situation in which people trust me, and feel I'm a good person, and listen to me. I can make a significant impact by what I do in the Jewish community. I can organize people who have points of view similar to mine, and I can bring some people together and have them be good for each other. I can encourage each of these people to be a little firmer in whatever attitudes they have that are already rational or close to rational. It's taken me several years to get to the point where I function that way.*

Yet, there is a universe of people who are at my disposal to work with. There are a lot of people I know who are busy doing different things, some committed activists, others with rational or partially rational ideas but without a commitment, still others who have good thoughts, but don't have any sense of having the power to do anything effective, or any plans for spending time trying. There are other people who are very committed to the Jewish community for a variety of rational and irrational reasons, but their ideas are colored by the terror that they have become locked into, so that they hold to quite-incorrect policies. There are also Jewish Co-Counselors who have sometimes expressed an interest in doing something effective for wide-world change inside the Jewish community, but have not yet moved to do much. These are the ones I am in contact with. These are the people I would like to take on leadership. There are a lot of organizations in my city that need some of these individuals to take good leadership within them, yet there is only so much that I can do as one person.

I need help with my own leadership in the Jewish community, but, even more so, in figuring out how to get other people to lead, so that to-

Appeared in **Ruah Hadashah** No. 6, 1986.

gether we can move things forward much faster than I can possibly do by myself.

Harvey: One problem we face is how to more effectively lead larger numbers of people. The heart of the solution is realizing that one has to lead leaders in order to have a very wide, effective influence. To lead people directly, one can never get beyond a small number. Perhaps armies have realized this in limiting the size of the combat platoon. An officer's direct leadership will not reach over a dozen or so men, or perhaps with a very stable, relaxed officer, twenty or thirty people at the most.

In order to lead widely, one must lead leaders. In order to have leaders to lead, in general, one must create them. This is because, although everyone is potentially a leader, and everyone is eager to become a leader, except where heavy patterns have been installed, the oppressive social cultures of current societies systematically discourage and invalidate the leadership ability of people from a very early age. The constant invalidation and the insistence that only a few elite people are able and competent to lead reinforces this incessantly.

You must turn people into leaders in order to have leaders to lead, in order to be able to lead widely yourself. This can be done, and we have at least the beginnings of knowledge of how to go about it.

First you raise the possibility with each one of her or his becoming a leader. You do this perhaps through asking them for assistance or telling them of the need for leadership, or creating positions with titles and asking them to fill them, or whatever other device you can think of. Second, you express confidence in the person's ability to lead, and this will have to be expressed over and over many times to penetrate the invalidation that has been put upon the person that has made the person feel that he or she can not do this and lacks information as to how to do it. Third, you will have to furnish some information about how to lead. You can do this either by communicating directly and individually, by lecturing to groups, by offering reading material on leadership, by preparing charts, or by your modeling, which is probably the most effective way of communicating. Fourth, you will have to provide some kind of an experience in which the person can practice leading in small increments and find, in the practice, that he or she is capable, that the role is rewarding, and that it is possible to learn to do it. Last, you will have to be lavish in your praise and appreciation and continual encouragement of the person's further progress. This will require the structuring of some kind of relationship with you and with the group that needs leadership that will be safe for the person to practice leadership in, a situation in which the person is in close touch with you and where it is impossible or nearly impossible to make a serious mistake. This way you will be able to continuously monitor the nurturing and encouraging of the person into leadership.

If one were to attempt this only through individual contact with each individual, the amount of time consumed would be very large. In bringing along very special individuals, some such time must be taken. A great violinist, for instance, will in general take only a small number of pupils from those who show the greatest promise. Most of what can be taught, however, can best be done in a group situation. A group situation is essential, in part, because the modeling needs to be done in an actual group relationship where the leadership of the learner will operate.

So, it will be necessary to hold *meetings* of the people whom you wish to become leaders in a particular field. Such meetings should be called when there is a situation that needs to be handled in the field of their leadership.

In such a meeting each person needs a chance, without scolding or criticism or having any obligation being placed upon him or her, to tell about what he or she has been doing and what he or she has been thinking about the particular problem or related problems in their field of leadership. Each person also needs a chance to share any information or opinions she or he has about the common area of concern or leadership. Each needs a chance to tell everything she or he knows or has heard. Each person also needs an opportunity to put forward his or her own goals, tell the things he or she would *like* to do, the things he or she intends to attempt in the next period.

They need to do all this while being listened to by people who share their concerns and share their backgrounds and information. They can think about their goals much better while being listened to in this kind of a group situation.

Each person also needs the opportunity to express their fears and misgivings about leadership and to discharge any distress which would interfere with their successful leading, whatever that distress is or wherever it comes from. With the interested attention and reassurance of the group and the assistance of the instructor or consultant (meaning you) they can shift attitudes and reduce and eventually eliminate difficulties. This last amounts to a demonstration session.

These four needs or agenda points for developing leaders constitute what we have called "Wygelian Leaders' Group" meetings. The principal points on the agenda of such a meeting are exactly: a report from each person on what they have done recently in leading in their area, a sharing of the information and opinions that they have about the situation and the people they are leading, the opportunity to present their intentions for leadership in the next period, and the opportunity to be counseled well on whatever difficulties are interfering with their leadership.

Such Wygelian leaders' meetings need to recur dependably but in general not on a regular basis. Regular meetings seem to me now to be clearly a bureaucratic expression of the oppressive society's inflexibility. I think they have interfered with learning to be a leader at least as much as they have helped. Good leaders' meetings will be held on a "called" basis, whenever there is a need for such a meeting, whenever there is a desire for consultation on something of common concern to the group.

M—: *I have another question. When I look at the people whom I see as being capable of taking leadership in the near future, they seem to me to have good intentions, to be reasonably intelligent, to have the ability to take action and initiate things:* but *to some extent their ideas are all colored by their fears and other distresses and I feel hampered in my mind by the fact that they don't have the background of counseling theory and information that I have. They don't have the discharge process to help clarify their thinking and help deal with their problems as they come up. Do you see this process taking place and people becoming clear with respect to policy and eliminating their fears in a non-counseling setting and environment?*

HJ: When you said that they don't have the discharge process, I think you mean they don't have a commitment to the discharge process.

M—: *I mean they don't have an understanding of the discharge process.*

HJ: I think even "understanding" is the wrong word. In my observation every person in the whole world is waiting for a chance to discharge. They "have" the discharge process. They are unaware, perhaps, of its importance, or they have been conditioned to try to repress it, but I am sure that, nevertheless, every person in the world is ready to discharge whenever a second person will do the basic three things that we list as the counselor's responsibility. These three things are: (1) to pay enough attention to the first person to see clearly what the distresses are, (2) to think of all possible ways to contradict those distresses, and (3) to contradict those distresses sufficiently. In such a case I am sure that any person will always discharge.

I don't think there is any way for a person to get to the level of awareness and commitment and clarity on policy that counseling leaders have reached except by going through the same process that these counseling leaders did. I don't think you would have your present clarity nor would any of the other present Jewish RC leaders had you and they not worked through a great deal of discharge in order to get there.

I think, however, that people in the wide world not only have to do the same thing, but that they are ready to do the same thing at any opportunity. They don't need to have it labeled as "counseling." They don't have to have it done with the separateness and sometimes the awkwardness that we sometimes unawarely assume to be part of counseling. They do need to have it done, I think, spontaneously and in a human way. The same three actions on the part of a second person will lead any person to discharge, and will lead to clarification of his or her policy. A Wygelian-type leaders' meeting with the four points of the agenda carried out without labels and simply as part of the leadership of a meeting will, I think, lead any group of individuals to development of a good policy and toward a commitment for carrying it out.

I think our assumption here has to be that the only thing holding any individual back from commitment for progressive action and effectiveness in taking such action is just exactly the lack of opportunity to converse and plan with others, the lack of information, and the presence of distress which they have not yet been able to discharge.

I think you have to deal with this through some kind of meeting whose content will be the same as the Wygelian Leaders' meeting even though it may take place in a cafeteria or even in a pub. I don't think there is any way to get around the need for the content of counseling or for the content of a Wygelian Leaders' meeting. These things, I think, have to be done. We have some counselors already who are very excellent at presenting this process in an easy, naturalized way which people grasp and participate in very quickly.

M —: One of the problems that's particularly true in the Jewish Community (I don't know how much this is present with other groups as well) is that you have a group of people whose intelligence has been allowed to remain free in a lot of ways and who are articulate, active people but who are often driven or motivated on Jewish questions by fear and terror. This fear comes across in all kinds of little hang-ups.

HJ: Then we must check on and work on the little hang-ups as well as the big ones.

M—: Certainly the fearful mannerisms and habits on little things are reflections of the big terror. It seems to me that a main goal would be to eliminate terror as a motivator and controller of actions and policies.

HJ: Yes, certainly.

M—: It seems to me to be that the goals of our wide-world Jewish liberation work is to have happen there what has happened in working out Jewish liberation policies in RC. I think that process needs to happen for policies in the wide world to really change as well.

HJ: Well, as the fear discharges the policies will improve, but you can criticize and contradict isolation as a policy even when there is still a lot of fear there. You can do this even though it's hitting your own fear. It's possible for people to see that isolation is non-survival, if you can get them to look at it, even if they're still afraid.

M—: As soon as you attack the isolation, people's fear comes right up and that's what gets thrown at you all the time. Whenever any good policy is put forth, the fear comes up.

HJ: And argues.

M—: Yes, and argues.

HJ: If you continue to contradict the fear when it comes up, however, the person will discharge.

M—: That might be the case all right (laughs). I'm trying to think as you say, if I've ever seen any examples of that in a non-counseling context, outside of an RC situation.

HJ: That may be where you are hung up, M—. It's important to realize that RC is just a subset of the wide world. With competent, confident counselors, that distinction or division between RC and wide-world situations no longer needs to be made. Early on, we put up a kind of a fence between the subset RC and the big set of the wide world, in order to give enough safety within RC to recover our ability to discharge and begin and learn to counsel, while we kept the patterns that usually operate to disrupt discharge in the wide world from spoiling the sessions. Now, however, at the level where you and I are supposed to be functioning, that fence is often no longer useful. It can become a distraction. It works better if you handle contacts in the wide world the same as you handle clients when you are counseling well in a session. (It's also probably true that you should handle a client in a session the way you would thoughtfully handle your daily contacts in the wide world.)

M—: Well, I don't actually make a distinction in terms of thoughtfulness or in the kind of attitude with which I treat Co-Counselors and treat other people.

HJ: Do you make a distinction in terms of the role you play?

M—: Well, perhaps. Where I'm stuck is in being able to be confident enough. I am not sure that I can have enough relaxed confidence myself that I can be effective in a room with five or ten or thirty Jews who are all to varying degrees rehearsing and exhibiting the fear and isolation. It's difficult for me to....

HJ: ...have enough confidence for all of them?

M—: ...to contradict that kind of thing. I can do it much more easily on a one-on-one basis.

HJ: Well, I can understand that. I have a little trouble when more than one person is screaming at me at a time, too (laughs). But, you know certainly that you are safe at this moment?

M—: Yes.

HJ: I can even guarantee you complete safety for the next minute.

M—: Yes.

HJ: Nothing bad will happen to you for the next minute, I promise you. Relax.

M—: *(laughs) I led a short Jewish liberation workshop yesterday.*

HJ: So?

M—: *I did a class on internalized oppression. We had a very amusing time around the statement "It's safe to be a Jew." That takes some explaining for Jews to hear.*

HJ: Yes, it does.

M—: *It seems to me safe to be a woman. It seems to me safe to be a worker. We have all kinds of oppression that we are involved in, but the safety question doesn't usually come up with them. It may seem that it's not safe to be a woman in some places. It may not be safe to walk on the streets at night. But one doesn't usually make a statement that it's not safe to be a woman in the same way that it's said that it's not safe to be a Jew. There is a different kind of feeling there.*

HJ: Was there discharge in the class?

M—: *Yes, there was good discharge (laughter).*

HJ: M—, is it safe to be a Jew?

M—: *Mostly (laughs)! I'm trying to figure out what is a real fear and what is not a real fear.*

HJ: They are *all* real fears. I think you mean justified or unjustified fears. Or do you mean useful and unuseful fears?

M—: *Yes. I mean there are some things that we need to be concerned* about and other things where there's an irrational level of anxiety. I mean, of course, now that I think about it, no fear is rational (laughs).

HJ: That's right, and no fear is useful, either.

M—: (laughs) No fear is useful?

HJ: It's hard to face that.

M—: (laughs) I had a little trouble yesterday saying things are better off now than they were a couple of hundred years ago. That is not really the point, I guess, because a couple of hundred years ago it wasn't rational to be afraid either.

HJ: No, fear is not any help under any conditions. Try saying a phrase to me, would you, M—? (M—: Okay.) "You mean my fear is not useful?" (in a humorous voice).

M—: (laughs) "You mean my fear is not useful?" It seems absolutely necessary.

HJ: The fear seems like it's the same as awareness, doesn't it?

M—: What do you mean by awareness?

HJ: Being alert to everything, including being aware of dangers.

M—: Right. The problem is to separate being aware and being afraid.

HJ: But they are completely different.

M—: I agree. They are completely different.

HJ: Now try, "None of my fear is useful."

M—: None of my fear is useful. The statement that it is safe to be a Jew is something that just strikes right at the heart of the fear. Every time I've said it to anybody in a Jewish situation, I immediately get back all the fearful concerns, all the awareness of danger.

HJ: It's a good contradiction. Say it to me, see what comes to your mind.

M—: *It's safe to be a Jew.*

HJ: Is it really?

M—: *I have a hard time thinking about what that actually means.*

HJ: Good. Let's just keep on that subject.

M—: *It's safe to be a Jew.*

HJ: Oh, really? I thought it was dangerous.

M—: *(Laughs) It's dangerous too. (Laughs)*

HJ: It's dangerous to be alive.

M—: *Yeah!*

HJ: Life consists of an unstable equilibrium.

M—: *That's right. Yes. Yes, but the fear is heavy.*

HJ: It is, isn't it?

M—: *That sort of implies that if it's safe to be a human being, it's safe to be a Jew.*

HJ: Really? There's no more danger in being a Jew than being a human being.

M—: *Well, there are some few more dangers that you might have by virtue of being Jewish, but there are also more dangers that people have by virtue of living in the state of New Jersey.*

HJ: Is it possible that other people are in more danger than Jews are?

THE LONGER VIEW

M—: Oh, there are a lot of people who are in a great deal more danger than Jews are.

HJ: Is that right?

M—: Yes.

HJ: So you're relatively safe, right?

M—: Actually, to be a white U.S. Jew living in my city is incredibly safer than life is for most of the world. (Laughs)

HJ: In other words, you might say that you are very safe?

M—: (Laughs) Yes, we're very safe! (Laughs)

HJ: You're doing fine. Every new thought that comes up in response to the statement that it's safe to be a Jew, you test out against reality. That's pretty good. Okay. So, you want to get this process started in the middle of a group who share a huge common anxiety?

M—: Yes. That's what I want to do.

HJ: Well, that should be challenging fun. If you take a confident position, they will all speak out, won't they? They will all start screaming at you?

M—: Yes, all at the same time. They'll feel that there's a lot of education that needs to go on. They'll all try to educate me (laughs) immediately as to all the dangers that there really are that I am being foolish about.

HJ: Okay. What would happen if you just kept on warmly asserting, in a confident tone of voice, your position that there is safety, and they all kept screaming?

M—: What would happen?

HJ: Yes, if you just kept on for a long time, being affable, unshakable, confident, just kept on reassuring them in a positive, confident tone of voice?

M—: *(Laughs) Something would happen. (Laughs) Something would have to happen.*

HJ: Yes. Do you know what it is that would happen?

M—: *I would imagine that I would pick up an ally or two. That's one thing that I think would happen. There would be people coming up to me afterwards or eventually, wanting to hear more about that.*

HJ: And all the people would be very thoughtful the next few hours about how you could possibly state and stick to such a position. They would do a great deal of thinking about it afterwards.

M—: *I do see. I know what you're saying is right, because I have this sense, this image of how powerful it is to be confident. I have this sense of how workable it would be to be sure that everything is possible, to be out from under that anxiety. That is the most liberating thing that could happen to a Jew, to be out from under that terror and the sense of impending doom.*

HJ: You would just as soon be out of that now, wouldn't you?

M—: *For me personally, to be outside of that would be the greatest joy I could have in my life.*

HJ: Okay. It won't take long. Let me read you something from **Present Time**. Fighting for ethical clarity is almost comparable to that. J—, who writes here in **Present Time**, is an ethicist. She writes, "I was a keynote speaker at a symposium in a hospital in San Jose for clergy and physicians. I put out a policy that 'Life is always worth living regardless of damage.' For the first time I could see clearly how difficult it was for people to hear that, and how they consequently kept insisting on how it would lead to inhumane consequences. I hung on to my own conviction that no rational policy could support abusive practices, and so I was sure some distress must be getting in the way of the people there, most likely in the context or sphere of death and disability. One woman in the audience knew intuitively I was right. She was a great asset. Two nurses cried telling horror stories, and a minister came up to me afterwards and cried re-telling the story of a man loving and caring for his comatose wife for two years. My ability to do this has qualitatively improved over the past years."

She takes this position that all life is worth living and people get up and scream at her. She is hitting into another very, very deep fear there, the fear of dying.

M —: It's probably the same fear. (Laughs) We're talking about it in a different context is all.

HJ: Okay.

M —: I am thinking now about Israel. For political Jews, and for a lot of the Jews whom I know who are involved in the community relations process, what their fear gets centered on is Israel, and threats to Israel. The logical extension to what you've been saying is a position that Israel is safe.

HJ: Oh, sure. Israel's safe.

M —: And Jews are saying that Israel is in great danger.

HJ: Oh, yes.

M —: Everyone feels danger from the trouble within as well as without for Israel.

HJ: Oh, Israel is safe. The Jews are safe in Israel. Yes, yes. Practice insisting on this. All the anxiety and all the fooferrah is about less terror than takes place in lower Manhattan in any one day. There's a certain amount of it, but it's just blown totally out of proportion by the propaganda, the manipulation of the fear, for political purposes. Jews are safe. Israel is safe and Jews are safe. Statistically, the chance of being hurt in Israel is less than it is for residents of many United States cities.

M—: Then what we require is separating the reality that there are problems that need to be solved from the fears that attach to them.

HJ: And from the feeling that all is lost!

M—: (Laughs) Right! From the panic associated with and deeply tied, by now, to the mere existence of problems.

HJ: Okay. This is turning into quite a good conversation.

M—: Well, based on what you said, it seems to me the kind of approach that I need to be taking is to look around at the people that I know who are in the best shape and who are at least somewhat committed to taking leadership or people in such a condition that in a relatively short period of time spent around other leaders, they would want to take leadership.

HJ: Which is everybody, if you look at them hard enough.

M—: I need to get these people together, based on some proposal. Have us get together for some reason or other.

HJ: Or have lunch with one or more of them to start with.

M—: And, basically, do a leadership group with them, asking them those four questions. (How have you been leading? How does the situation seem? What do you propose to do next? Where do you find it difficult to lead?)

HJ: Yes, to bring it up in some way. I do such leadership groups with one person often, in order to get started. Just like that.

M—: And, if I do it well, people will like it or be intrigued by it, and eventually, the people will see it as something that is being helpful.

THE LONGER VIEW

HJ: They may not tell you they like it, but they will come back for more. Don't expect praise or encouragement too quickly. If a person can beat one clay pot off his head by pounding it on you, you see, it doesn't lead to immediate gratitude. There's not usually any communication such as, "Oh, thank you. I'm sorry I hurt your head. It's so good to have that clay pot off." It's much more likely to be, "Let me hurry back with two more clay pots to beat on your head." So don't expect quick reassurance and appreciation. But the person will be moved, and he or she will come back to you. They'll be back with more questions. You may get to feeling like an anvil, but keep saying, "Yes, go ahead, pound away."

M—: And then, I'll need to call another meeting at some point in the future.

HJ: Have several lunches with individuals or small groups of them. Then you can say to them, "You know, you have very interesting ideas and there's a number of people I've been talking to that I think would benefit from hearing your ideas. How about having dinner with me if I can get the others to join us? I'll check with the others and confirm it." Do it very informally. Don't rush it and don't formalize it. What will happen is that suddenly M— is somebody that people like to hang out with. They don't yet know that it's because they got some encouragement or that they got some discharge. They don't know that it's the discharge that makes you so attractive; but they keep coming in to "argue" with you.

The first time you have a meeting they may all join in arguing against you. You may temporarily wish that you had not called the meeting, if they all start yelling at you at the same time, and seem to reinforce each other. But if you remain relaxed and smiling and tough it out, finally one person will decide that you are possibly right and the move over to your ideas will begin.

M—: I already have done a lot of that homework with people, so I think I'm past the point of just getting together with people one at a time. There are numbers of people that I've already done that with who would come to such a meeting because of the relationship that I've already established with them.

HJ: Yes. Good, but remember the organizing of the meeting itself isn't going to do it for you. The meeting is just a pretext for *you* to do it. You will have to have and furnish not only all the reassurance needed to encourage the ones who want encouragement, but also the chutzpah to counsel the ones who want to dramatize in the unaware hope that you will get them to discharge.

M—: Is there anything else I should know about the development of leadership at this point?

HJ: I think the present job for those of us in leadership is to clone ourselves. We have to bring people up to our level of leadership in great numbers, and do it in a way that will move us ahead, too, so that it will be an ongoing process. We can't be satisfied with people who take a little leadership and then stay stuck there. We need to have a general process of all our leaders growing into more and more general leadership, more and more powerful leadership.

What I'm doing with leaders in RC at the present time involves a three-pronged attack. Whenever I work with them I first ask for a commitment to complete individual responsibility *for everything*. This sounds fantastic at first, but it turns out that this just challenges a bunch of irresponsibility patterns and hurts hidden under the guise of "group leadership" or "committee leadership" or "limited leadership" or other concepts like that. I ask them to make a commitment that reads "From now on I am in complete charge of absolutely everything, including the entire RC Community." Then I model saying "Ha ha ha ha ha," in a powerful voice, so that they get a chance to practice tone of voice without confusing it with the meaning of the words. Then I ask them to keep thinking of new implications each time so that they finish with, "This will mean _____," and then fill in the blank with new implications that they have thought of each time they say it.

In general this will mean that as each one of them understands, accepts, and embraces this commitment (and discharges a lot in the process) that each one will take complete and total responsibility for everything. This replaces the previous attitude of accepting limited responsibility in the mistaken notion that leadership by a group of people each taking limited responsibility is something that works.

I then have them work on getting completely close to each other. I proceed on that by asking them what gets in the way of their being completely close to *me* and completely open with *me*. Always, each person immediately thinks of something and is ready to discharge on it. Each person always has a good session on that. Apparently there's only one set of patterns that gets in the way of closeness, and the people I'm working with become very close to each other after they have worked on and discharged the blocks on being close to me. I previously tried to work with two of them on being close to each other, but that gets very difficult. If I'm in one end of the relationship, I at least know what's going on there in my own end and I can handle it. So far, everyone discharges easily and well in response to such a question.

The third prong (which is fairly recent) is offering to stand guard for people against their anxieties so they can rest. Of course I want them to do this for each other, and people seem very receptive to doing it, but I demonstrate it first. This deals with the fatigue and the anxiety which glues the fatigue in and which helps it accumulate. Observably, fatigue tends to accumulate on people who take responsibility and are responsible leaders. I find that if I offer to "stand guard" for a person for even one minute (if that's all the time I've got) or for five minutes if I have that much time, and promise that I will see that nothing bad will happen anywhere, that they don't have to worry about anything, that I will take care of everything and give them safety for that long, people discharge voluminously. Some of them just explode with grief discharge about how tired they are. Others start shaking. Others start talking about how tired they are and yawning and in a group everyone else starts yawning with them. Some of them just go to sleep on my shoulder standing up. I put my arms around them and they go to sleep, just like that.

That's a fairly new tool. It turns out to be simple and workable, but I didn't figure it out until recently. I needed it myself, but I was slow to be able to think about it.

These are the three things that I am doing with leaders currently.

Counseling Between Jews and Gentiles

Harvey: Joan's letter came out at the same time as the open letter from Cherie and me to the RC Communities which pointed out that the work on ending Jewish oppression had lagged. Cherie had noted a number of things before that, but I was shocked at a Midwest teachers' and leaders' workshop on the way people reported on their efforts to end anti-Jewish oppression in the world. Joan's letter appeared in the same issue of **Present Time** and received a wide response. There was a great surge of relief because she said that Gentile RCers should learn to patiently, pleasantly listen to Jews complain. That wasn't her only point. She said many important things in that letter. Thinking about it before this workshop, I thought that was an important point to make to Gentile RCers, but I wouldn't like it to be left there for Jewish RCers. I wouldn't like *them* to get stuck in the complaining. I thought of raising slogans that would take them right past that on to glorious self-confidence and being in charge of everything. I've tried to do this at this workshop. I'm not retracting these slogans. I think they are correct.

The point has been well-made to me today that although what I'm suggesting Jewish leaders do — step clean outside your patterns right now — is useful, I have missed dealing with what would make it possible for them to do it. I think this is what people have been trying very tactfully to tell me. Probably not very many people are disagreeing that it would be nice, but the question of how is rolling around there somewhere.

Joan: In coming to the workshop it seems to me that we need help with

From a discussion at the Jewish Leaders' Workshop, November, 1982. Appeared in **Ruah Hadashah** No. 6, 1986.

how to discharge a lot of our difficulties that are attached to being Jewish. That's what has been hard to do at home. A lot of Jews have a hard time discharging on anything effectively in sessions. I've noticed in the last period of time that Harvey and other people who have been our good allies have gotten impatient, particularly with the manifestations of our distress. Yet, although we may be able to discharge on them, we just can't discharge out of them. For instance, we can complain or take charge, but to get rid of the chronic distress that sets us up in a complaining relationship to the world has been hard to do, so we struggle our way through with difficulty. It seems to me that there are three major areas that we need help discharging on dependably. One is being liked, being liked as Jews. For a lot of us, the anti-Jewish oppression says, "I don't like you because of the way you are, because you are a Jew."

(Harvey: This includes times when I've said that I can't stand your patterns?)

Joan: Right. We need to know we are liked as Jews with whatever manifestations we have that allow people to recognize us as Jews. That's one major area: to know we are likable as Jews, that a non-Jew likes us, even with whatever patterns we may carry. They aren't, after all, any worse than the patterns Gentiles carry. They just stand out more because they're different from the regular cultural patterns. For example, most people don't often get impatient with Gentile women who are in pattern because they fit with the culture.

The second problem is our difficulty in trusting. This keeps our heavy feelings of isolation in place. Jews who are having trouble discharging in sessions need to be able to trust their counselor or they can't work on anything very effectively. So we need dependable ways to work on this distrust. It is helpful for us to realize that it is our relationships that enable that trust to build up, not a technique or a particular contradiction in a particular session at a particular moment. It is the building up of a trustworthy relationship that enables people to discharge well in their sessions. To people who have said they have had difficulty in their sessions, I always recommend: take time to work on building up a relationship with a Co-Counselor that you can trust even if that takes a year or longer. There don't seem to be many shortcuts, and techniques often get in the *way, although they may be valuable for many people.*

The third problem is despair. We do work on it, but it's still difficult to work on. There seems to be some combination of despair and lack of trust that is behind our complaining. We need different ways of looking at it instead of just the old "we feel like victims." Cherie has done an excellent job of giving people a chance to discharge on despair. Discharging insecurity is even harder. Where the Communities are stronger and more established it's easier for people to hold the direction out for us against despair, but it's still difficult to do. Despair works like an anchor for any other difficulties that we have in our life; we might be able to clean up a particular hurt, but the general despair related to being Jewish doesn't seem possible to emerge from fully. Holding out a forward-moving direction is that much more difficult, and any particular distress becomes more difficult to contradict because we are weighted down with this despair. We need to know that we can and will personally get rid of the load of distress on us as Jews, as well as that the oppression will end. I have more confidence in the oppression ending than I do in getting rid of the feelings of internalized oppression. To have some confidence that it is possible to fully recover personally from the effects of the oppression would make everything move much more quickly. It's something like getting a glimpse that it really is great to be female. When I got that glimpse, it made everything else easier. It gave me a dependable handle with which to move me and everyone else forward against that particular distress. I think we need something like that here, only it must include a sense of personal hope. It is good to be a Jew, but that doesn't seem to be enough.

Harvey: I would like to add something that struck me about a year ago that I've been sharing with workshops since for the benefit of Gentile RCers. In general, members of an oppressed group who love someone in the oppressor group have to get outside the oppression to do it. A black person who loves me will pretty much have to regard me as an ally to do it. But Jews have had to learn to love a member of the oppressor group without trusting. To clarify this with our Gentile Co-Counselors will make a whole lot of difference. They have been misled by the warm affection that many Jewish Co-Counselors give to them, the warm, free, thoughtful, caring affection, to think that there must be trust there as well and they can't understand why counseling doesn't work so well.

Joan: There's one other thing: The way Harvey has been working with me over the last period of time may be helpful for lots of other Jews. Basically, most of us struggle all the time to do the right thing, and we are using every ounce of energy we have to try to do the right thing at all times. So, for somebody to tell us to do better is hard on us. Many of us tend to beat ourselves anyway. What Harvey has been doing with me very effectively, no matter how much I hate it at times, is to urge me to pay attention to how hard things have been. When I get into a situation where I go numb, or when I have trouble in my sessions, I remember that. I hold such a strong direction outside of how hard things are, to do what I do. I sometimes have to acknowledge how hard things are first in order to discharge. We are already pushing ourselves as hard as we can; we need some people from the outside to say, "You're doing a good job, relax, take a look at how hard things have been." Many of my difficulties operate like the oppression itself—they are hard to notice.

Harvey: I'd now like to call on people who lead Communities and have to solve this and ask for their comments and thinking.

JAAP: THE THING ABOUT LOVING WITHOUT TRUSTING HITS IMMEDIATELY. THAT SEEMS VERY TRUE. WHAT CAME TO MIND WAS WHAT YOU SAID YEARS AGO ABOUT THE INVISIBLENESS OF JEWISH OPPRESSION, THE INVISIBLE STAINLESS STEEL NOOSE THAT EVERY JEW WEARS AROUND HIS THROAT, THAT IMAGE.

Harvey: I work with many oppressed groups, and, for example, if you work closely with blacks, you see how they are denied any knowledge, any skills, any hope, from the beginning, nothing to support them. If you look at Jews, well, my gosh, they have got a tradition of knowledge, and great leaders, and taking leadership, and international connections and— what oppression?!! But every Jew has an invisible stainless steel wire noose around his or her neck ready to be jerked any time they get out of line with the ruling forces at all. They don't need any other symbols of oppression; they can appear to be free and still be forced to toe the line as long as that fear is there.

Gene: The only thought that I had was that there seems to be no way out. I can't think of a way out, that's the feeling that I have about it. Also, I've begun to feel recently that the oppression of being Jewish comes from two sides: from non-Jews and from Jews. I am a Jew because my family was Jewish, it goes way back, 3000 years. I never had the opportunity as a human being to make a decision about being Jewish or not being Jewish or being anything else. It was totally imposed upon me. That's what makes it seem as if there is no way out. The people who love me the most and the people I love the most took away my power and made me Jewish. Something like that. Not that I have any objection to being Jewish, I just wish they had let me decide.

Diane: Much of the content of anti-Semitism is reproach and blame and scapegoating, and that is something that has happened to us as a people. That's an historical condition of Jews that came from the outside. We have been blamed and scapegoated for economic crises and the world's problems. The outside messages are that something is wrong with us and that the world would be better off without us. When that message gets repeated in subtle forms in RC, it is absolutely paralyzing. Every attempt to fight back is obviously a patterned response to something that doesn't seem real and in the present. Then the message is given that it is imaginary, that there is no real threat in the present, that you are safe and the situation is safe. So you end up feeling crazy. One thing that needs to be understood which I have had difficulty communicating well in counseling is that this is an historical collective experience.

When something happens it isn't just to an individual; we experience it as a group, even if it happens to us

only as an individual. If you are a Jew, there is always a "we" context. And I always experience others not just as individuals, but as part of a group. That's part of us, and at least for me so far I have not been able to emotionally separate that out. It always gets forgotten in our individual interactions with any non-Jew in the Community, especially those with Protestant backgrounds. In my head, it is always a collective experience. But I know in their head, they may have a picture of me as a Jew but they're trying to relate to me as an individual and I don't know how to make the personal connection. Then I feel blamed when I can't make that personal connection because I want to tell them that when they are dealing with me, they are dealing with my people, not just dealing with me.

It has to be understood in the International Community that there are subtle forms of anti-Semitism that are as devastating as overt forms of anti-Semitism. I don't think that has been understood. These are not times when people in the International Community will call me a Yid or a kike; no one has done that yet and I would be quite shocked if anybody did.

Part of the reason is that much of the population, at least in the United States, has been trained in politeness. That cultural training and background is also difficult for Jews. I think that politeness has to be understood as a difficulty, although not to condemn people who have had that training. Because although the overt anti-Semitism doesn't come at you, the very subtle forms of anti-Semitism do. I don't need to repeat all of them here, but I certainly experience them everyday in the International Community. The question isn't, is that my distress or is it real? That constantly goes on in my head. What we need is some real space to be heard out, for those experiences to be shared at least in a Co-Counseling session with non-Jews just listening and for us not to worry about what we say. Every moment we censor ourselves, is this the appropriate thing to say?, because the forms of Co-Counseling are not the cultural forms that we grew up with. Again, it's not right or wrong. Many of the cultural forms appear to be much more similar to the dominant culture, and there is some way that I have not been able to speak out as an oppressed person yet within the Communities. Yet as a leader in the Communities I am continually giving help to other oppressed groups. I would like to see that format really, where we just get heard out about what it is like for us and have a good and skillful Co-Counselor to be there and interrupt if it gets critical and attacking. I think the other additional difficulty has been when the brunt has been on us to interrupt the criticalness, when we're trying to find a way to have our own voices and to speak up for ourselves.

The last thing I would like to say is a personal thing, that as an International leader in the Community I receive a tremendous amount of admiration and respect. I think that is wonderful and healthy. I do have difficulty receiving it, and I'm doing the best I know how. But I know that a lot of the admiration comes from non-Jewish women who respect me and respect my cultural patterns, are in awe of them. What people respect is the fact that I can talk. Well, I don't think for a woman it is a particularly big deal to be able to talk. I talk well, and that's good. But the awe almost comes on as anti-Semitism. It's their difficulty, not my difficulty. I need to be proud of it as a strength, but some responsibility needs to be taken on the other end. That awe and admiration can be interpreted and has been used as a form of anti-Semitism. Basically, I can also be abandoned because I'm articulate. The not-talking and the non-speaking-up on the part of non-Jewish women has always been used to put me down historically, at least in the U.S. Their patterns have always been used against me. That's something that I person-

THE LONGER VIEW

ally need help and assistance with.

Louise: The good news is the bad news. What we do so well gets turned back on us. What we put out that is our best stuff, the best news that we have to offer, somehow gets put out into that culture and comes back at us as not okay and not safe. I agree with what Diane is saying. I have the feeling we need to keep telling our story of what it FEELS like to us, we have to have the safety (certainly within the RC Community) of telling our story over and over and over again. To all of the concerns that Joan mentioned — being liked, loving without trusting, all of that, there needs to be a safe forum for us so that non-Jews can hear what it feels like to us. I think if they hear it, and if we keep telling them, especially in the context of the RC Community where we have a vehicle for communication that is so good, that they'll hear it, and we won't have to take the responsibility all the time for it.

Keith: For years the message has always been that I have incorrect patterns. In Philadelphia "incorrect" is a big word, "correct" is an even bigger word. For example, when you worked with me last week you spent a long time just giving me enough room so I didn't have to defend the way my stuff is set. It was around hopelessness. That evening you told a nice hopeful labor story and two people looked at me as if to say, "See, Keith, there's hope, you are wrong for being hopeless." I had enough slack from that afternoon that I noticed it and talked to them later. But it's that kind of thing, that "no, there's no reason to be hopeless, don't be hopeless." And you internalize it. The other thing I thought about is, have we learned to be lovers and not trust as a survival mechanism, or did we do it in a very pro-human way, even if we couldn't trust, we loved.

(Harvey: Pro-human, there's no question about it.)

Keith: I know for myself, I'm probably the best "lover"

in Philadelphia, that there is something good about being able to connect with people in that way, but it's true, you don't trust them, you love 'em.

CORINNE: WELL, I'M REALLY EXCITED. I'VE HEARD A LOT OF THIS BEFORE, BUT THERE IS A PIECE THAT IS JUST MAKING SENSE TO ME NOW. MY FAMILY MADE ME FEEL NUTS FOR MY PERCEPTION OF THE WORLD, AND IT'S JUST FINALLY MAKING SENSE TO ME THAT THEY HAD TO DENY THAT ANYTHING WAS WRONG BECAUSE OF JEWISH OPPRESSION. IT WAS NOT OKAY TO TALK ABOUT BEING OPPRESSED AS JEWS. THAT'S BEEN THE MAIN REASON IT HAS NOT BEEN OKAY TO DISCHARGE, TO FEEL BAD; IT WAS ALL FROM THERE. THE THING THAT I COULD USE SOME HELP ON IS THE TRUST PIECE. IT'S CLEAR IN MY COMMUNITY THAT WE DON'T TRUST EACH OTHER AND WE'RE MAKING PROGRESS ON IT, BUT IT'S SLOW. ANY SUGGESTIONS ON HOW TO MAKE THAT PROCEED A LITTLE FASTER WOULD BE APPRECIATED.

Jeremy: Most of what has been said so far makes sense to me. I was thinking about what Joan said about the difficulty Jews have in discharging in their sessions. For me the most dependable source of discharge about Jewish distress is going to the movies rather than counseling. Certain movies enable me to feel certain things that I have trouble feeling in sessions. It seems that most of the time I'm inside the feelings so much that it's very, very difficult to get outside them in order to discharge. Something about movies makes it possible for me to get really beyond. It has to do with the "invisible noose" thing. I realize that I am in it all the time, and that a lot of what I do in counseling is being polite to keep up the forms. But I'm not getting outside this distorted viewpoint enough and the various things that have already been mentioned make it hard for me to get outside. A couple of months ago I went to a movie with a Co-Counselor as a way of getting to this particular distress.

ANN: IT OCCURS TO ME THAT OUR HISTORICAL EXPERIENCE IN THE UNITED STATES IS A FAIRLY RECENT ONE, AND A LOT OF THE RECORDINGS I CARRY ARE IN YIDDISH EVEN THOUGH I DON'T SPEAK YIDDISH. I DON'T KNOW YET WHAT IT WOULD MEAN TO NATURALIZE RC IN A JEWISH WAY, BUT I DON'T FEEL THAT IT HAS HAPPENED FOR ME YET. I THINK PART OF WHERE I GET STUCK IN DISCHARGING IS THAT I'M TRYING TO FIT DOING IT IN TERMS OF THE DOMINANT CULTURE AND THAT I DON'T NOTICE THAT THERE IS A DIFFERENCE. SOMEHOW I NEED TO FIND A WAY OF MAKING IT JEWISH SO THAT IT CONNECTS BACK TO THE OTHER THOUSANDS OF YEARS OF HISTORICAL EXPERIENCE RATHER THAN THE MORE RECENT YEARS OF BEING IN THIS COUNTRY. SO I THINK ONCE WE COULD CONNECT BACK TO WHERE THAT ANCESTRY COMES FROM, MUCH MORE PROFOUND DISCHARGE WILL HAPPEN.

Karen: I think that we also need to think about how we take on reproaching ourselves. It's part of the internalized oppression. We too play out that impatience with the pattern because it is so painful to see and because we don't know how yet to offer hope outside of it, that sense of what would it really be like to not have that around our necks. In terms of being a Jewish woman, what Diane is saying is important.

Cherie: A lot of times things get told to us, and I look around and see that everybody else seems to be doing the same things, but somehow we seem to get targeted for them, like — we huddle. Well, I've seen more huddling in some Communities that have very few Jews in them. Or being noisy — I don't know why we would want to be more quiet. One of the things that happens for us as Jews is that we are constantly told that there's nothing threatening until it's too late. We know it's there, we feel it's there, and our counselors look at us and go, "Oh no, everything is just fine." But we know that there is anti-Semitism going on in spite of the denial. What hurts me is NOT hearing that people have attitudes, when they think we're too smart, or they're scared of us, but having them denied while feeling them very subtly.

The third question is about functioning. It was an eye-opener to me this summer, when Harvey stopped me at the leaders' meeting and tried to get me to say "I'm a Jew" and I couldn't say it. Here I am the International Jewish Liberation Reference Person and I couldn't say it. Nobody, Jew or non-Jew, until this summer, had seen that. I get up, and I do it, but that has nothing to do with where I live inside. I think that's true for all of us, how we talk, what we say, how we communicate, what we look like, has been very confusing and we can confuse each other, because *we* don't know. I had no idea. The only way I know I am scared here is that I'm not sleeping and I usually sleep. So chances are that I'm probably scared. I knew that I was scared but unless something smashes me up against being terrified so that I shake, I have a sense that it's there but I can go on. The way that I know is that my back will hurt, I'll get sick, I'll get asthma. (We die early.) People get sick more at a Jewish workshop.

Harvey, I can feel your love for us so strongly and that you want us out so much. You see us, we're so powerful, you want so much for us, you can't quite figure out why we just don't DO it. The other day you kept giving me these directions and I kept trying to say, "Well, it seems to me...." And you kept on, "No, no, trust me, if you really did it, if you held this direction, it would work." And I tried because we try hard. The thing that seems so important for Jews amongst ourselves and has to be true in terms of others working with us, is taking a look at what we look like, at what's in our eyes. The stuff is there, no matter how well we function, the stuff is on our faces, it's in our eyes. The point is that it's hard for us to look at each other. I have been told at more workshops things like, "If you just didn't look so scared," "you do everything well, but why do you look like that?" "Just get the look out of your eyes." Or "Thank God you don't look like a Holocaust survivor any more." Jews tell each other this all the time. The Jews that get scapegoated are the ones that look like the pictures that everybody saw. The strongest thing that we need is that it's okay, that there are good reasons we look that way. Let us really show that we are that scared. We need to know that you are willing to go in there with us and look at it. You've been telling us that all the other people in the world have had awful tragedies, but we're so great because we've survived. We need that. It's been vital that you've said all that, it's given us a balance and reality check and all that. But we also need to know that you are willing to get in with us and go back to the camps, that you would be willing to go with us to Auschwitz, to Bergen-Belsen and look with us and look in our eyes and look at our families the way that they looked, and look at the terror because it is right there. It's not that hidden. It's just that we keep getting these directions that we're already supposed to be out of it, and nobody in the world wants to see it. And the Jews that look that way are the Jews that are killed and the Jews that are persecuted.

Leah: The people that I taught counseling to in Birmingham know the theory well and know about the pattern and the person, but when it comes to my blaming, they can't see it as a pattern. It isn't a pattern in their eyes. I'm really struggling with that. Everything else they can accept, but on this they don't counsel me well and I'm not discharging. This they can't see at all. I'm just some kind of crummy person.

And they don't help me see it as otherwise. It took me ages to realize that that's the nature of the anti-Semitism. It really is that subtle. This, tonight, has been good for me, it's really good for me to hear. I need people to say that they are with me. That it's all right to put the blame on them rather than blame myself. A lot of it is really self-destructive. This is all good information to take back with me and deliver joyously.

SIDNEY: WHAT I REMEMBER ABOUT OUR RELATIONSHIP ARE THE

times when you acknowledged what things were really like for me, how hard things have been. It wasn't that I was trying to get at something that said I had been hurt worse than anybody else, but that people treated me differently because I was hurt that way.

GALE: In my particular Community which I am building as rapidly as I can, I'm the only Jewish person on the Area Reference Committee, the only Jewish teacher, and what I was thinking when I came to this workshop was, "Gee, I wonder what I'm here for." I think what I learned was the isolation part of my pattern is part of my culture, and it's the part that makes me very vulnerable. When I go to the Area Reference Committee meeting and say that our Community's been growing well but nobody's teaching, the people on the committee turn around to me and say "You're just saying that because you're a Jew, you're criticizing just because you're Jew, you've read Joan Karp's article." And I say immediately, "Well, gee, I guess you're right" and I haven't ever figured out how it worked so that I could say, "Well, look now, I'll bring another Jewish ally in and they'll speak for me." One reason I came was that I think I'm at the limit of my effectiveness in my Community and I realize that the reason why I feel that way is that every time I say something in the most even, quiet way I can find, and it's not often I can find it, people say to me, "You're just saying that because you're a Jew. You're never happy with anything because you're a Jew." Maybe if I work hard enough on being a Jew with all my Gentile Co-Counselors, not seeing another Jewish person except for one in my Community, I'll get out of it so that I can communicate well. But from what people have said here tonight that's not the issue.

Mitzi: Now I understand what happened at the workshop with Cherie last year. I need to look Cherie in the eye because I've been afraid to look at her since I came. About every two or three months I've told members of my class, ten nice, Christian Co-Counselors, to go off and work on anti-Semitism. I give them all the issues of **Ruah Hadashah** *and I give them Joan's article. Then they come back and they give me a direction. They really think they are very happy for me, because I am always light and I never let anything get heavy, including myself. So if that gets validated all the time, I don't see where the space is for us to get out of it. Do you know what I'm trying to say? Do you think this is the type of thing that can get worked out in an all-Gentile Community?*

Harvey: I think it can now. I think we had to do what we did which was to bust up the Community and let the pieces settle first. But I think it can now. With a little outside intervention, maybe.

David: Right about the time that Joan had written her letter and talked about it at the teachers' workshop, I went home and thought about how it applied to me, and I thought about all the attacks I was under in my Community. People had attacked me for a whole bunch of different reasons. I thought about it and saw it as anti-Semitism and also internalized oppression. I'm still not sure exactly how it's going to shift. At this point, I'm still trying to build a Community, but I'm not sure that the same things aren't going to happen again.

Becca: Harvey, you letting me off the hook last summer let it be all right for me not to have to do anything, not to have to keep doing more and more and more. I can't talk, it's so frustrating, I can't stand not being able to talk, it feels so non-Jewish. This is what so often happens to me in my Community, every time I get up and can't talk, people come up to me saying, "Why are you so incoherent?" Anyway, what I am thinking is that the effect of you not continuing to expect more from me was to open up a whole nice green pasture for

me, and to start looking at Jewish issues again. The other thing that I am worried about is that it also made me feel completely isolated from everyone else who was doing anything.

ARIANNE: I GUESS SITTING HERE LISTENING MADE ME WANT TO SPEAK OUT AS A YOUNGER PERSON ABOUT WHAT IT'S BEEN LIKE FOR ME, TRYING TO MOVE FORWARD AS A YOUNG PERSON WHERE IT'S VERY HARD TO FIT INTO AN ADULT COMMUNITY AS WELL AS BEING JEWISH. I HAD TO ASK JOAN TO ASK DIANE TO SAY MY NAME BECAUSE I CAN'T STAND UP FOR MYSELF. IT FEELS LIKE FOR ME TO IMPOSE IN ANY WAY IS TO NOT TAKE RESPONSIBILITY. THE WAY IT FEELS THAT THINGS HAVE COME AT ME IS THAT I HAVE TO BE RESPONSIBLE FOR EVERYTHING THAT I DO. NOT ONLY BECAUSE I'M YOUNG AND SO HAVE TO CONFORM AND LOOK RESPONSIBLE (AND BELIEVE ME, IF YOU ARE GOING TO BE YOUNG IN COUNSELING YOU HAVE TO LOOK DAMNED RESPONSIBLE OR ELSE YOU WON'T BE LISTENED TO BY ANYBODY), BUT ALSO BECAUSE I'M JEWISH AND I CARRY STUFF THAT LOOKS NASTY. IF I LET IT SHOW ANYWHERE I GET IT FROM MY BEST ALLIES. FOR THE LAST EIGHT OR TEN MONTHS, I HAVEN'T BEEN ABLE TO LEAD AT ALL. I SIT WITH MY PILES OF LITERATURE TO GO THROUGH FOR **Young and Powerful**, AND EVERY ONCE IN A WHILE I KNOW THAT I OUGHT TO PICK IT UP AND LOOK AT IT AND THINK HOW I OUGHT TO EDIT IT OR OUGHT TO DO SOMETHING, AND I CAN'T MOVE. THERE ARE A FEW PEOPLE WHO COUNT ON ME VERY MUCH AND I CAN'T DO ANYTHING. I FEEL LIKE I DON'T WANT TO OPEN MY MOUTH IN FRONT OF AN RC GROUP FOR FEAR THAT I WILL DO SOMETHING WRONG. I THINK THAT PEOPLE HAVE TO LEARN TO NOTICE WHERE SOMEBODY IS. THE FACT THAT I'M YOUNGER MEANS THAT THERE'S SOMETHING DIFFERENT GOING ON. I DON'T HAVE THE KIND OF SELF-CONFIDENCE THAT OTHER PEOPLE DO. I DON'T KNOW WHAT'S GOING ON. YOU ALL TALK ABOUT NOT KNOWING THAT YOUR STUFF'S YOUR STUFF, BUT I HAVE LESS EXPERIENCE WITH IT. I FEEL VERY BAD THAT I CAN'T DO WHAT I WANT TO DO RIGHT NOW. I CAN'T MOVE THROUGH IT AND I CAN'T ASK FOR HELP ANY MORE. SO I JUST COME AND BE QUIET.

THE LONGER VIEW

Harvey, I feel a real difficulty is to move into being a Jewish woman. Living in a rural area *is* different. We counsel that Jews can live anywhere and we're doing it, but the Gentiles there look at us and go off to the woods. There's a real hard feeling that areas like St. Johnsbury and Claremont and Freeport, Maine and Montana aren't places for Jews to live. We have a long history of living in our ghettos and we know where the appearance of safety is. It's a real hard expectation to go up to Jewish people and say to them, "We want you to feel safety outside of a large Jewish community." Of course it should be expected. The non-Jewish people in RC— all the ones in the rural areas—can read the thing and they pick up the words and they pick up our patterns. It's extremely hard for us to get any feeling of support up there, one, because there's one other Jewish person in my community. There are so few Jews in the areas to reach out to them. There are people living seventy miles, eighty miles away from another Jew. The isolation is very real. When we encounter anti-Semitism from other Jews or non-Jews, we need to have ways to open up to people. We need other Jews who can give us support. We feel the isolation from Jews outside of the ghetto.

Sheila: You said that for most oppressed groups, if you love someone outside your group, you're also trusting them but that that doesn't apply to Jews. It certainly also doesn't apply to women. I've thought a lot about Jewish oppression. There's something that's gone on in RC which everybody knows shouldn't happen and is totally against the theory, but which happens anyway. That is acting out patterns. That's happened a lot to leaders. I didn't put two and two together about that until listening to people's comments just now. That practice is absolutely demolishing to Jews and *has* to stop. There is never any excuse for that. That is against everything that we know about theory.

One thing I come to Jewish workshops for, that I get from Cherie that just thrills me and moves me terrifically every time she opens her mouth is that the basic RC theory comes out in Jewish terms. There are certain basic things in the RC theory that we can apply to ourselves as Jews, but it usually never comes out in those terms. It's never applied to our specific case. When Cherie talks, the examples are always in terms of Jewish history. The particular understanding, the particular loving that we need always comes out as Jewish examples. That's something that has been missing from a good deal of this workshop. The other point I had — which I just realized about five minutes ago — is that I function well in my leadership in the RC Community. I function well in my job. I function well with my friends, and both friends and Co-Counselors are totally amazed that my picture of myself has nothing whatsoever to do with the outside world's picture of me. I just always assume that's standard RC theory that we've all internalized all the invalidations. It didn't dawn on me until just about five minutes ago that it had anything to do with survival as a Jew.

Bob: In some ways my experience with non-Jews in Co-Counseling has been pretty benign. There have been a fair number of contacts I've had which have been unaware in terms of patterned admiration that doesn't recognize my distress, in terms of non-Jews communicating to Jews about what it means to be Jewish and about Judaism in a way that is upsetting to me, in effect telling us what being a good Jew is, what being a good Jew isn't.

But most of the experiences that I've had have been with internalized oppression. I feel very much that the relationship of most religious Jews towards other Jews is very much like the relationship of Jews towards non-Jews. What has come to me has been very explicit criticisms of my patterns by other Jews, that my patterns are too restimulating for other people to continue working with, or that I should stop communicating that I feel that nobody's out there for me, or that I'm not getting support, that I feel like I'm being abandoned. Even the isolation that goes for me — there's a lot of it. I have very frequently felt that it was something that I was doing. I still feel that it's something that I'm doing, and the message that I got repeatedly from people in my Community has been "Yes, it's something that you're doing."

I have the feeling that nobody sees my distress as a Jew simply because I walk around wearing a Jewish identity that looks a little bit firmer than other people's identities. I have the sense that it's almost impossible for me to work with Jews on anything religious. The issues for me about being religious are what I sense most people are bothered by. Being religious is not something that is on my mind all the time. It's not problematical. Being unemployed is. There are lots of other issues that are much closer to me. But there are very heavy issues around my relationship with other religious Jews that I haven't found any space to deal with. There's a sense in which I feel very marginal, from the first experience that we had. In that first contact I wasn't able to find space to say prayers at night because it was after hours when everybody is supposed to be quiet. Even at this workshop it's like struggling to make space for myself as a religious Jew. That whole dimension of my life is a problem only in Co-Counseling.

Co-Counseling is a problem for me more than being religious. My wife is uneasy about my involvement in Co-Counseling. It's not something I can easily talk to other people about.

The issue that has been raised around love and trust has been extremely difficult for me to work on in any context. I've been cut off each time I've started working on it in Co-Counseling. The sense of isolation builds up more and more and more and my sense of desperation, my sense of nobody really being out there. I haven't felt a sense of being connected up with the Jewish Co-Counseling Community. If it weren't for Cherie reaching out to me over and over again saying, "We're out here. There's somebody concerned" (and for you), I don't think I'd be in counseling at this point.

The thing, aside from all the Jewish stuff that everybody has, that piles everything else up for me is the experience of over and over again raising expectations that something's going to be out there. And it's like the image I have of the Peanuts' cartoon every fall, where Lucy is saying, "I really want to hold the ball." (Laughter) Last Jewish workshop I left early, I walked out, I didn't say anything to anybody. I sent a letter saying I was never going to come back to a workshop again. I came back and I have the same feeling. That's not what I need to work on. I don't need to spend the whole workshop (nor does any other religious Jew) on restimulations around the way we carry our Jewishness. There are so many other issues, the issues you're talking about, that it becomes impossible to get to.

Pat: I'd like to echo what Karen said about the isolation. I've lived in the South for twenty years. Last year when I came to the Jewish women's workshop I realized that being in the Northeast with Jewish women I felt more at home in that workshop where I knew only a handful of people than I did in my own Regional workshop. In the Regional workshop I was one of three Jews. The problem for me is that I'm often the first Jew that my Co-Counselors have ever talked to. I happened to grow up in an assimilated place, very assimilated. My reclaiming my Judaism is because of RC. I don't have the kind of information about the oppression of Jews that people that grew up in large Jewish communities have. I was not given that information as a child, for better or for worse. I mean I got some good things too. So it's especially hard for me when I go back to my Region, when I go to Regional workshops, and I feel like I don't belong there. What I hear is "Ah! Jewish pattern! Don't belong? Well, that's your Jewish pattern." It was a great relief to realize that there really is oppression.

The point is there are so few Jews in the Region that it's very important that we have a strong Jewish support group. It's also very important that the non-Jewish counselors take the situation seriously and learn about the oppression on their own so that we don't have to be teaching them all the time.

I have one other thing that I'd like to say that has to do with the counseling community. I'm just going to say how I feel: **The holocaust is not a Jewish issue.** *The only time people discharge in counseling on the holocaust is at a Jews' workshop or a Jews' and allies' workshop. If you go someplace else you don't ever hear anybody counsel on it. The holocaust happens to be a major, cataclysmic, historical event that would not have occurred if everyone else hadn't colluded. Other people need to be discharging on that so they can understand it and assimilate it and use the knowledge so that it doesn't happen anywhere to anyone ever again.*

Esther: Things are heavy in Israel. When someone from the United States comes and says, "It's internalized Jewish oppression. It's hard to listen to." Well, everything is hard, so we say to each other, "Okay, it's internalized Jewish oppression," but it's hard to define what the truth is and it's very confusing. For me it's very difficult.

GAIL: FIRST OF ALL I THINK IT'S REALLY CLEAR BOTH HOW WHERE YOU'VE BEEN A PERFECT ALLY FOR ME IS WHERE I'VE BEEN JEWISH AND ALSO WHERE WE'VE HAD TROUBLE IS WHERE I'VE BEEN JEWISH, BUT IT'S MOVING VERY WELL. I REALLY THINK THAT WHAT YOU DID WITH ME LAST NOVEMBER ON THE COMMITMENT WAS ONE OF THE MOST INCISIVE MOVES AGAINST JEWISH INTERNALIZED OP-

PRESSION THAT YOU'D DONE UP TO THAT POINT. WE DIDN'T KNOW IT. WE DIDN'T CALL IT JEWISH DISTRESS, BUT IT WAS. I WANT TO SAY SOMETHING ABOUT MYSELF. WHAT'S GOING ON FOR ME IS "SHOULD I CLIENT? SHOULD I GIVE INFORMATION? SHOULD I DISCHARGE? HE'S NOT GOING TO CALL ME ANYWAY. I ALWAYS RAISE MY HAND, BUT HE'LL NEVER CALL ON ME. THIS IS WONDERFUL AND WE'RE GOING TO MOVE ON THIS WITH EVERY OTHER JEW BUT ME. I'M STILL GOING TO BE THE JEW THAT GETS TRASHED. (CRIES) I'LL BE THE LAST JEW." I'M HEARING ALL THIS INFORMATION THAT'S PERFECT, BUT I'M SAYING, "IT'S NOT GOING TO WORK FOR ME." I GET JUST AS MUCH HURT FROM JEWS AS I DO FROM NON-JEWS. I GOT IT WORSE FROM JEWS. I HATE JEWS. (LAUGHTER) SOMEHOW I'M JUST DIFFERENT. I'M GOING TO STILL GET TRASHED, BY MYSELF AND EVERYBODY ELSE. I'M THE ONLY JEW YOU SHOULD CALL ON IN THIS GROUP. I MEAN THAT.

THERE'S A GROUP OF US THAT MET ON COMBATTING JEWISH OPPRESSION, AND WE DID A LOT OF THINKING. THAT FINALLY HAPPENED. FINALLY IN THIS WORKSHOP WE'RE GOING TO DO A REPORT. I THINK WE COVERED A LOT OF IT.

I THINK THE DIRECTION NEEDS TO BE TO RELAX AND LOOK AT THE OPPRESSION. LOOK AT THE OUTSIDE OPPRESSION, NOT ONLY AT OUR PATTERNS. LOOK AT WHAT HAPPENS TO EACH OTHER. LOOK AT THE OPPRESSION, HOW IT RUNS IN RC AND OUTSIDE OF RC. TELL STORIES. TELL INCIDENTS. LOOK AT THE DETAILS AND DISCHARGE. THAT'S ALL WE HAVE TO DO. WE DON'T HAVE TO DO ANYTHING ELSE. BECAUSE IF WE WILL DO IT, WE WILL GO OUT AND WE WILL FUNCTION BEAUTIFULLY. WE'LL DO ALL THAT. THAT'S BEEN SAID ALREADY BUT I WANT TO REPEAT IT. THE REST IS UP TO OUR ALLIES. IT'S THEIR JOB NOW.

David: I want to speak as a Jewish man, particularly as a U.S. Jewish man. It seems that the more progressive lead that I've taken, the more visi-

ble leadership in counseling, the more numb I've gotten. When I was an assistant teacher I was doing well, as a Jewish support group leader I was doing well. When I became a teacher it became a little worse. When I became an Area Reference Person, I dove. Cherie and Joan in particular have made important, key steps in the direction of acknowledging that for Jewish men things sit a little differently. I can't exactly tell you how it sits. One reason is that I can't feel it all that well; I know that the one thing that Joan did that really worked (and I cried for an hour and a half afterwards about how I wished it would work) at a workshop where allies were not in the room at the moment she had the women cheer the men. That was one of the most profound experiences in RC for me. I have never felt cherished as a Jewish man in RC. As you know, Harvey, it's been very difficult to move past the enormous amounts of shame that I feel for being a Jewish man. It's been difficult to even tell people that this is what I most want — just to be cherished and to have a place to discharge. What I want from you, and from allies, is for other non-Jewish men to reach out and to hold out to us that we are beloved and that we are cherished, just as Jewish men, not as men and not as Jews but as Jewish men. I need to hear that being a Jewish man is, of itself, a cherishable thing to be.

Vicki: I want to say one thing about our functioning. I don't know for how many other Jewish women the question that prevents us from taking complete leadership in the world is this question. The theory misses me in some way. I have sat through seven years of leaders' meetings absolutely numb thinking that I should find an answer that fit me into the theory.

I got a glimpse of it at the world conference this summer through something somebody did. I realized that we need to ask a different question for me and for Joan. Obviously there's more. I haven't quite figured out what the question is, so I can't give you the answer. There's something about our functioning so well. Cherie said part of it when she said that people are relieved that we function. They say, "You're not scared. You function so well." Then they run. It feels

like I have to stop functioning in order to get help. I know that's not right.

Something happened at the Santa Cruz workshop when we were talking about our relationships and you asked some of the Gentile people at the table how it is that they relate to you or you relate to them. One of them said to me (she was a woman), "Harvey doesn't look at me as a fighter." I thought, that's true, he doesn't look at you as a fighter. David said it. Some of us are fighters and we need to be loved for being fighters or in spite of it. Don't be afraid of us. We won't hurt you. I feel that sometimes in order to be loved by you I have to stop being Jewish and be a nice, timid, white, Gentile female. That feels hopeless because I'm never going to be that way.

(Name unintelligible): I left New York because of internalized oppression around being a Jewish woman and tried the non-Jewish Communities. One of the reasons I came back was because I was told to come back. People in the RC Community that I was in said my patterns had gotten in the way or gotten to be a problem. I was told to go back where I came from and learn humility. That ran right into my internalized oppression, so I came back. Everything that's been said here has helped me to understand that my own feelings are not just my own. I guess there are three crucial things for me. One is to be outside the client role and counselor role. I've been hooked inside that for eight years. I've worked with many people here in front of workshop groups and not felt any ongoing relationship with them and not felt any ongoing community. That's been a lot my distress, but that's how it's gone. I haven't recognized it before as particularly Jewish. The second thing that I came upon about five years ago is that as a Jew I need to hear from non-Jews simply that my existence is important to you. Not my skills, not my work, not the way I articulate, not what I can do; just my *existence* as a Jew. The third has to do with expectations. I've been looking a lot at confusions around language and the word "expectations" is one source and the word "I" is another. "Expectations" used to be a very negative word to me. It came out of people expecting things from me that were out of their own frozen needs and I would disappoint them and disappoint myself. The kind of expectation that I experience you as holding forth is the kind of expectation that helps me move out. So I encourage you to keep on holding out that expectation.

Margaret: On this goal of re-emerging completely, I don't yet seem to be determined to do it no matter what. I live in such an isolated way that I don't even know that I'm isolated. I just seem to travel all over the world in order to try to find a place that's mine. (Begins to cry)

Harvey: You're at one such place now. Let the tears come.

Margaret: Nobody in my Community would criticize Jewish patterns. They would feel far too timid, like they didn't know enough about it. I know that people on the Area Reference Committee read Joan's article. It's okay for me to complain and, reluctantly, I do. I complain very entertainingly. I think I'm the funniest complainer. That's the way in which I keep managing to carry on, that I really save up all those things I need to do. I have refused consistently to do the usual kinds of leadership, and I haven't known why people have just tolerated it and haven't really dealt with it. I'm hearing that people are talking, but maybe there are some good reasons why they haven't dealt with it.

Laurie: I'm sitting here listening and trying to sort out stuff for myself. That's okay. For a long, long time I've been very confused about being Jewish and being physically different. It seems to me that Jewish workshops are the only places where my physical difference is not the main issue. Even though other people might get uptight, to me it always feels like it's "their" Jewish distress. That's important for me. This makes me believe that perhaps the physical difference intensifies what's buried underneath that — the feelings about what kind of background we come from. I'm not sure, so don't quote me. It's what I feel I'm experiencing. That's that physically different people need very much to be together to create the safety to look at what's neat about being physically different. Time will tell. It might change in a year.

Cherie said to me once, "Why don't you start looking at being Jewish?" This summer I began looking at it and after the summer, I began to feel different. More and more they call me uppity. That started happening.

In my Community there's a tendency for us to become absorbed with all kinds of other issues. Once in a while when we start really getting sunk and feeling unsupported, someone will say, "That could be anti-Semitism," but we haven't really allowed ourselves to look at that for a long time. I think it's important because a lot of us are Jewish. There are Jews in my Community and we need to be there for each other. That's all.

Betty: First of all, it feels like everyone else has said everything much better than I could say it. I've gone in and out of thoughts of what I want to say. I started counseling in the United States as a Jew in U.S. and then moved to Israel. It's interesting because of what I saw going on for me as a Jew in a very non-Jewish Community in Portland, Oregon and then going to a totally Jewish Community. All the feelings of isolation I was having in Oregon got changed around in Israel. I didn't feel isolated as a Jew any more, but I felt a lot of our not really supporting each other in our best possible way, something like what Esther said of the internalized oppression. That's why it was helpful for me when you came.

In the last workshop, right at the beginning, Harvey

told us that we weren't allowed to criticize. He even put a sign up on the wall and that was helpful. Harvey acted angry at us a lot about our talking and criticizing between each other, but I realize now that it would have been more helpful if it was done in a more loving way. We really need someone to come in and interrupt our internalized oppression that we are doing to each other, but it has to be done in a loving way. We have to hear it coming from a loving space.

(*Tape runs out. Next tape begins in the middle of someone's turn. Person speaking is a woman.*)

(Name unknown): I'm aware and would like you to be aware that all of us who are forty or over have directly experienced some very colorful anti-Jewish experiences in the world. If you think about the events in our lives, they're not all anti-Jewish because among them is the foundation of the state of Israel, but there are some direct experiences of the Second World War and the Holocaust. A number of historical events are ones that we have known first-hand. One of the ways we tend to feel in a particular way as older Jews is that the future belongs to young people. We're all too willing to give it over without insisting on our right to re-emerge. It's where we get hooked with the despair. As people who have lived for the number of years that most of us have, we have become extremely adept at doing the best we can and smiling and telling you that it was really quite easy. We're often hoping against hope that you would insist that we take time to really be in touch with and tell what those experiences have been like for us. I think that there's nothing essentially different about the experience of older Jewish counselors, but it may be multiplied by some factor.

Harvey: Two more, no matter how unreasonable the limitation is.

S—: I WOULD LIKE TO SAY A WORD FOR LESBIAN, GAY, AND BISEXUAL JEWS. I'VE BEEN THINKING ALL WEEKEND THAT WE'VE REALLY GOTTEN TERRIBLY VISIBLE. IN JEWISH CULTURE THERE'S THE WORD "ABOMINATION." IT MAKES IT VERY HARD. I THINK THAT WE NEED SOME HELP FROM EACH OTHER AND FROM JEWS AND FROM NON-JEWS ABOUT THIS, UNLESS WE WANT TO ACCEPT THAT OPPRESSION. IF WE'RE GOING TO CHALLENGE EVERYTHING ELSE, WHY NOT CHALLENGE THAT, TOO? SO I'D LIKE PEOPLE TO THINK ABOUT THAT BECAUSE THAT MAKES OUR LIVES VERY, VERY HARD. WHEN I STOOD UP TODAY AND TALKED ABOUT INCEST, I KNEW THAT THERE ARE A LOT OF PEOPLE HERE THAT HAVE MATERIAL ON IT. WE ALL HAVE MATERIAL ON IT, SINCE WE'VE ALL COME OUT OF FAMILIES OF ONE KIND OF ANOTHER. THE MYTH IS "NOT IN NICE JEWISH FAMILIES. THIS DOESN'T HAPPEN. NEVER DOES A MAN BECOME GAY, NOR DOES A WOMAN BECOME A LESBIAN, NOR DO WE EVER SLEEP WITH BOTH SEXES." IT'S JUST "IMMORAL" AND IT'S AN "ABOMINATION." WE WANT TO CHALLENGE THAT. WE NEED SOME HELP.

Randi: There are two main things that I want to say. When I hear what's been said I keep thinking, "Oh, it's not only me," which has been very reassuring, but then there are other places where I think, "Maybe it *is* only me." Perhaps all the common experiences means that everybody's thinking that. When Gail spoke I thought, "Oh, maybe it's working class." Because I'm thinking maybe I'm not Jewish, I'm only working class or something. Anyway, the idea of really counseling is part of it. If you remember what happened last June, we had the leaders' meeting at the teachers' workshop and you were asking different oppressed groups how it was. Then you started asking the Jews and every single one of us started crying because we were sure you wouldn't ask us. That same agonizing has been going on for me. I sat there thinking, "He won't call on me because I know he doesn't think I'm important. But am I?" You know, back and forth. Which was confirmed. What it actually confirmed was if I push so hard that I don't even want to push anymore, then maybe I'm important. I keep getting the sense that when push comes to shove, I'm not really important enough. I tell myself to stop acting out of frozen needs. I've got the theory down so well I use it against myself better than any non-Jew could use it. What that does is it makes me paralyzed to actually try to think about what to do because I'm so sure I understand distress and I shouldn't act on it.

The other thing about that is expectation. I don't know if this is a little like what Ricky was saying. It's different from her for me. I'm dying—oops—forget that word.

Harvey: Yearning.

Yearning, thank you. I'm yearning—sounds like a national anthem. I'm wishing—I told this to Cherie today and I thought maybe it would suffice, but I think maybe I ought to tell it to you, too. I'm wishing you'd put expectations on me, so high that I wouldn't be able to achieve them, because what happens to me is I set my own goals and my own challenges as best I can figure out and then I go for it and I do what I need to get there. Everyone's so impressed that nobody bothers to think maybe I'm not really doing what I want or maybe what I can. I don't know what happens. I don't know what they see, but I know I've been trying to figure out all weekend what it is that I'm wanting here. I couldn't even think about it until I saw the work this morning and realized if it was true for Debbie and Corinne, I could at least think about it. I'm trying to be succinct.

There's something inconsistent. I think I'm so fragile in my belief about being liked, I think particularly by non-Jews, particularly by non-Jewish men, particularly by non-Jewish men whom I respect.

(Harvey: She's getting it narrowed down, isn't she?)

That, if there's sixteen examples that you like me, it only takes one-half example that could in any way be interpreted as negative. I take a sentence out of a letter that you write me and I take it to session and say, "How *dare* he say — you'll know what I'm talking about, too — how dare he call my mind fertile?" I can't make sense of it, which I guess gets to mistrust. It's inconsistent, because when you did the work with me in June with Judy Muench and you asked her what she would see if the Jewish shackles were removed, she didn't know what at all, but *you* knew. You almost said it in the words that I had going in my head and I thought, Well, if he *sees* that so clearly, what's wrong here? I don't understand. Anyway, it's this feeling that I don't understand — somehow because of the way RC works. If you don't have expectations of me, then I must not count to you in your view of what it's going to take to move the world from where we are now until the next step. So, I think, when I write to you, I don't know what you are. I would love to find out. I really would, because somehow I'm writing to you all the things I'm doing well, but I'm wanting you to tell me either to find out what's hard so I can go further or to tell me what I'm doing wrong because at least that would be showing you care.

(Harvey: Will you make a note of that, Patsy?)

Note? What note?

(Harvey: All that's necessary is that I *remember* that. That's why I said that. That's what my crack about a note was.)

Oh. Okay, that's one other thing. I have a good sense of humor, but somehow when you make jokes it throws me every time. Every time I try to talk to you and you come back with any kind of a joke, it's like my mind just goes blank. It's too close to ridicule, even if it's as far from ridicule as it could be. I feel like this difficulty has gone on long enough. It's not productive for either one of us at this

point. We should be great friends and I would cheer your life up, as well. So there's something in it for you.

Seeking An Effective Gentile Voice

The following documents may be useful for allies of Jews in organizing to be effective against anti-Semitism.

The project was launched in Seattle, largely among leaders of the Christian churches, and met an initial warm response.

As it developed, a number of these Christian leaders felt they must consult the "official" leaders of the Seattle Jewish Community with whom they had been working on "joint" bodies of Christians and Jews. These Jewish leaders expressed anxiety about any independent body of Gentiles taking any positions which they, the Jewish leaders, were not in a position to veto, and some of the crucial Christian leaders felt they could not continue against this opposition. The anxiety was primarily about possible criticism of the "official" Jewish leaders' anti-Arab and anti-Palestinian positions.

These difficulties were not unexpected, and in fact a primary purpose of the project was to establish an effective Gentile voice against anti-Semitism that would be more believable and supportable because it would not be contaminated by the anti-Arab, anti-Palestinian, or "support-the-Israeli-Government-policies-no-matter-how-oppressive-and-wrong-they-are" positions with which joint Gentile-Jewish bodies have often been associated in the public mind in the past.

The project is still feasible, but personal overwork, health, and shortage-of-help problems have delayed my taking more vigorous initiatives recently. People in other cities have asked

Appeared in **Ruah Hadashah** No. 6.

THE LONGER VIEW

for information about getting started, however, and so I am offering **Ruah Hadashah** the draft documents.

— Harvey

PROPOSAL

Proposal:

That we and/or others constitute ourselves (or in the near future form or assist to form) a committee or public body of some sort composed entirely of non-Jews

who will speak out and organize against all instances or practices of anti-Semitism (directed against either Jews or Arabs) and in particular against all oppression of, discrimination against, or defamation of Jews

not primarily or only because of the injustice of such practices to Jews but primarily because such practices are an insult and injury to Gentiles and to the viability of the society of which we are a part and serve as an entering wedge and evil model for oppression and unfair treatment and attitudes to be visited upon all other groups of the population through racism, discrimination, and slander.

That we expose to the general public the evils, dangers, and sources of all mistreatment of Jews.

That we maintain friendly relationships with *all* sections of the Jewish community but that we set our own policies and take our own actions independently of any other group, seeking to be the best expression of Gentile opposition to oppression of Jews, *in the interests of Gentiles*.

In particular that we not require nor expect that any sections of the Jewish Communities agree with us or approve of our positions, and that we feel free to differ with any of our Jewish friends where we conclude that their policies are in error and are weakening the battle again anti-Semitism or anti-Jewish oppression.

That we designate a spokesperson whom we can trust to react quickly and publicly in our name to events, without having to clear a consensus for his or her particular statements but who will confer individually and in occasional meetings, to keep a general consensus clear among us.

That we initiate and publicize any appropriate actions against anti-Semitism freely as individuals and seek to draw other persons into support of such actions. That we inform our designated spokesperson of such actions as time permits and share experiences when we meet.

That we seek a volunteer worker to handle the necessary correspondence and other work that may be entailed, at least until the volume of activity justifies a full-time paid assistant for such work.

That our policy be uniformly to end the isolation of Jews from the other groups in the population and to end all forms of discrimination, prejudice, and slander against them.

Letter sent to interested parties with the third draft of the policy statement after the provisional committee had become inactive.

Dear Friend,

The Committee Against Jewish Oppression was proposed as a body of non-Jews who would speak out and act against all instances of anti-Jewish oppression (anti-Semitism), primarily because of the deleterious effects of such oppression on society generally and on non-Jews in particular. It was also intended to permit the inclusion of many people who are against Jewish oppression but who have not felt comfortable with joint bodies of Jews and non-Jews where they had in the past felt pressure to take an anti-Arab or anti-Palestinian position with which they could not agree.

Some individuals who assumed leadership at the first, founding meeting of the Committee later found themselves unable to proceed, and the organization of the Committee was halted for a time.

Others of us felt, however, that it was, historically, time for such an effort and such an organization and intend to continue in this direction. I enclose a copy of the third draft of a policy statement for the Committee. It can still be revised and improved as our role develops, but if you feel in accord with it generally, please sign it and invite your like-minded friends and associates to sign it, and return it to me.

When a substantial number of signatures has accumulated, a meeting will be called, of which you will be notified, and the organization of the Committee will proceed.

Sincerely,
Harvey Jackins

POLICY STATEMENT OF THE COMMITTEE AGAINST OPPRESSION OF JEWS

NAME

This body shall be known as "The Committee Against Oppression of Jews."

MEMBERSHIP

The Committee shall consist of individual Gentiles who have associated themselves together to speak out and act against all expressions or practices of oppression or discrimination or defamation against Jews.

We welcome other non-Jews from all walks of life to join our Committee, to add themselves to our forces, and to participate in whatever we do. Such additional people shall be accepted upon application and approval at a meeting of the Committee.

PURPOSE

We are engaging in these activities in the interest of all peoples and in the particular interest of non-Jews or Gentiles. Oppression of Jews is not only harmful to Jews. It is not only wrong, shameful, bigoted, and a threat to the viability of the society of which we are a part. It is harmful to the real interests of all non-Jews or Gentiles, who are injured by it in many general and specific ways.

Discrimination against, defamation of, or oppression of Jews (often called anti-Semitism) serves as an entering wedge for such practices against *all* members of society. Black people, people from the various Asian and Latino cultures, Native Americans are injured by racist discrimination in ways that are modeled on the oppression of Jews and for which the oppression of Jews has served as a precedent. If the oppression of Jews is not combatted and stopped, the members of these other groups suffer also: Oppression of Jews leads to other oppressions as well. Once a model of oppression of one group of people is tolerated, then it can be easily applied to working-class people, women, trade unionists, elderly people, young people, and all other groups which can be differentiated within the population and marked out for persecution. All members of oppressed minorities (nearly everyone belongs to such a minority in some sense) have a real stake in insisting that Jews not be mistreated or oppressed in any way.

History repeatedly reveals that the oppression of Jews is the signal and precedent, an "early warning system" for the oppression of other groups. Pastor Martin Niemoller, the great Lutheran pastor who was imprisoned by Hitler, said afterwards that "When the Nazis came to imprison the Jews, I was not a Jew, so I did not speak up. When they came to imprison the trade unionists and the communists, I was not a trade unionist or communist and I did not speak up. The same happened with many other groups. When the Nazis came for me, there was no one left to speak up."

Thus, while recognizing that Jews are obviously hurt by oppression, defamation, and discrimination directed against them, we emphasize that non-Jews are equally victimized by and suffer from the results of such practices. Therefore we take our stand and conduct our activities primarily in the interest of non-Jews, of Gentiles.

POLICIES

We will set our own policies and take actions on our own judgment. We will not expect or require that any sections of the Jewish communities agree with us or approve of our positions. We shall feel free to differ with any of our Jewish friends whenever we conclude that their policies are in error and are not effective against anti-Jewish oppression.

We do intend to keep close contact with all sections of the Jewish communities and appreciate being alerted or warned by them of anti-Jewish activities when they become aware of them.

We welcome the existence of Israel as the national homeland for Jews everywhere and support the continued existence of Israel as a basic fundamental righting of centuries of wrongdoing. This does not mean that we approve of any specific policies of the Israeli government nor that we would not feel free to differ with such policies or criticize them. In particular the fact that we are supportive of Jews and support the existence of Israel does not mean that we oppose the interests of the Palestinians or other Arabs or that we condone any oppression of Palestinians by anyone, including the Israeli government.

ACTIONS

We seek to arouse the general public to the evils, dangers, and sources of all mistreatment of Jews and seek to have non-Jews act effectively against such mistreatment.

We will not limit ourselves to any specific form of action but feel free in the future to take any action which will be effective.

ORGANIZATION

We designate a Spokesperson to speak publicly for our Committee who will react quickly and publicly in our name to any events without first having to clear a consensus for his or her particular statement. This Spokesperson will confer individually with us as possible. There will be occasional meetings of our Committee to keep a general consensus clear among us.

Each member of this Committee at present and such as join us later shall feel free to initiate and publicize any appropriate action against the oppression of Jews and seek to draw other people into support of such actions, but will not speak in the name of the Committee unless he or she is the designated Spokesperson. Each of us who undertakes such individual actions will inform our designated Spokesperson of such actions so that he or she may be informed of whatever we do. We will share experiences in our occasional meetings.

We may designate a volunteer worker to handle routine activities (correspondence, etc.) and may provide a full-time worker later if the volume of activity justifies this.

GOALS

Our goal is to end the isolation of Jews from other groups of the population and to end all forms of discrimination, prejudice, oppression, and slander against them.

RESTRICTION

We recognize that many other groups in our population suffer from discrimination and oppression and we welcome the formation of committees similar to ours, such as by whites to combat white racism, by Caucasians to end the oppression of Asians, and so on. We hope that other committees such as ours will arise to function in a parallel manner. Many of us, as individuals, would be willing to participate in such other committees. As a group, however, since the oppression of Jews is such a precedent and opening wedge for the oppression of all other minority groups, this Committee shall deal only with the oppression directed against Jews.

Reports

A General "Upbeat" Report

Our Communities appear to be in a time of decisive change. It is plain wherever I go that a very different atmosphere is surrounding our active Co-Counselors than formerly. Decisive numbers of people, including most leaders, are taking charge of their lives and of the environment around them in ways that we have talked about in recent years, but which has never before been so widely modelled. Every day's mail contains letters saying things like, "It has made a huge difference to me to realize that I *can* have things in my life just the way I want them. I am proceeding to do so." There's a confident, upbeat tone both in the large and in the small Communities. This is in spite of the continuing pressure from a collapsing society, recession, general financial difficulties, and war danger.

Some key principles are being grasped and held in awareness in this period. These certainly have something to do with the almost triumphant tone of many leading Co-Counselors at the present. Among them are the realizations that *deciding* does not have to follow discharge, but can precede it; that discharge is enhanced and accelerated by putting the decision first (in the form of decisions, directions, commitments, and actions); and that our lives can be much more the way we want them without waiting for discharge; that attention away from distress is an efficient route to discharge and that we can discharge as we act. Everywhere, people are realizing that they *can* have everything the way they want it and are enjoying triumph after triumph as they proceed to put this principle into action. These people are no longer being stopped by old feelings of discouragement or the actions of the oppressive society.

Appeared in **Present Time** No. 63, April 1986.

The enormous complexity of our central nervous systems (one thousand billion neurons in intimate contact with each other and capable of making more uniquely discrete responses than the number of atoms in the observed universe) brought us *intelligence* and *awareness* as qualitatively different functions than those possessed by simpler forms of life. We are now quite sure that this complexity also brought us *complete freedom of decision* (we can decide anything we want to, any way we want to, any time we want to, under any conditions) and complete power (all of us were conceived and most of us were born with the justifiable expectation that the universe would be responsive to our wishes). Even though this inherent complete freedom of decision and total power have been almost totally obscured by individual hurts and the great mass of distress piled up by the operations of oppressive societies, it is at last becoming clear that all that interferes with our reclaiming complete power (we mean rational, benign power, of course, not the oppressive pseudo-power that is visible in the oppressive societies) is an accumulation of powerlessness patterns. Since we know how to discharge patterns, we are slowly but determinedly finding effective tools to discharge the powerlessness ones. Reclaiming our powerful tones of voice is the one that's received most attention to date, and it is helpful. We now also have a commitment which seems to work well in the same direction. This commitment, "From now on, I will see that everything that I am in contact with works well and I will not restrain my contacts or inhibit their continual expansion."

PRESENT TIME **SUBSCRIPTIONS**

Subscriptions for **Present Time** now represent a central channel for community building work. Now that we can offer **Present Time** on a subscription basis, the securing of subscriptions puts a powerful, consistent source of crucial information in the hands of every subscriber. The silly myth that used to circulate that our journals could only be understood by the "in-crowd" is belied by the fact that whenever a journal escapes from the confines of the "in-crowd" and a stranger finds it and reads it, the stranger writes to Seattle excitedly requesting more information and more access to the literature.

To secure **Present Time** subscriptions in large numbers is the single most effective and the easiest way of building the very large Communities which the near future will require for the survival of humankind. We will have subscription blanks available very soon on card stock for RCers to carry with them, but there is a blank printed in this **Present Time** and you can make up your own. Thousands of new subscriptions to **Present Time** is a crucial task. Regardless of what else we are doing and how much we are doing, this is a central operation.

NEW ZEALAND AND AUSTRALIA

My long trip to New Zealand and Australia in January of this year was a remarkably fine experience and a thoroughgoing success. The last time I was in New Zealand, I met with about five people and the last time in Australia with about forty-one. This time, the workshop on the South Island, at Christchurch, had twenty people present and the one at New Plymouth on the North Island, had twenty-four people present. The one at Sydney, Australia, had one hundred thirty-five people present. Forty-one attended the one in Tasmania and there were twenty at the one in Perth. A great deal of fine work was done at each workshop and the eagerness of people to hear the most advanced concepts of our new theory and to take on the job of each individual building his or her own world community was quite electrifying. There is fine leadership emerging everywhere in the two countries. In some particular ways, the Communities there are the most advanced in the world.

I was delighted to find many Maoris participating and taking leadership in New Zealand, particularly on the North Island. I was very pleased to find many of the white Australians in contact with and determined to be effective allies for Aboriginals. I was reassured to find close contact with the trade union movement and the labor movement throughout Australia. In both

THE LONGER VIEW

countries there was a *determined* commitment to model opposition to nuclear arms and warfare for the rest of the world.

Diane Shannon is a tower of strength to everyone in New Zealand, particularly on the South Island. Julie Lambie, the organizer of the North Island workshop and a Maori leader, has a fine group of Maori RCers around her and the support of my old friend, Wiremu Solomon from Auckland. Jonathan Shaw's role as Regional Reference Person for all of Australia is working well. Both the old leaders and much new leadership are working extremely well together around Sydney. Anne Smith, in spite of many old Community problems and in spite of ill heath, has done an exemplary job of fighting for correct policy in Tasmania and has been rewarded with a powerful and effective Community. Smaller groups in Newcastle and the Blue Mountains and Adelaide and Canberra and Melbourne, etc. are healthy and growing. Perth is as far away from the beginning Communities in Sydney and Hobart as Seattle is away from New York, but the group of sturdy pioneers in Western Australia are doing well and show every sign of having a strong Community growing rapidly around them in the near future.

I thoroughly enjoyed all the New Zealanders and Australians that I was in contact with, thoroughly enjoyed every aspect of their varied and beautiful countries, and was treated royally by everyone there. On the way home I met with the RC leaders in Hawaii and enjoyed our profitable interactions. RC is effective in wide world affairs there in many ways.

Two open workshops, in Vermont around the 1st of March and in Santa Fe, New Mexico around the middle of March, have been very, very encouraging. Large numbers of RCers turned out (from long distances in some cases) and grasped the job of building world communities around each individual with great enthusiasm.

It's a very exciting time in RC and to be able to visit and participate with these people is a great privilege.

As **Present Time** goes to press, I am leaving for the General Liberation workshop in Leicester, England and will make Community visits to the RC Communities in West Berlin, Warsaw, and Salzburg before I return home shortly after the middle of April.

A COMMITMENT FOR ACTIVISTS

At the Santa Fe workshop, a new "Commitment for Leftists" was worked out that I think will mean a great deal to the many activists who are seeking support and personal nurturance from their contact with RC. It is as follows:

"I have chosen the responsibility to change society, but I also choose to be intelligent in the way I do it.

The future needs *me*, well-rested, well-nourished, and well-exercised.

The past is useful for information, but never as a substitute for my own fresh thinking. Mao respected Marx but did his own fresh thinking. I will respect all past thinkers, but my thinking will necessarily be more brilliant than theirs because I stand on their shoulders.

If I am not enjoying what I am doing, then there is something wrong with what I am doing and I will correct it."

Report on Recent Activities

As this **Present Time** prepares to go to press, I am looking forward with great eagerness to the trip which Mary Ni, Tim, and I will be making in early October to Beijing, China. Li Mei Ge, who attended the World Conference in 1985, has arranged for an official invitation by the Chinese Association for Mental Health. We will be having conversations with various individuals and groups in Beijing. This contact with the nation which includes one-fourth of the world's people is a very exciting prospect.

I have just returned from Europe. On September second, near Newcastle-upon-Tyne, I attended a conference of RC leaders of university and college faculty in the eastern hemisphere. The conference was attended by an impressive array of faculty. It was organized by Doug Miller and was co-led by Pam Roby, the International Liberation Reference Person for Colleagues. Pam met me there, coming around the world from the other direction. She had led workshops in Hong Kong, Singapore, and in Delhi, India on her way as well as attending a world conference of sociologists in India.

Dramatic improvement in the activity and numbers of RC colleagues was reported and the conference itself was marked by excellent, frontier counseling.

From Newcastle, I went to Amsterdam for a meeting of Regional Reference Persons and Liberation Reference Persons of the eastern hemisphere, led by Joke Hermsen. Not all of the Regional Persons were able to attend, but there was a substan-

Appeared in **Present Time** No. 65, October 1986.

tial group there and fine discussions, planning, and coordination. Daniel LeBon, the Regional Reference Person for Francophone Europe, was able to attend for one day and the discussion he led on the importance of the redefinition of restimulation as a basis for advanced development of theory will be remembered by all of us.

Ulla Sjögren was not able to attend the conference because of previous commitments, but came to Amsterdam the next day and we had a very fine two-way conference on RC in Scandinavia. Ulla is well and working effectively. She undertook certain commitments that will mean a lot to the Scandinavian and Polish Communities.

I flew next to Budapest. The beginning of RC in Hungary consisted of three meetings and some counseling with groups of artists, professionals, and students. Interest is very clear. A lending library of literature will be established; discussion groups will begin to meet; translation of some of the literature from English is beginning; and there are plans to bring people who take the greatest interest to workshops in other parts of Europe for accelerated training in becoming RC teachers.

Budapest is an impressive city and the Hungarian people obviously have a remarkably rich culture. There will now be a contact person for Hungary in the lists at the back of **Present Time**. RCers in other countries who have friends, relatives, or contacts inside Hungary are urged to put them in touch with the contact person for a wider development of RC there in the future.

From Budapest, I flew to Athens. The Greek Community has changed and grown a great deal since I was last with them. I led a weekend workshop involving twenty people, all of whom are Co-Counseling at an advanced and responsible level. There is now a male teacher, Thanos Zarangalis, and men are beginning to share leadership in what had been a woman-led Community. Thanos has translated **The Human Side of Hu-**

man Beings and The Fundamentals Manual into Greek and these are already in use. There will be a significant increase in the numbers of teachers in Athens and individual communities are going to be built around many of the presently active members.

On Sunday evening, after the workshop was over, I led a discussion on new developments relating to men's oppression and liberation for a largely non-RC group which RCers had organized.

My final stop in Europe was in Split, Yugoslavia. Split is a town of about a quarter million population with many ancient buildings, streets, and squares still functioning after 2,000 years of use. I had two meetings with groups assembled on short notice by Mrs. Branka Drascic, who had heard about RC from a friend in London. In the group were engineers, social workers, psychologists, and a considerable variety of other people. We met first in the courtyard of my hotel, shaded by palm trees on the shores of the Adriatic Sea. Later that afternoon I met, in a social service agency where a number of the people in the morning meeting worked, with other members of their staff.

A very alive interest was shown in RC at both meetings. Discussion groups will begin; a lending library of literature will be established there and translations, into Croatian at least, will be worked on.

At the end of August the Regional Reference Persons and Liberation Reference Persons of the Western Hemisphere met in Albuquerque, New Mexico. Thirty-one leaders attended. Discussion was good, morale was high, and there was marathon counseling.

This group and the meeting in Amsterdam have agreed on a world-wide meeting of Regional and Liberation Reference People for 1987. The dates set are July 24-28th. The place will be somewhere in the Northeast United States.

Latin American RC!

The first Conference of Latin American Leaders of RC was held in Buenos Aires November 14-18th. Twelve people were present from Argentina, six from Mexico, five from Peru, two from Sweden, one from Nicaragua, and one from the United States.

It was an excellent conference. The translation was handled as described by Margaret Grammer-Vallejos in another part of this **Present Time** with one person translating from Spanish to English and one person from English to Spanish. Much of the proceedings were videotaped, and some very fine discussions and demonstrations occurred as well as the lectures. A number of people decided to begin teaching RC in their countries. Francisco Lopez-Bustos undertook overall responsibility for developing new leadership in Argentina as an Apprentice Regional Reference Person, and Rogelio Acosta undertook the same overall responsibility for Mexico as an Apprentice Regional Reference Person there. There will be teachers in Mexico City, Puebla, and Irapuato in Mexico, in Managua in Nicaragua, in Lima, Peru, and in Buenos Aires.

RCers who wished to attend, but were unable to, plan activities in Equador and Brazil. Maribel Arrelanes from Irapuato is undertaking to develop a network of women leaders in Mexico.

A next planned overall activity will be a series of workshops in different locations in about a year, which I have promised to lead. These workshops will be of about two days duration each and should involve many more people than we can afford to

Appeared in **Present Time** No. 66, January 1987.

bring together in one conference.

I want to express my warm appreciation to all the participants in the conference and especially to all the translators and organizers who helped the work go forward and helped bring people together.

Jewish Leaders' Conference, 1986

On October 31st, and November 1st and 2nd, a hundred RC Jewish leaders from five countries gathered in New Hampshire with Cherie Brown and myself to review Jewish liberation policy, Jewish participation in RC, and the placing of RC theory and tools in the hands of the wide-world Jewish communities. It was a splendid conference and there will be many reports of its effects in the future, both in **Present Time** and **Ruah Hadashah**.

We were saddened that the expected Australian RCers could not attend because of the sudden illness and death of Stephen Minz, and we send our condolences to his family.

Some very controversial problems were dealt with and complete unity and working consensus was achieved. In behalf of the whole RC Community, I congratulate Jewish RCers everywhere for the splendid leaders they have developed.

Appeared in **Present Time** No. 66, January 1987.

Organizing

Understanding and Using Organizational Forms

In other places we have discussed the fundamental actions which you, as an individual, can take to begin the formation of a world-class community around yourself and the assumption by yourself of world-wide leadership and influence.

STEPS TO WORLD LEADERSHIP

These have been summarized as:

(1) Giving up permanently and completely the ancient and universal (until now) habit of seeking to claim other people's attention and their listening to you when with them (the only exceptions being when the other person or persons understand *how* to be an effective counselor and *has or have agreed* to be counselor to you at that particular time);

(2) Substituting for the ancient habit a new active attitude, whenever with other persons, of paying attention to them, and listening to them, of enhancing their functioning (and possibly their re-emergence) by approval of them, validation of them, interest in them, confidence for them and in them, high expectations of them, contradiction of their distress (and directing their attention away from their distress) and, sometimes, assisting them to discharge;

(3) Teaching, expecting, and assisting the most responsible of the people around you to become leaders to the people around them by following your model of how to do it;

(4) Teaching these leaders how to teach the other people to

Appeared in part in **Present Time** No. 65, October 1986.

be leaders, in the same way as they are learning to be leaders from you; and

(5) Communicating to these successive spheres of influenced and informed people the theory and practice of recovering our occluded intelligences and leading, inspiring, and organizing people to eliminate all practices by which humans harm humans, the theory and practice that we have called Re-evaluation Counseling.

Theory, policy, goal-setting, organization, decision, and action are all necessary to attain the full re-emergence and the benign societies we all desire. Organization, in particular, is a field in which we have operated intuitively and without much rigorous discussion in recent periods. We have certainly been making organizational progress, however, and have accumulated many good experiences from which we can deduce useful generalities.

ORGANIZATIONAL FORMS

As we experienced Co-Counselors proceed with the construction of our individual world communities, we will need to *organize* our community members, will need to understand and use effective *organizational forms*.

Let us look at some of the basic forms that we have been using in our work. We have familiar labels for them in many cases (and I think these labels will remain useful for us in defining them and in communicating with each other about them); but clarification and understanding of the *content* of these forms will be more useful than simply settling for the *labels*.

THE SESSION

One form can be called the SESSION. Its content is *two (or more) persons paying helpful, interested attention to one of the persons*. Most of the action in the fourth paragraph of this article will qualify as a SESSION. We already know of the possibility of, and already use, *Co-Counseling sessions (two-way sessions), one-way sessions, three-way sessions, mini-sessions, telephone sessions, intensive sessions, correspondence-by-mail sessions, formal sessions, informal sessions, supervised sessions,* and many others. The ten-second exchange in which one person says, "I feel depressed this morning," and another replies, "I'm sorry. You *look* fine. Have a nice day," qualifies as a SESSION, in my opinion. *Two or more persons paying helpful, interested attention to one of the persons.*

THE CLASS

Let's call a second organizational form the CLASS. Its content is *communication to one or more persons of some of the knowledge of what people are like, what they can do and how they can do it (how they can recover their inherent intelligence and power) which we collectively have called Re-evaluation Counseling theory and practice.* This knowledge has been hidden from people by patterns, by mis-information, and by the oppressive practices of societies. We have recovered a great deal of it out of occlusion and continue to learn more and more. Every bit of this knowledge is precious to every person who learns it. It has already dramatically changed the lives of hundreds of thousands of people.

We are familiar with fundamental classes, ongoing classes, advanced classes, a great variety of special-purpose classes. I would include the informal communication of even one piece of information under this label. "I've heard it's good to let babies cry. Let me hold her while you shop," qualifies as a CLASS. So does loaning a piece of RC literature. *The communication of RC knowledge to one or more persons.*

THE SUPPORT GROUP

The SUPPORT GROUP is a widely-used form. The basic content of the SUPPORT GROUP is *each person in a group having a turn at being listened to without interruption.* An RCer may have to insist on the "no interruption" practice the first few times in a wide-world group, but the "no interruptions" will then be insisted on by the members as they experience the two great benefits of (1) actually being listened to and (2) actually hearing what other people are saying.

We already have women's support groups, men's support groups, support groups of every kind of commonality, within RC and without. Support group forms have spread from RC to wide sections of the population that have never yet heard of RC.

In general, every RCer should organize the *content* of a SUPPORT GROUP whenever she or he finds herself or himself with two or more other people. This includes at the bus stop, driving to work, on the work break, the lunch hour, at other meals, on all social occasions. This is what all people hope for from each other when together, but, because of the ancient habit of trying to be client always when with others, don't know how to bring it about or how to take turns.

Each person in a group having a turn at being listened to without interruption.

THE LEADERS' GROUP

The WYGELIAN-TYPE LEADERS' GROUP* is an organizational break-through. Its content is *each leader in a group of leaders who share a commonality of purpose, having four basic needs of rational leadership met.* Each leader needs a chance to review his or her past leadership before peers, needs to share information with peers, needs to set goals in the hearing of peers, and needs to receive counseling assistance where distress is limiting his or her leadership. These are the four points of the Wygelian leaders' agenda.

Such a leaders' group format eliminates the traditional "group programs," "checking up on each other," "arguing," "clienting," and "dramatizing at each other" which has been traditional in the best of previous functioning of leaders in the same field.

*See **Present Time** No. 54, pp. 3-5 and No. 55, pp. 13-14.

The WYGELIAN-TYPE LEADERS' GROUP works well in coordinating the work of RC leaders. It works well in leading, and developing leadership for, the special background and special liberation groups within and without RC. It works well in the wide world with leaders who know nothing of RC, providing an RCer uses RC skills as the Consultant to the group. *Each leader being listened to while reviewing his or her past leadership, while sharing information, while setting future goals, and while being counseled on difficulties with leadership.*

THE WORKSHOP

An RC workshop involves many highly developed practices which guarantee these workshops almost uniform success. The "Organizer's Guidelines for International and Regional Workshops," which is in the possession of most RC leaders, covers many details of these forms. I shall not try to summarize them here, but, instead, I ask readers of this article to send me lists of the organizational forms they see present in an RC workshop, and the contents of these forms.

THE PANEL

The PANEL is an organizational form that has evolved steadily and has lately proven very effective at ending misunderstandings between the women and the men in RC. Part of the oppression of men is to condition them not to talk about themselves and never tell of their hardships or hurts. In general, women have not known this. At recent workshops I have asked four to twelve men to appear as a panel in front of the workshop, where I question each one in turn as to "what it has been like to be a male" at each period of his life, as an infant, as a toddler, early grade school, later grade school, middle school, college, young adult, and at present. As each period's hurts are recalled I ask, "Where did you go for comfort?" The answers reveal to women listeners a reality of males' lives they have never suspected and open the door to much better communication between women and men.

THE LONGER VIEW

Some questions that the panel moderator will find useful with panels of oppressed groups are: "What has been great about being a _____ (Wygelian)? What has been hard about being a _____ (Wygelian)? What do you wish other people knew or understood about your kind of Wygelians? What do you wish non-Wygelians would never say again? What would a non-Wygelian who was a perfect ally for Wygelians be like? How do you wish Wygelians would relate to each other?" *Representatives of particular populations being helped to communicate the realities of their lives and their oppressions while the general population listens with respect.*

THE "TOPIC GROUP"

The "TOPIC GROUP" is a kind of discussion group that has evolved at RC workshops, gather-ins, and conferences. It has several distinctive characteristics, any one of which, or combination of which, will tend to improve the discussion process in any organization or conference.

In its most complete form the RC "topic group" includes the following features:

1. The topic is proposed by a person interested in that subject, who also designates the time and place of the meeting and posts these publicly or before the whole workshop or conference. This person becomes the "Convenor."

2. Attendance at the topic group is completely voluntary. Only people who are interested in that topic attend. If no one attends except the Convenor, he or she usually joins another topic group. (The usual rule at an RC workshop is that at least two people must attend for a report to be given to the whole workshop *except* in the case of an oppression-liberation topic in which case the Convenor can claim time for a report to the whole body even if no one else attended.)

3. When the group convenes, the Convenor sees that a Chairperson and a reporter (if possible, *two* reporters) are

chosen. The Convenor may or may not be Chairperson or reporter.

4. The job of the Chairperson is to see that good discussion is held, that important ideas and proposals are occasionally summarized and re-summarized to keep the discussion coherent, that issues are discussed and not personalities, that no person speaks twice before everyone has spoken once (no matter how much patience, time, and encouragement are necessary to help an inhibited person speak), and that no person speaks four times before everyone has spoken twice.

5. The job of the oral reporter is to prepare a (usually four-minute) report of the parts of the discussion that will be important for the larger body to hear and make the report orally to the large body at the next appropriate session.

6. The job of the written reporter is to prepare a succinct written report of the discussion and forward it to the appropriate newspaper, newsletter, or journal for publication. (In RC, usually to **Present Time** or one of the other RC journals.)

7. If necessary the Chairperson and reporter jobs can all be filled by one person.

THE PLANNING OR PROBLEM-SOLVING MEETING

When some problem or project needs wide consensus of Community members to be solved or carried out effectively, a meeting is called by the leader or leaders who will have to take action and all interested Community members are invited. The leader(s) state the problems clearly (in writing accompanying the meeting notice is best, but for certain at the beginning of the meeting) and *propose his, her, or their best solution or best thinking about the project so far.* (If only the problem is stated, with no proposed solution, the insecurities of those attending will be triggered and much dramatization will ensue. If a solution is proposed, even if not a good one, the meeting attenders will tend to respond thoughtfully.)

THE LONGER VIEW

The consensus of the discussion should be summarized by the people or leaders who will be responsible for taking action, and agreement with their summary expressed by the meeting.

If there remains disagreement or lack of consensus, the project should only proceed by the decision of the Area Reference Person or the International Reference Person (who are delegated this responsibility by the Guidelines) in RC affairs, or by such people as "Executive Officers" in the wide world. No leaders should be expected to carry out projects which they disagree with.

THE THINK-AND-LISTEN GROUP

This is a device for enhancing the boldness and clarity of people's thinking. In it each group member has a turn thinking (usually out loud, although the person may choose to think silently) while the other group members pay close, respectful attention but do not indicate in any way any response or reaction to what the thinker says. Each group member agrees at the beginning of the meeting to never afterwards refer to anything said by any other person in the meeting to any person, present or not. If any group member wishes to later express any ideas he or she heard in the meeting, he or she must express them as his or her own and not attribute them to the speaker of them.

The goal is to enhance each person's thinking by: (1) being listened to with full attention by the other group members, and (2) being completely free of any pressure from actual or anticipated responses by the others.

For a first meeting an introduction by the Convenor reminding people of what diversity of things there are to think about (the macroscopically large, the microscopically small, the simple, the complex, life, people, art, science, beauty, the past, the future, etc.) is helpful.

Groups need to be small. A group of four, each having a half-hour turn, works well.

Until one has experienced such a think-and-listen group, one can hardly credit the relief and freedom one feels at being able to think freely without anticipating having to cope with others' responses. One's thoughts amaze one, flying bold and free.

Discharge often accompanies the thinking and is accepted but not responded to by the other group members.

THE WORK PARTY

Meetings of Co-Counselors (or in the wide world, of members of groups or organizations) are planned with the Area leaders and calendar-keepers to avoid conflicts in scheduling. The person who wants a particular topic for a gather-in will organize it or secure an organizer for it, or will lead it or secure a competent leader for it. The Community is notified by flyers, announcements, or a telephone tree, and those who are interested attend.

A donation at the door will cover rent and expenses and possibly support some Community project. A full variety of literature will be diplayed and on sale.

The leader will ask each person to introduce herself or himself and give some quick item of information relating the person to the topic for the evening. The leader makes a presentation on the topic for an hour or less. Discussion groups are then set up on various sub-topics proposed by individuals who become the leaders of the discussions they propose and, after the groups meet and discuss, the groups report to the whole meeting *or* Co-Counseling pairs Co-Counsel on what they have heard and then express the thoughts they had after the meeting re-convenes.

The leader answers questions, summarizes the meeting, people announce any ongoing or upcoming activities, the gather-in adjourns.

Each RC Area organization is required by the Guidelines to

have at least two gather-ins each year, at one of which the Area Reference Person and the Alternate Area Reference Person must do self-estimations before the gather-in and be confirmed or replaced in their jobs.

THE WORKSHOP

The RC workskhop combines almost all of the above organizational forms. Detailed discussions of its organization are already available in the literature.

A Realistic Conference
For members of organizations or enterprises

(Questions are asked by the Consultant of each person in turn, by paragraphs, except where comments are asked from each of the others.)

What is something new and good in your life?

What, from your point of view, are the goals, at present, of the enterprise you work in? Which are you comfortable with? Which would you like modified or extended?

What, at present, are the important goals of your life? Which seem satisfactory to you? What parts of the work environment or procedures would you like to change?

What has the enterprise been doing? Details?

How is the enterprise working well, in your opinion? How is it ineffective? In potential trouble? In trouble? Where can it expand or work better?

In which ways do you feel you are a fine, satisfactory, admirable person? (What do you like about yourself?) In which areas would you like to change or improve? (What changes, what improvements?)

What are your special functions in the enterprise? (To the others) What does each of the others think this person's functions are?

Appeared in **RRP** No. 5.

THE LONGER VIEW

What have you done recently as a participant in the enterprise?

How have you done well? Where would you like to improve?

(To the others) What does each of the others think this person has done well?

Where does each of the others think this person can improve? How?

How is each of the others willing to assist him or her?

What do you plan and propose to do and accomplish in your life in the near future?

What do you plan and propose to do and accomplish in the near future as a participant in the enterprise?

Where are you blocked? Where would you like counseling assistance from the Consultant? (Counseling is given.)

What about this conference has been useful to you? How would you like the next conference to be different?

What was the one best thing about the conference?

(Adjourn)